FOREWORD

This anthology, which includes all the poems prescribed for the Higher and Ordinary Level English Leaving Certificate Examinations of 2008, has been prepared by three experienced teachers of English. Each of the contributors has been able to concentrate on a limited number of the prescribed poets and their work, thus facilitating a high standard of research and presentation.

Guidelines are given which set each poem in context. In addition, each poem is accompanied by a glossary and appropriate explorations, designed to allow the student to find his/her authentic response to the material. Relevant biographical details are provided for each poet. A range of general questions is set on each prescribed poet at Higher Level to aid in exam preparation.

Guidelines are included for students on approaching the Unseen Poetry section of the course. There is also advice on approaching the prescribed question in the examination. Students will also find the glossary of poetic terms a valuable resource in reading and responding to poetry.

The poetry course for Leaving Certificate English demands a personal and active engagement from the student reader. We hope that this anthology makes that engagement possible and encourages students to explore the wider world of poetry for themselves. Due to the poet's wishes, we have not included guidelines or questions with the poetry of Adrienne Rich.

CONTENTS

denotes poem included for Ordinary Level English Leaving Certificate

EDCO
THE EDUCATIONAL COMPANY

newdiscovery

**Leaving Certificate Poetry Anthology for
Higher and Ordinary Level 2008**

Patrick Murray
Kevin McDermott
Mary Slattery

SYLVIA PLATH

ADRIENNE RICH

MAYA ANGELOU

ACKNOWLEDGEMENTS

The poems in this book have been reproduced with the kind permission of their publishers, agents, authors or their estates as follows;

'The War Horse', 'Child of our Time', 'The Famine Road', 'The Shadow Doll', 'White Hawthorn in the West of Ireland', 'Outside History', 'The Black Lace Fan My Mother Gave Me', 'This Moment', 'The Pomegranate', 'Love' from *Collected Poems* (1995) by Eavan Boland, published by Carcanet Press Limited

'The Tuft of Flowers', 'Mending Wall', 'After Apple-Picking', 'The Road Not Taken', 'Birches', '"Out, out—"', 'Spring Pools', 'Acquainted with the Night', 'Design', 'Provide, Provide' by Robert Frost from *The Poetry of Robert Frost* edited by Edward Conner Lathaem, Copyright 1928, 1969 by Henry Holt and Company, Copyright 1936, 1942, 1956 by Robert Frost, Copyright 1964, 1970 by Lesley Frost Ballantine. Reprinted by permission of Henry Holt and Company, LLC

'Grandfather', 'Day Trip to Donegal', 'Ecclesiastes', 'After the Titanic', 'As It Should Be', 'A Disused Shed in Co. Wexford', 'Rathlin', 'The Chinese Restaurant in Portrush', 'Kinsale', 'Antarctica' by Derek Mahon from *Collected Poems* (1999) by kind permission of the author and The Gallery Press, Loughcrew, Oldcastle, Co. Meath

'Killing the Pig', 'The Trout', 'The Locket', 'The Cage', 'Windharp', 'All Legendary Obstacles', 'The Same Gesture', 'The Wild Dog Rose', 'Like Dolmens Round my Childhood', 'A Welcoming Party' by John Montague from *Collected Poems* (1995) by kind permission of the author and The Gallery Press, Loughcrew, Oldcastle, Co. Meath

'Pheasant', 'Finisterre', 'Mirror', 'Child', 'Morning Song', 'Elm', 'The Arrival of the Bee Box', 'Poppies in July', 'Black Rook in Rainy Weather', 'The Times Are Tidy' by Sylvia Plath from *Collected Poems* (1981) published by Faber and Faber Ltd

'The Uncle Speaks in the Drawing Room', 'Our Whole Life' from *Collected Early Poems: 1950–1970* by Adrienne Rich. Copyright © 1993 by Adrienne Rich. Copyright © 1967, 1963, 1962, 1961, 1960, 1959, 1958, 1957, 1956, 1955, 1954, 1953, 1952 by Adrienne Rich. Copyright © 1984, 1975, 1971, 1969, 1966 by W. W. Norton & Company Inc. Use by permission of the author and W. W. Norton & Company Inc.

'Storm Warnings', 'Aunt Jennifer's Tigers', 'The Uncle Speaks in the Drawing Room',
'Living in Sin', 'The Roofwalker', 'Our Whole Life', 'Trying to Talk with a Man',
'Diving into the Wreck', 'From a Survivor', 'Power' by Adrienne Rich from 'Storm
Warnings', 'Aunt Jennifer's Tigers', 'Power' by Adrienne Rich from *The Fact of a
Doorframe: Selected Poems 1950-2001* by Adrienne Rich. Copyright © 2002 by
Adrienne Rich. Copyright © 2001, 1999, 1995, 1991, 1989, 1986, 1984, 1981,
1967, 1963, 1962, 1961, 1960, 1959, 1958, 1957, 1956, 1955, 1954, 1953,
1952, 1951 by Adrienne Rich. Copyright © 1978, 1975, 1973, 1971, 1969,
1966 by W. W. Norton & Company Inc. Use by permission of the author and
W. W. Norton & Company Inc.

'Wedding Wind', 'At Grass', 'Church Going' from *The Less Deceived* (1955), 'An Arundel
Tomb', 'The Whitsun Weddings', 'MCMXIV', 'Ambulances' from *The Whitsun
Weddings* (1964), 'The Trees', 'The Explosion', 'Cut Grass' from *High Windows*
(1974) by Philip Larkin, published by Faber and Faber Ltd

'Phenomenal Woman' by Maya Angelou from *And Still I Rise* (1978) published by
Virago Press, reproduced by kind permission of Random House Inc.

'It Ain't What You Do It's What It Does To You' by Simon Armitage from *Zoom!*
(Bloodaxe Books, 1989)

'Valentine' by Carol Ann Duffy from *Mean Time* (1993) published by Anvil Press Poetry

'Going Home to Mayo' by Paul Durcan by kind permission of the poet

'May' by Kerry Hardie from *A Furious Place* (1996) by kind permission of the author
and The Gallery Press, Loughcrew, Oldcastle, Co. Meath

'Postscript' by Seamus Heaney from *The Spirit Level* (1996) published by Faber and
Faber Ltd

'The Ladybird's Story' by Elizabeth Jennings published by kind permission of
David Higham Associates Ltd

EAVAN BOLAND

B. 1944

BIOGRAPHY

Eavan Boland was born in Dublin in 1944, the daughter of diplomat Frederick Boland and artist Frances Kelly. As a child she moved with her family from Dublin to live in London and later in New York, where her father had been appointed Ambassador to the United Nations. On her return to Ireland in her mid-teens, she completed her secondary school education at the Convent of the Holy Child, Killiney. Afterwards she studied English and Latin at Trinity College, Dublin.

In 1966 she was awarded a first-class degree in English. For a time she was a junior lecturer at Trinity College, but in 1967 she left the academic life, becoming a literary journalist with RTÉ and the *Irish Times* as well as concentrating on her career as a poet. In 1969 she married the novelist Kevin Casey and moved to the suburb of Dundrum at the foothill of the Dublin mountains. The couple have two daughters.

Eavan Boland's first book of poems, *New Territory,* was published in 1967. *The War Horse* followed in 1975. In 1979 she lived with her family for a year in Iowa, USA, where she lectured at the International Writing Program. Her next collection, *In Her Own Image* (1980), with its explicitly feminist themes, reflects her exposure to the North American women's movement. In 1980 she was also a co-founder of Arlen House, an Irish feminist press. *Night Feed* (1982) and *The*

Journey (1986) celebrate the reality of many women's lives, looking after children and tending the home.

The two collections *Outside History* (1990) and *In a Time of Violence* (1994) broadened the scope of these issues, exploring the place of women in the past. *Collected Poems* was published in 1995, followed by *The Lost Land* in 1998 and *Code* in 2001. She has written a number of stimulating prose essays about poetry and the role of the woman poet in society, in particular *Object Lessons* (1995). She is now Professor of English at Stanford University in California.

SOCIAL AND CULTURAL CONTEXT

In her poetic career, Eavan Boland has engaged with many interesting and controversial issues. As an undergraduate in Trinity College she was part of a gifted group of young poets that included Brendan Kennelly, Michael Longley and Derek Mahon. When she became a full-time poet, she was for a time involved in the Dublin literary scene, meeting poets such as Padraic Colum and Patrick Kavanagh. Later, when she had married and moved to the suburbs, she began to examine critically the Irish poetic tradition as represented by these male poets. Sensing that this tradition was primarily 'bardic and male', she has said: 'I couldn't find my life in poetry'. For her, she says, the kettle, the baby's bottle, the kitchen 'were parts of my world. Not to write about them would have been artificial.'

In the 1960 and 1970s, the influence of the feminist movement, arguably the most influential movement of the second half of the twentieth century, began to be felt in Ireland. Questions about the relationship of gender and power were being asked in the field of poetry as well as in the political sphere. Internationally, the example of poets like Sylvia Plath and Adrienne Rich offered scope to women to write about their experiences of marriage and motherhood. Eavan Boland has said that, for her, feminism has been an enabling perception. Her involvement with the feminist publishing house Arlen Press and creative writing workshops for women stemmed from her interest in women's issues. However, she has pointed out that though she is a feminist she is not a feminist poet: 'Poetry begins where the certainties end …Women writers have struggled to be heard … and it is very important that they are not part of silencing anyone else.'

In later years her interpretation of feminism broadened to include an examination of the position of women in the Irish poetic tradition. She has concluded that the complexity of real women's lives has been diminished by the association of femininity and Irishness in poetic emblems such as Caitlín Ní Houlihan and Dark Rosaleen. This, she contends, has ignored the lives lived by ordinary women in the past, by what she terms the 'lost, voiceless, the silent' women who were victims of the Irish famine or, like her own grandmother, who died in a fever hospital in Dublin in 1909.

Her engagement with these issues has strengthened her assertion that there has been, and will continue to be, change in the role of women in Irish literature. She has said that 'over a relatively short time – certainly no more than a generation or so – women have moved from being the subjects and objects of Irish poems to being the authors of them'. In this context, she became involved in the debate about the under-representation of women writers and editors in *the Field Day Anthology of Irish Literature* in 1992.

The nature of Irish identity and how it is portrayed in history and literature has been a subject of intellectual and political controversy in recent times, particularly since the onset of conflict in Northern Ireland in the 1970s. Eavan Boland has dealt with these issues in her work and in her public life. Her autobiographical collection of prose essays, *Object Lessons: the Life of the Woman and the Poet in Our Time*, gives valuable insights both into her development as a poet and into her perceptions of the challenges that she faces as a woman poet in our time.

THE WAR HORSE

This dry night, nothing unusual
About the clip, clop, casual

Iron of his shoes as he stamps death
Like a mint on the innocent coinage of earth.

I lift the window, watch the ambling feather   5
Of hock and fetlock, loosed from its daily tether

In the tinker camp on the Enniskerry Road,
Pass, his breath hissing, his snuffling head

Down. He is gone. No great harm is done.
Only a leaf of our laurel hedge is torn –   10

Of distant interest like a maimed limb,
Only a rose which now will never climb

The stone of our house, expendable, a mere
Line of defence against him, a volunteer

You might say, only a crocus, its bulbous head   15
Blown from growth, one of the screamless dead.

But we, we are safe, our unformed fear
Of fierce commitment gone; why should we care

If a rose, a hedge, a crocus are uprooted
Like corpses, remote, crushed, mutilated?   20

He stumbles on like a rumour of war, huge
Threatening. Neighbours use the subterfuge

Of curtains. He stumbles down our short street
Thankfully passing us. I pause, wait,

Then to breathe relief lean on the sill   25
And for a second only my blood is still

With atavism. That rose he smashed frays
Ribboned across our hedge, recalling days

Of burned countryside, illicit braid:
A cause ruined before, a world betrayed.   30

GLOSSARY

5 *ambling*: moving at an easy pace

6 *hock*: joint on hindleg of a horse

6 *fetlock*: part of horse's leg just above hoof

13 *expendable*: can be done without

15 *bulbous*: swollen

22 *subterfuge*: an evasive device

27 *atavism*: reverting to ways of past

29 *illicit braid*: the members of the Irish secret society known as the 'Ribbonmen' founded in the nineteenth century in opposition to the 'Orangemen' wore a green ribbon as a badge

GUIDELINES

'The War Horse' is from the collection *The War Horse*, published in 1975. It was written at a time when the conflict in Northern Ireland, the so-called Troubles, was at its peak. It was a time when, as Eavan Boland herself reminds us, the 'sounds of death' were heard daily from the television. The poem is one of her first attempts to tackle a public or political theme.

The poem had its origins in an actual incident in which a stray horse, probably belonging to Travellers nearby, made its way into the front garden of Eavan Boland's new house in the suburbs. The horse is described as he makes his way down the street, damaging lawns and flowers as he goes. The setting is reassuringly normal. The speaker's response, observing the horse from the safety of her window, seems natural: 'we are safe'.

From the beginning, however, even from the poem's title, the horse is given a symbolic significance. His progress is described in terms of violence and war. Images of suffering, and military metaphors add to the increasing intensity of feeling. In this context, the speaker's attitude may be seen as indifferent or even callous. Might there be a suggestion of political evasion, a fear of becoming involved?

The poem, literally and metaphorically, makes us pause with the line 'I pause, wait', before leading us to the insight of the final lines. This insight may not be realised by the mind but instinctively in the blood. Images of the tattered flowers on the hedge disturb the speaker because of the associations with a more primitive experience of violence, hidden in Irish people's ancestral memory. In this manner the poem links the present situation with the past, and seems to imply the impossibility of real detachment from the conflict in Northern Ireland.

You may notice that the form of the poem is very controlled. Rhyming couplets – sometimes full-rhyme as in 'feather' / 'tether', 'head' / 'dead', or half-rhyme ('death' / 'earth', 'fear' / 'care') – echo a desire for order implied by the suburban attitudes and the well-kept gardens, but these attitudes are ultimately at variance with the irrational destructiveness of the war horse, expressed in the images of violence.

QUESTIONS

1 Trace the development of the horse as a symbol through the poem.
2 How does the poet make use of contrast in the poem?
3 Does the response of the observer in the poem change as the poem progresses?
4 What insights are contained in the poem's final lines, in your view? You might focus in particular on the word 'atavism' and on the connotations of the phrase 'illicit braid'.
5 In what sense might the final lines alter our perspective on the theme of the poem?
6 The poet has referred to 'The War Horse' as her first 'political' poem. What political point is she making? Can it be applied to the Irish situation only, or does it have a universal significance?
7 Explore the language of the poem – the imagery, sound effects, metaphors and similes.
8 How did you respond to this poem?

CHILD OF OUR TIME

for Aengus

Yesterday I knew no lullaby
But you have taught me overnight to order
This song, which takes from your final cry
Its tune, from your unreasoned end its reason;
Its rhythm from the discord of your murder   5
Its motive from the fact you cannot listen.

We who should have known how to instruct
With rhymes for your waking, rhymes for your sleep,
Names for the animals you took to bed,
Tales to distract, legends to protect   10
Later an idiom for you to keep
And living, learn, must learn from you, dead,

To make our broken images rebuild
Themselves around your limbs, your broken
Image, find for your sake whose life our idle   15
Talk has cost, a new language. Child
Of our time, our times have robbed your cradle.
Sleep in a world your final sleep has woken.

GUIDELINES

'Child of Our time' is taken from *The War Horse* (1975). The precise date of the poem is 17 May, 1974, almost immediately after the bomb blasts that took place in Dublin in 1974.

Eavan Boland describes the genesis of the poem:

I wrote it inspired – and I use the word with care – by a photograph I saw two days later on the front of a national newspaper whose most arresting feature was the expression on the face of the fireman who lifted that child, an expression of tenderness as if he were lifting his own child from its cradle to its mother's breast.

She also writes of 'that greatest of obscenities, the murder of the innocent' and refers to her poem as 'one among many other statements of outrage'.

From the beginning, the two qualities of tenderness and outrage are evident in the tone of the poem. The formal elegy or lament, which the poem is, becomes in the first stanza a lullaby suitable for a child. But the musical imagery does not allow us to forget the utter horror of the child's death. Although the world of the child is lyrically evoked for us, there is a contrasting note of moral severity to be heard throughout. Adults should have known how to protect this child. Images of language, as of music, are significant: the 'idiom' of a society, the culture and values that it holds, should have been transmitted to this child. But now the roles are reversed, as the poem makes clear, and it is the adults who must learn from the child.

The image of language, of speech, takes on a further urgency in the final stanza. A new way of communication must be found if any progress can be made, if healing can take place. Maybe, paradoxically, the innocence of the child's death, his final sleep, might 'wake up' the world he once lived in.

Traditionally, an elegy had three main functions: to lament, to praise and to console. All three elements are to be found in 'Child of Our Time'. Rhyme and sound patterns add to the formality of the poem's intention. The poem also has a political dimension. The response is to a public tragedy that has occurred because of a breakdown in political relations. The undoubted anger in the poem is not directed at individuals, but at the irresponsibility of a society which has allowed such things to happen. What sort of 'times' do we live in, the poem implies, if an infant can be arbitrarily killed? How can we in Ireland find a new way of communicating with each other that does not include violence and murder? Although the poem is rooted in the conflict in Northern Ireland, the question nevertheless applies to the suffering and damage inflicted on children in all wars.

QUESTIONS

1 Would you agree that the poem expresses feelings both of tenderness and outrage? Where in the poem can we locate these contrasting feelings?
2 How is the world of childhood innocence evoked in the second stanza?
3 Trace the imagery of song, language and speech as used in the poem.
4 How does the sound of the poem contribute to its effect?
5 A political poem usually seeks to bring about change. Is 'Child of Our Time' an effective political poem, in your view?
6 Compare this poem with Boland's other 'political' poem, 'The War Horse'. Which poem do you prefer, and why?
7 As a poem, 'Child of Our time' communicates its theme by aesthetic means. Using the language of argument/persuasion, write out the speech you would make for or against the view that violence can never be justified.

THE FAMINE ROAD

'Idle as trout in light Colonel Jones
these Irish, give them no coins at all; their bones
need toil, their characters no less.' Trevelyan's
seal blooded the deal table. The Relief
Committee deliberated: 'Might it be safe,   5
Colonel, to give them roads, roads to force
from nowhere, going nowhere of course?'

    "One out of every ten and then
    another third of those again
    women – in a case like yours."   10

Sick, directionless they worked; fork, stick
were iron years away; after all could
they not blood their knuckles on rock, suck
April hailstones for water and for food?
Why for that, cunning as housewives, each eyed –   15
as if at a corner butcher – the other's buttock.

    "Anything may have caused it, spores,
    a childhood accident; one sees
    day after day these mysteries."

Dusk: they will work tomorrow without him.   20
They know it and walk clear. He has become
a typhoid pariah, his blood tainted, although
he shares it with some there. No more than snow
attends its own flakes where they settle
and melt, will they pray by his death rattle.   25

    "You never will, never you know
    but take it well woman, grow
    your garden, keep house, good-bye."

'It has gone better than we expected, Lord
Trevelyan, sedition, idleness, cured   30
in one; from parish to parish, field to field;
the wretches work till they are quite worn,
then fester by their work; we march the corn
to the ships in peace. This Tuesday I saw bones
out of my carriage window. Your servant Jones.'   35

> "Barren, never to know the load
> of his child in you, what is your body
> now if not a famine road?"

GLOSSARY

title *Famine*: In the 1840s the potato crop in Ireland was affected by blight which
prevented the sowing of a new crop. The consequence was starvation and
destitution. In all, over a million people died during the years of the Famine.
See the note to lines 4–5 for an explanation of the term 'Famine Road'

1 *Colonel Jones*: Colonel Harry Jones, an English officer of the Royal
Engineers, appointed Chairman of the Board of Works in Ireland during
the time of the Famine

2 *no coins at all*: perhaps a reference to the demands from some localities for a
'dole' to keep people working on their farms

3 *Trevelyan*: Charles Edward Trevelyan (1807–86), had final responsibility for
Irish relief policy. He defended, on economic grounds, the export of food from
Ireland during the crisis

4–5 *Relief Committee*: groups established in 1847 to help organise famine relief.
They were comprised of magistrates, clergy and significant rate-payers.
The government lent money to them for public works schemes, such as
building of roads, piers, etc. These schemes often had no real purpose,
resulting in roads that went nowhere, for instance (a 'Famine Road')

17 *spores*: minute germs or organisms

22 *typhoid*: from 1847 there was a typhoid epidemic in Ireland

22 *pariah*: a social outcast

22 *tainted*: contaminated

25 *death rattle*: breathing sounds made by dying person

30 *sedition*: rebellion against government

33 *fester*: rot

33 *corn to the ships*: corn was exported from Ireland during the famine

GUIDELINES

'The Famine Road' is from the collection *The War Horse* (1975). The poem is an imaginative recreation of a bleak period in Irish history – the Famine. The response of the British government was to establish Relief Committees under the directorship of Charles Trevelyan, Lord of the Treasury. He organised and oversaw schemes for relief e.g. elaborate building schemes that would give 'employment' to the starving. Many of these schemes, as mentioned in the glossary, had no real practical purpose. A 'Famine Road', therefore, is a pointless road.

A certain familiarity with the historical background of the poem is necessary. The poem crystallises, in vivid images and within a short space, a historical event of great magnitude. It also takes the risk of linking a tragic public experience with a more private one, namely a woman's experience of infertility. It sets up a daring analogy between the Famine Road of the title and the barren woman. The poem suggests that a sense of uselessness and defeat is common to both.

There are several 'voices' to be heard in the poem. At first we hear the voices of the governing classes in the form of Trevelyan, writing to Colonel Jones and the Relief Committee, expressing a stereotypical and dismissive view of the Irish and suggesting the idea of the Famine Road. This voice is heard also in the seventh stanza. The writer of the report to Trevelyan, Colonel Jones, is smugly triumphant. The dehumanisation of the Irish is accepted, almost casually.

In the italicised words – the second, fourth, sixth and final stanzas – a different voice can be heard. At first it is not clear exactly what the problem is. It seems to be one of statistics. The dismissive tone echoes that of the earlier speakers. It becomes clear that this is the voice of a doctor, explaining, without much compassion or even interest, that these 'mysteries' happen i.e. some women are infertile. His patronising attitude may be inferred from his advice to her to accept her lot, to involve herself in her work. In an ironic reflection of the attitude of the Relief Committee, physical work is seen as a solution. The individual woman, like the Famine victims, is almost invisible. This is the voice of the powerful raised against the powerless. The link between this 'barren' woman and the Famine Road is made clear in the final lines: both experiences suggest powerlessness and defeat.

The voice in the third and fifth stanzas may be said to be the voice of the poet, narrating, in a series of vivid and horrifying images, the reality of the Famine experience. Work on the Famine Roads was backbreaking and pointless. Starvation dehumanised them; according to legend, Famine victims began to look upon each other as possible food, as the poem implies. The fifth stanza outlines how normal human standards have been lost. All social networks and rituals that make us human, such as family ties, grief and prayer for the dead, are now non-existent.

This is a complex poem that raises questions of a link between gender issues and the defeated, unrecorded lives of the people of the Famine era. Eavan Boland has outlined her sense of discovery of the history of the Famine and the real lives that were lost there in her prose essay 'Outside History'. In choosing to make an analogy between female barrenness and a traumatic event in Irish history, the poet bears out her thesis that womanhood and Irishness are metaphors for one another.

QUESTIONS

1 In the first stanza we are given an insight into the attitudes of the governing classes to the victims of the Famine. What precisely are those attitudes?

2 How does the poem succeed in indicating the gradual dehumanisation of the Famine victims? Look in particular at the images of bodily parts.

3 Do you think the poem succeeds in conveying the horror of the Famine?

4 In what way do the tones of the different speakers resemble each other?

5 Why, in your opinion, is the woman's voice not represented here?

6 Do you find the analogy between the experience of the Famine and the childless woman successful? Explain your view.

7 What is this poem saying about the status of women? How do you respond to the viewpoint expressed?

8 If you were asked to compile an anthology of your favourite poems by Eavan Boland, would you choose to include 'The Famine Road'? Give reasons for your response.

THE BLACK LACE FAN MY MOTHER GAVE ME

It was the first gift he ever gave her,
buying it for five francs in the Galeries
in pre-war Paris. It was stifling.
A starless drought made the nights stormy.

They stayed in the city for the summer.   5
They met in cafés. She was always early.
He was late. That evening he was later.
They wrapped the fan. He looked at his watch.

She looked down the Boulevard des Capucines.
She ordered more coffee. She stood up.   10
The streets were emptying. The heat was killing.
She thought the distance smelled of rain and lightning.

These are wild roses, appliquéd on silk by hand,
darkly picked, stitched boldly, quickly.
The rest is tortoiseshell and has the reticent,   15
clear patience of its element. It is

a worn-out, underwater bullion and it keeps,
even now, an inference of its violation.
The lace is overcast as if the weather
it opened for and offset had entered it.   20

The past is an empty café terrace.
An airless dusk before thunder. A man running.
And no way now to know what happened then –
none at all – unless, of course, you improvise:

The blackbird on this first sultry morning,   25
in summer, finding buds, worms, fruit,
feels the heat. Suddenly she puts out her wing –
the whole, full, flirtatious span of it.

GLOSSARY

2 *Galeries*: department stores in Paris

13 *appliquéd*: work laid on another material

15 *tortoiseshell*: the shell of a tortoise used for ornament

15 *reticent*: uncommunicative (as a tortoise is)

17 *bullion*: gold or silver underwater treasure

20 *offset*: set off as an equivalent of something else

25 *sultry*: hot, oppressive

28 *span*: measure

GUIDELINES

'The Black Lace Fan My Mother Gave Me' is from 'Object Lessons', part one of the collection *Outside History* (1990).

The poem was inspired by a black lace fan that had been a gift from the poet's father to her mother when they first met in pre-war Paris. In the past, a fan was traditionally an erotic object, given by a man to a woman and often used as a complex signalling system between them. The poem recreates an incident from her parents' past. As it progresses, the fan seems to become a metaphor for their relationship.

The poet imagines a little scene, or perhaps recalls hearing about it from her parents. She sketches the atmosphere of pre-war Paris in vivid, sensuous images. The weather forms a backdrop to the progress of the relationship, perhaps reflecting the human feelings involved. When the poet does focus on the fan itself, in the fourth stanza, it is as it is now – her mother's gift to her, handed down from the past – rather than as it was then. She describes it in unusual images that have complex connotations. The reader must decide whether the images contain reflections of suffering and fragility. The fan may then be seen as an emblem of human relationships, with all their precariousness and liability to change. It has gone beyond the traditional, static object often celebrated in poetry.

The poet is aware that it is impossible to recreate particular moments of the past. The essential truth about any relationship may never be known. But an artist may 'improvise', as the final evocative image shows. Birds have always been associated with love. The blackbird spreading its wings recalls the opened fan. The final lines of the poem are celebratory in tone, although there may also be more sombre implications: a 'span' is after all a measure of time as well as space. As such the poem both celebrates her parents' relationship and perceives its vulnerability.

QUESTIONS

1 The first three stanzas offer an imaginative recreation of the past. What aspects of the description appeal to you?

2 How would you interpret the descriptions of the weather in the poem?

3 Would you say that the fan was an important gift from the poet's father? Explain your view.

4 What impression of the fan do we get from the metaphors and similes used to describe it in Stanzas Four and Five?

5 What sort of relationship might Boland's parents have had? How might the fan reflect this?

6 What do you think is conveyed by the metaphor in Stanza Six, 'The past is an empty café terrace'? How is the idea developed in the rest of the poem?

7 Explore the image of the blackbird in the final stanza. Take into account words such as 'worms' as well as 'fruit'.

8 How would you respond to the view that the poem deals with the mystery of human relationships?

9 What does this poem say to you about love?

10 Compare the poem with Boland's poem 'Love'. Which poem do you prefer and why?

THE SHADOW DOLL

*(This was sent to the bride-to-be in Victorian times, by her dressmaker.
It consisted of a porcelain doll, under a dome of glass, modelling the
proposed wedding dress.)*

They stitched blooms from the ivory tulle
to hem the oyster gleam of the veil.
They made hoops for the crinoline.

Now, in summary and neatly sewn –
a porcelain bride in an airless glamour –   5
the shadow doll survives its occasion.

Under glass, under wraps, it stays
even now, after all, discreet about
visits, fevers, quickenings and lusts

and just how, when she looked at   10
the shell-tone spray of seed pearls,
the bisque features, she could see herself

inside it all, holding less than real
stephanotis, rose petals, never feeling
satin rise and fall with the vows   15

I kept repeating on the night before –
astray among the cards and wedding gifts –
the coffee pots and the clocks and

the battered tan case full of cotton
lace and tissue-paper, pressing down, then   20
pressing down again. And then, locks.

1 *tulle*: fine silk netting

2 *oyster*: an off-white colour

3 *crinoline*: a hooped petticoat

9 *quickenings*: stage in pregnancy when the mother becomes conscious of the child's movements

12 *bisque*: unglazed white porcelain

14 *stephanotis*: a white flower, used for weddings (and sometimes funeral wreaths)

GUIDELINES

'The Shadow Doll' is from 'Object Lessons', part one of the collection *Outside History* (1990). The author's note at the beginning of the poem explains the function of the shadow doll to model the proposed wedding dress for the prospective bride.

The focus of the first two stanzas is on the doll itself. It is described in a series of vivid images. We become aware of the connotations of the language used, expressing ideas of passivity and restriction. As in 'The Black Lace Fan My Mother Gave Me', Boland allows her imagination to move beyond the concrete object – the doll – so that it becomes symbolic of the female experience of marriage, especially in the context of the past.

One of the main attributes of the doll is its silence. This silence, the poet implies, has characterised such experience of marriage and childbirth, and indeed the whole lives of women, those whom Boland has referred to as having lived 'outside history'. The theme is developed in the poem as the focus alters from the doll to the poet's imagining the thoughts of a Victorian bride contemplating her wedding, and finally focusing on the poet's own experience as a prospective bride. The final imagery gathers together all the suggestions of restriction that have been indicated from the beginning.

The poem suggests that marriage for women has meant silence and submission, not necessarily literally, however, but as an area of experience reflected in poetry. (We should recall here Eavan Boland's statement about her early years as a poet: 'I couldn't find my life in poetry'.) Objects such as the shadow doll presented women in an artificial way, without recognising their real flesh-and-blood qualities and desires. The imaginative recreation of the past highlights even more intensely the depressing perception that little has really changed over the years, despite the obsolete function of the 'shadow doll'. It has survived as a symbol of the silence of the unexpressed lives of women in the past. Eavan Boland has written: 'We have to take that great theme, that silence, and command it as a human theme'. This is something that Boland has returned to many times, particularly in the poems of the sequence 'Outside History'.

QUESTIONS

1 What characteristics of the doll are emphasised in the poem's title and in the first two stanzas?
2 Explore the language used to describe the doll in Stanzas Two and Three. Are the implications suggested positive or negative?
3 What aspect of the Victorian bride's experience does the doll also reflect?
4 Why do you think the poet refers to her own marriage in the last two stanzas?
5 What does the poem say to you about the experience of marriage?
6 How would you define the tone of this poem? Is it angry? Regretful? Pessimistic? Accepting? Perhaps you would suggest another term?
7 Compare 'The Shadow Doll' with 'The Black Lace Fan My Mother Gave Me' in terms of theme and technique. Which poem do you prefer?
8 Would you describe 'The Shadow Doll' as a feminist poem? Explain your view.
9 You wish to include this poem in a short talk entitled 'Introducing Eavan Boland'. Write out the talk you would give.

WHITE HAWTHORN IN THE WEST OF IRELAND

I drove West
in the season between seasons.
I left behind suburban gardens.
Lawnmowers. Small talk.

Under low skies, past splashes of coltsfoot,   5
I assumed
the hard shyness of Atlantic light
and the superstitious aura of hawthorn.

All I wanted then was to fill my arms with
sharp flowers,   10
to seem, from a distance, to be part of
that ivory, downhill rush. But I knew,

I had always known
the custom was
not to touch hawthorn.   15
Not to bring it indoors for the sake of

the luck
such constraint would forfeit –
a child might die, perhaps, or an unexplained
fever speckle heifers. So I left it   20

stirring on those hills
with a fluency
only water has. And, like water, able
to re-define land. And free to seem to be –

for anglers,   25
and for travellers astray in
the unmarked lights of a May dusk –
the only language spoken in those parts.

Hawthorn: a small tree of the rose family, originally used for hedges. It grows wild throughout Ireland. There is a great deal of folklore and superstition around hawthorn. It can be associated with good luck, but to bring white hawthorn inside a house was to risk death or other misfortunes

5 *coltsfoot*: a large-leaved, yellow-flowered plant

6 *assumed*: took on

7 *Atlantic light*: the changeable weather conditions near the Atlantic coast causes the light to vary, a fact that makes it very popular with painters

20 *heifers*: young cows that have not yet had a calf

GUIDELINES

The poem is the fourth of a twelve-poem sequence, 'Outside History', part two of the collection of the same name published in 1990.

The poem is structured in a dramatic way around the image of a journey that the speaker makes from what is clearly her usual environment to the west of Ireland. As the journey progresses, the poet feels herself assimilated into the landscape of the west, as she indicates with some striking visual images. Her joy in the unfamiliar surroundings, in particular the white hawthorn she sees, is checked by her awareness of the superstitions associated with the plants.

In this context the speaker, in what would correspond to the resolution of the poem's dramatic structure, must leave the hawthorn alone. She sees it as having a mysteriousness, almost the life force, of an element such as water. It also has a 'fluency' – the word, and the images of language that continue, seems to imply the communicative power of hawthorn. It appears to offer what amounts to an alternative commentary on human actions that may displace the power of language in the usual sense of the word. Like language, it has the power to affect human behaviour. We could interpret the poem as suggesting that the 'language' of superstition , as well as the 'language' of landscape, has superseded the actual language of the place. Bearing in mind that the poem is set in the west of Ireland, this insight has further possibilities of meaning.

If we consider the title of the sequence of poems, 'Outside History', its relevance to this poem may be that as part of the natural world, hawthorn itself is outside the influence of history. It has, however, in an oblique way, exerted an influence on the course of history, as it has influenced the actions of human beings. Perhaps this 'history' has not been recorded in any official version but it nonetheless remains part of the hidden lives of the past. In this way it is a symbolic language, a sign of communication.

Like the poem which follows, 'Outside History', 'White Hawthorn in the West of Ireland' seeks to explore the abstract concept of history, looking at what it has recorded and, even more importantly, what has been excluded from it. (If you are interested in these ideas, you should read Eavan Boland's prose essay, 'Outside History'.)

QUESTIONS

1 What sort of environment does the speaker leave behind? How does it contrast with the landscape of the west?

2 What desire does the poet express in the third stanza? What obstacles does she encounter?

3 Explore the possibilities of meaning implied by the word 'luck'. What does it suggest about the power of the hawthorn?

4 Why does she decide to leave the hawthorn outside?

5 How does the speaker's mood change as the poem progresses?

6 Do you think the specific setting of the poem – the west of Ireland – has any significance to the theme of displacement in the poem?

7 In what sense do you think the hawthorn seems to be 'the only language in these parts'?

8 It has been said of Eavan Boland that while she is a 'poet who works with concrete images', she is also a poet who is 'unafraid of thought'. Discuss this viewpoint with reference to the poem.

9 Eavan Boland's poems have been called 'painterly'. Would the adjective apply to the images in this poem, in your opinion?

10 How did you respond to the poem?

OUTSIDE HISTORY

There are outsiders, always. These stars –
these iron inklings of an Irish January,
whose light happened

thousands of years before
our pain did: they are, they have always been   5
outside history.

They keep their distance. Under them remains
a place where you found
you were human, and

a landscape in which you know you are mortal.   10
And a time to choose between them.
I have chosen:

out of myth into history I move to be
part of that ordeal
whose darkness is   15

only now reaching me from those fields,
those rivers, those roads clotted as
firmaments with the dead.

How slowly they die
as we kneel beside them, whisper in their ear.   20
And we are too late. We are always too late.

GLOSSARY

2 *iron inklings*: intimations, hints. The adjective 'iron' refers metaphorically to the
   coldness of the stars, especially in the context of an 'Irish January'

17 *clotted*: clustered

18 *firmaments*: the skies

GUIDELINES

'Outside History' is the twelfth and final poem of the sequence of the same name taken from the collection *Outside History* (1990). The theme of the sequence is the exclusion from history of those who have been voiceless and forgotten, in particular the women of the past. Eavan Boland's own comments are helpful in reading the sequence:

> *As a poet I have one register, if you like, one area I return to … perhaps it's a sense of the lives that haven't been lived … How emblematic are the unexpressed lives of other women to the woman poet, how intimately they are her own … silence is … part of her tradition.*

It is in this poem that the theme is expressed most explicitly. As in 'White Hawthorn in the West of Ireland', natural imagery is used in a symbolic way. Stars have often featured as symbols of timelessness and myth. As such they have remained far removed – 'outside history' – from human suffering and change which the notion of history implies. But the speaker, as a human being and as a woman, affirms her desire to claim her place as part of the painful experience of history ('the ordeal') rather than remain in the traditional mythic role hitherto assigned to women. In these lines, too, there is a suggestion of continuity with the past. The image of suffering in the last three lines is accompanied by a sense of grief and collective responsibility. There is a need to recognise the wrong that has been done to those who have died, whose lives were forgotten and unexpressed.

The author's position as a woman poet is relevant to the poem. One of Eavan Boland's main contentions as a critic of poetry written by Irishmen is that women have been diminished by their depictions as mythical creatures such as Caitlín Ní Houlihan or the Sean Bhean Bhocht. The tradition of Irish poetry as, in her words, 'bardic and male' must be challenged and examined from a feminist perspective. She would see the contemporary Irish woman poet as redressing the balance by according women the same rights to full humanity (their rightful place in history) as men have had. In order to do this, it is necessary for the woman poet to reposition herself and her consciousness of the world within poems as their author, rather than as an object of poems written by men.

Eavan Boland has also written that the past is the profound responsibility of the woman poet. The defeated and the marginalised (not exclusively women) must be reclaimed for inclusion in poetry.

QUESTIONS

1 What point do you think the poet is making when she asserts that 'there are outsiders, always'? How is it related to the images of the stars which follow?

2 To whom is the poet referring in the third stanza when she says 'you found / you were human'? What do the words 'human' and 'mortal' suggest in contrast with the image of the stars?

3 What do you think the difference is between 'myth' and 'history'? Why would the poet choose 'history'?

4 History is referred to as an 'ordeal' in the fifth stanza and is associated with 'darkness' in the following line. What does this imply about history?

5 Why does the poet change from 'you' to 'I' and later to 'we', in your opinion?

6 How did you respond to the images of the 'dead' in the final stanzas?

7 'And we are too late. We are always too late.' What is the tone of these lines, in your view?

8 Boland has put forward the interesting thesis that 'over a relatively short time – certainly no more than a generation or so – women have gone from being the subjects and objects of Irish poems to being the authors of them'. Do you think this statement is relevant to an understanding of 'Outside History'?

9 To what extent does the poem succeed in making a complex and abstract theme accessible, in your view?

10 'Outside History' and 'White Hawthorn in the West of Ireland' are part of a sequence of twelve poems. Which of them do you prefer, and why?

THIS MOMENT

A neighbourhood.
At dusk.

Things are getting ready
to happen
out of sight.   5

Stars and moths.
And rinds slanting around fruit.

But not yet.

One tree is black.
One window is yellow as butter.   10

A woman leans down to catch a child
who has run into her arms
this moment.

Stars rise.
Moths flutter.   15
Apples sweeten in the dark.

GLOSSARY

7 *rinds slanting around fruit*: an unusual image, almost kinaesthetic in its sense of
movement. Even the rinds (peel) of the fruit appear to be 'getting ready' to
change as the moment will change

GUIDELINES

'This Moment' is from 'Legends', part two of the collection *In a Time of Violence*
(1994). The poem captures the essence of a particular moment in time in vivid,
sensuous images. The effect has the clarity of a painting.

The moment takes place at dusk, in itself a fleeting time of day. The setting
is a suburban neighbourhood. The focus is on what is actually happening at that

particular moment, but the intensity of the perception is heightened by an awareness, almost from the very beginning, that the moment will not last.

The only human figures in the poem are a woman and her child, running into her arms. The image reminds us, perhaps, in its timelessness, of the Madonna and Child. The language in the final stanza has rich connotations: 'sweeten' appeals both to our sense of smell and taste but it also has associations with the sweet smell of decay. If we remember too that an apple has Biblical associations (Adam and Eve ate from the Tree of Knowledge, traditionally an apple tree, and so lost Paradise for ever), we can see further associations with change and loss of innocence.

QUESTIONS

1 Would you agree that the poem is effective in evoking a particular moment? How does it do so?

2 Which of the adjectives best describe the atmosphere in this poem, in your opinion: peaceful, tender, strange? Perhaps you would suggest another word?

3 How does the poem make us aware of change?

4 Look at the form of the poem with its varying line lengths and stanza lengths. What effect do they contribute to the poem?

5 Eavan Boland has spoken of her desire to 'bless the ordinary, sanctify the common' in her poetry. To what extent does this short lyric succeed in this?

6 If you were to make a short film of this poem, what music/special effects would you use? What atmosphere would you try to create?

LOVE

Dark falls on this mid-western town
where we once lived when myths collided.
Dusk has hidden the bridge in the river
which slides and deepens
to become the water   5
the hero crossed on his way to hell.

Not far from here is our old apartment.
We had a kitchen and an Amish table.
We had a view. And we discovered there
love had the feather and muscle of wings   10
and had come to live with us,
a brother of fire and air.
We had two infant children one of whom
was touched by death in this town
and spared: and when the hero   15
was hailed by his comrades in hell
their mouths opened and their voices failed and
there is no knowing what they would have asked
about a life they had shared and lost.

I am your wife.   20
It was years ago.
Our child was healed. We love each other still.
Across our day-to-day and ordinary distances
we speak plainly. We hear each other clearly.

And yet I want to return to you   25
on the bridge of the Iowa river as you were,
with snow on the shoulders of your coat
and a car passing with its headlights on:

I see you as a hero in a text –
the image blazing and the edges gilded –   30
and I long to cry out the epic question
my dear companion:

Will we ever live so intensely again?
Will love come to us again and be
so formidable at rest it offered us ascension   35
even to look at him?

But the words are shadows and you cannot hear me.
You walk away and I cannot follow.

GLOSSARY

1 *mid-western town*: Eavan Boland attended the International Writing Program at the University of Iowa, USA, in 1979

6 *the hero*: Aeneas, the hero of Virgil's *The Aeneid*. In Book 6, Aeneas visits the underworld, crossing over the river Styx. There he sees his dead companions, but they are unable to communicate with him

8 *Amish*: a strict American Mennonite sect. An Amish table would suggest a sturdy, unadorned piece of furniture

29 *hero in a text*: Aeneas, as before

35 *ascension*: a sense of uplift

GUIDELINES

'Love' is from 'Legends', part two of the collection *In a Time of Violence* (1994).

The myth behind the poem 'Love' is that of the journey undertaken by Aeneas to the underworld in Book 6 of *The Aeneid* by Virgil. In the story, Aeneas meets the ghosts of his former companions, who are both pleased and frightened to see him. However, despite their best efforts, they fail to communicate successfully with him because their voices have become feeble, almost a mockery of what they had once been. The essential point of the myth is the pain of separation and loss.

Eavan Boland has written of the importance to her of this particular moment in the Aeneas myth, when reading it as a student she came to realise the ultimate powerlessness of language to recreate experience: 'The heroes had spoken and their voices had not carried. Memory was a whisper, a sound that died in your throat.'

In this poem, as in 'The Pomegranate', myth is a way of exploring real experience and concerns. Addressed to the poet's husband, it retrieves their shared married history and memories. Personal details recall their time in Iowa – their apartment, furniture, the illness of their child. But the poem goes beyond the personal to meditate on love itself and how it is affected by time and change. The past is recalled as a time of great emotional intensity that the present cannot recapture. Love still exists between them, the poem makes clear, but something has been lost or diminished. This perception heightens the sense of longing in the poem.

You may notice the image of language used throughout the poem, appropriate to the significance of the underlying myth. The final lines seem to express the perspective of the comrades of Aeneas, who wish to speak but fail to do so. They seem to suggest that words are only a shadowy reflection of reality and can offer no consolation in the face of the erosions of time and feeling. There are possible implications of final separation in death in the last line: 'You walk away and I cannot follow'.

Boland has written of myth as: 'a beautiful important way of organising the wounded, of bandaging the wounded knee of things …'. By focusing on moments of sadness in the old stories, she relates them to her perceptions of change and loss in her own life.

QUESTIONS

1 'Love' is clearly an autobiographical poem, addressed to the poet's husband. How does the imagery used convey a sense of intimacy?
2 What is the effect of love, suggested in the second stanza?
3 Why do you think she makes the analogy with the Aeneas myth in the stanza describing her child's illness?
4 How has the poet's experience of love changed?
5 How is her beloved 'dear companion' presented in the fifth and sixth stanzas? Examine the language in which she describes him.
6 How do the questions the poet asks in the penultimate stanza, and the sense of finality in the couplet at the end, affect the theme and tone of the poem?
7 Do you think Boland's use of the Aeneas myth is effective in 'Love'?
8 What does the poem reveal about the personality and outlook of the poet?
9 What does the poem tell us about memory?
10 What does this poem tell us about love? Do you find its insights interesting? Explain your response.

THE POMEGRANATE

The only legend I have ever loved is
the story of a daughter lost in hell.
And found and rescued there.
Love and blackmail are the gist of it.
Ceres and Persephone the names.   5
And the best thing about the legend is
I can enter it anywhere. And have.
As a child in exile in
a city of fogs and strange consonants,
I read it first and at first I was   10
an exiled child in the crackling dusk of
the underworld, the stars blighted. Later
I walked out in a summer twilight
searching for my daughter at bed-time.
When she came running I was ready   15
to make any bargain to keep her.
I carried her back past whitebeams
and wasps and honey-scented buddleias.
But I was Ceres then and I knew
winter was in store for every leaf   20
on every tree on that road.
Was inescapable for each one we passed.
And for me.
      It is winter
and the stars are hidden.   25
I climb the stairs and stand where I can see
my child asleep beside her teen magazines,
her can of Coke, her plate of uncut fruit.
The pomegranate! How did I forget it?
She could have come home and been safe   30
and ended the story and all
our heart-broken searching but she reached
out a hand and plucked a pomegranate.
She put out her hand and pulled down

the French sound for apple and   35
the noise of stone and the proof
that even in the place of death,
at the heart of legend, in the midst
of rocks full of unshed tears
ready to be diamonds by the time   40
the story was told, a child can be
hungry. I could warn her. There is still a chance.
The rain is cold. The road is flint-coloured
The suburb has cars and cable television.
The veiled stars are above ground.   45
It is another world. But what else
can a mother give her daughter but such
beautiful rifts in time?
If I defer the grief I will diminish the gift.
The legend will be hers as well as mine.   50
She will enter it. As I have.
She will wake up. She will hold
the papery flushed skin in her hand
And to her lips. I will say nothing.

GLOSSARY

title *Pomegranate*: an oriental fruit, cultivated in warm climates

4 *gist*: the essence

5 *Ceres*: the Roman name for the Greek goddess, Demeter. Ceres was the goddess of foliage and corn. She was also known as the goddess of motherhood and fertility

5 Persephone: daughter of Ceres

9 *city of fogs and strange consonants*: London, where as a child Boland was aware of different accents to her own

17 *whitebeams*: small trees

18 *buddleias*: a type of shrub

48 *rifts*: openings

GUIDELINES

'The Pomegranate' is from 'Legends', part two of the collection *In a Time of Violence* (1994).

The legends tells how Persephone, daughter of Ceres, was carried off by Pluto, god of the underworld, to be his wife. The desolate mother threatened to interrupt the fruition of the earth until the king of Eleusis, Celeus, told her the name of her daughter's abductor. Ceres went to reclaim her daughter. However, during her stay in the underworld (Hades), Persephone had eaten six pomegranate seeds, which gave Pluto a magic power over her so that she had to spend part of the year with him and could only rejoin her mother for the remaining months. While she is with Ceres, everything grows; during her time in the underworld, everything remains barren.

As in 'Love', Boland makes use of a myth as a framework to illumine her own personal experience – in this case her changing relationship with her (then) seventeen-year-old daughter. In using myth she gives her experience a universal appeal. The underlying psychological truth of the myth suggests the vulnerability of all human relationships, especially that of parent and child.

The poem is narrated in the form of a single long stanza, unrhymed. By telling us from the beginning that 'love and blackmail', two contrasting ideas, are the 'gist' of the story, the poet prepares us for the tensions within the poem between the tender feelings expressed and the acute fear of parental loss which underlies them.

The poet has found parallels between the myth of Ceres and Persephone at different stages in her life. As a child in London, she was the exiled Persephone. As a young mother she experienced great love for her child, as well as an awareness of how vulnerable this love was. Now, at this point of their lives, the Ceres-Persephone relationship takes on a further significance. Images of her teenage daughter, asleep, with her plate of 'uncut fruit', remind her of a new phase upon which they are poised. Like Persephone, her child may reach out and eat the fruit, a metaphor for entry into the adult world and thus separation from the mother. (In many myths, plucking and eating of fruit has connotations of sexual knowledge and loss of innocence.) The mother's perception of her daughter's situation is tinged with sadness, but she comes to accept that it may be a mother's role to relinquish a daughter to the world of adult experience – as Ceres was ultimately forced to do. The separation that will entail may be a source of grief, but its very poignancy may also be a measure of its value as a source of happiness.

QUESTIONS

1 How does the poet identify with the myth of Ceres and Persephone?

2 From line 24, the poem becomes more dramatic: we are aware of a particular setting, a time and place. What effect is created by these changes?

3 What do the images of mother and child in lines 26–28 suggest to you about their relationship at that particular point?

4 Would you agree that a sense of loss pervades this entire poem? Explain your answer.

5 What insight does the poem offer us about the mother-daughter relationship?

6 Are these concerns uniquely female, in your view?

7 Do you think the use of myth adds to or takes from the poem's impact?

8 Does the poet blend myth and contemporary life successfully?

9 'The Pomegranate' dramatises the mother-daughter relationship in poetic form. Write a narrative (short story or personal essay) about the relationship between parents and children.

10 Write a letter to Eavan Boland in which you talk about 'The Pomegranate' as one of your favourite poems.

GENERAL QUESTIONS ON EAVAN BOLAND

1 'In many of her poems, Eavan Boland confronts the violent history of Ireland with honesty but always with compassion.' Would you agree?

2 In the words of Anne Stevenson, Eavan Boland is a poet who, although 'unafraid of thought', nevertheless 'works with concrete images'. Examine the poetry of Eavan Boland from this point of view.

3 Her personal experience as a wife and mother living in the suburbs enriches the poetry of Eavan Boland. Would you agree with this view?

4 'A sense of the past pervades Eavan Boland's poetry and she recreates it in an imaginative and dramatic way.' Examine at least three of Boland's poems in the light of this statement.

5 Eavan Boland herself has said that as a lyric poet she works with themes of 'time, perception of loss, down-to-earth disappointments or irretrievable segments of human experience'. Explore the treatment of these themes in her work.

EXAMINATION-STYLE QUESTIONS

6 'The poetry of Eavan Boland appeals to the reader for many reasons.' Write an essay in which you outline the reasons why poems by Eavan Boland have this appeal.

Guidelines

Your answer might include the following points:

- the domestic and suburban settings of her poems are attractive and accessible
- the themes (e.g. relationships) are sensitive and human
- her political and historical themes are complex and thought-provoking
- her use of myth and legend is unexpected and fresh, and gives a universal quality to her poems
- she is interested in the voices of those who have been powerless in society
- her use of language is evocative and painterly, etc.

You must support your points with reference to, or quotation from, the poems on your course.

7 Imagine you have invited Eavan Boland to give a reading of her poems to your class or group. What poems would you ask her to read and why do you think they would appeal to your fellow students?

Guidelines

You are obviously free to choose any of the poems on the course and make a case for their appeal to the group. Possible points you could include may be:

- you may feel the group would respond to those poems which deal with the poet's personal experience as wife or mother, e.g. 'This Moment', 'Love', 'The Pomegranate'
- as a contrast, the poems which deal with more public and political themes might appeal, e.g. 'The War Horse', 'Child of Our Time', 'Outside History'.
- poems with a feminist theme might be popular e.g. 'The Shadow Doll'
- you may respond well to Eavan Boland's recreation of the past in her poems, so request her to read 'The Black Lace Fan My Mother Gave Me' or 'The Famine Road'
- you may feel the group would respond to the language of the poems, for example the precise and evocative imagery and the lyrical tone she creates, etc.

You should support your points with reference to, or quotation from, the poems on your course.

8 'Introducing Eavan Boland.' Write out the text of a short presentation you would make to your class group under the above title.

Guidelines

Your presentation might include some of the following points:

- Eavan Boland's position as one of Ireland's best-known woman poets
- the link between her life and her poetry
- her choice of themes, public and private
- her general vision and viewpoint – of history, of women's experience, of the past etc.
- her use of language and imagery
- the impact her poems make upon the reader, etc.

You should support the points you make by reference to, or quotation from, the poems on your course.

Domestic and suburban
settings in poems.

Makes use of myth
and legend.

Feminist concerns, but not a
'doctrinaire' feminist.

Evocative, 'painterly'
language.

Recreates the past
in poems.

Eavan Boland

Personal experience
reflected in poems.

Interested in the voices of
the powerless in society.

Themes may also be
public and political.

Lyrical and imaginative
descriptions in poems.

Poems explore family
relationships.

JOHN DONNE

1572–1631

BIOGRAPHY

Donne (pronounced 'done'), the son of a prosperous London merchant, was one of the most learned men in an age remarkable for learned men. His learning is constantly reflected in his poetry. He spent three years at Oxford and three at Cambridge. He was a student at the Inns of Court in London, where he studied law, languages and theology from four in the morning until ten.

Donne was born into an age of fierce, often deadly, religiously controversy. During the long reign of Elizabeth the First (1558–1603), Catholics were regarded as enemies of the state and many suffered torture, imprisonment and death for upholding their faith. Donne was brought up a Catholic. His mother was related by marriage to Sir Thomas More, the Lord Chancellor of England, who had been martyred in 1535 for refusing to acknowledge the claim of Henry VIII to be head of the English church. Four hundred years after his death, More was declared a saint by the Catholic Church. Donne's family suffered for their religion. His brother Henry died in 1593 after being arrested for concealing a priest. When he was about thirty, Donne abandoned his Catholic faith and became an Anglican. In 1615, he was ordained to the ministry of the Church of England.

As a young man, Donne was extremely ambitious, attaching himself to influential patrons as a means of advancing his career. He travelled in Europe and took part in two naval expeditions. He became secretary to Sir Thomas Egerton, a man of great power and influence. His hopes of worldly advancement were blighted when he secretly married Anne More, Egerton's niece, in 1601. She was seventeen, he almost thirty. Her father, who was Lieutenant of the Tower of London, used his power to ruin Donne's career, compelling Egerton to dismiss him and have him imprisoned. On his release, Donne had to take legal action to be reunited with his wife. He summarised the consequences of his imprudent marriage in a rueful, witty epigram ('John Donne – Anne Donne – Undone').

During his Anglican phase, Donne was a champion of his new religion, and wrote a good deal of anti-Catholic propaganda. His literary career has two broad divisions. His memorable secular poetry (love poems, elegies and satires) belongs to the first half of his life, when he enjoyed the society of women, and was especially fond of the theatre. Almost all his poetry, even the *Holy Sonnets*, was written before his ordination in 1615. This latter event marked a new phase in his literary career. He abandoned poetry for the composition of sermons, achieving fame as one of the outstanding preachers of his time. Fragments of these sermons, divorced from their original contexts, have long been part of popular discourse (for example, 'No man is an island' and 'never send to know for whom the bell tolls; it tolls for thee'). Donne's sermons are intensely personal, expressing remorse for past sins and, above all, his obsessive interest in his own death, which was the subject of his last sermon, preached before King Charles I. The point of the sermon was reinforced by what his first biographer called 'a decayed body and a dying face'. Death is also a major theme of his poetry.

Donne became Dean of St Paul's Cathedral in London in 1621. This promotion, as he himself put it, marked the rejection of 'the mistress of my youth, Poetry' for 'the wife of mine age, Divinity [Religion]'. The evidence suggests that Donne regarded himself as a writer of sermons rather than a poet. He published virtually nothing of his poetry and took no steps to collect or preserve it. On the other hand, he saw to it that his sermons were carefully preserved for publication. His literary contemporaries saw things differently. When his poems were published after his death, some of the principal writers of his time composed impressive tributes to his originality and his inventiveness. For over two centuries, his poetry was not highly regarded. In the eighteenth century, when elegance and grace were among the desirable features of poetry, Donne's verse was seen as awkward, primitive and inelegant, partly due to the fact that his work was available only in poor, inaccurate versions. The first good text of Donne's poems was that of Grierson (1912). Following the publication of T. S. Eliot's celebrated essay 'The Metaphysical Poets' in 1923, Donne came to be regarded as a major poet, admired above all for his unique blend of thought with feeling, his exciting use of argument and analogy, his mastery of a lively, colloquial idiom. Donne was now valued for his wit, expressed in what became known as the metaphysical conceit, which depended for its success on his ability to discover resemblances between apparently unrelated facts and ideas. There was also the delighted recognition of his constant readiness to surprise — his use of learned ideas in support of the most daring conclusions.

The Donne revival became a cult. Some important twentieth-century poets and critics, among them Eliot and Pound, were profoundly influenced by his poetry. The daring conceit with which Eliot opens 'The Love Song of J. Alfred Prufrock' is a famous example of this influence. Donne's poetry is necessarily élitist; given his tendency to exploit his massive, wide ranging store of knowledge. Donne appeals to the intelligence and knowledge of his readers, as well as to their imaginations. An appreciation of his poems depends ultimately on our ability to work at them in order to discover what their astonishingly broad range of reference meant to their author, and what it can mean almost four centuries later.

SOCIAL AND CULTURAL CONTEXT

Since Samuel Johnson's discussion of their work in his *Lives of the Poets* (1779–81), it has been customary to describe Donne, Herbert, Vaughan and Marvell (to mention only the greater figures) as the English Metaphysical poets. To give an account of some of the distinctive features of Donne's poetry is a convenient method of describing the outstanding characteristics of Metaphysical poetry.

One of the most remarkable things about Donne's poems is the extent to which they are taken up with arguments or attempts to persuade. Many of them are exercises in the use and abuse of logic. An astonishing example is 'The Flea', which consists of twenty-seven lines of witty, closely-knit argument on the signif-icance for two lovers of a flea-bite. It is an argument designed to prove that if the speaker's mistress kills the flea, she will be committing murder, suicide and sacrilege. In his love poems, the speaker argues constantly with the woman he is addressing, trying to persuade her to share a point of view. In his religious poems, the 'Holy Sonnets' for example, he cannot refrain from arguing with God, to whom he addresses some outrageously witty and paradoxical appeals, such as in 'Batter my heart':

> *That I may rise and stand, o'erthrow me, and bend*
> *Your force, to break, blow, burn, and make me new.*

Much of Donne's poetry is dramatic, dealing vividly and directly with actual or imaginary experiences, situations and attitudes. His arresting, often startling openings are one aspect of his dramatic manner, illustrated for example in 'The Sunne Rising' ('Busie old foole, unruly Sunne'). Other dramatic features are the reader's sense of a situation, a speaker and someone being spoken to. As we read Donne's love poems and many of the sonnets, we have, more distinctly than in the case of almost any other poet, the impression of a living voice speaking from the page to us. The rhythms of Donne's verse are closer to those of living, colloquial speech than to those of most lyrical poems. Many of his poems are like performances by an actor enormously enjoying his brilliant displays of showmanship and virtuosity. The dramatic gifts displayed in the poems make it easy to understand why he was regarded as the greatest preacher of his age.

Donne is consistently witty, even in his very serious poems. Wit, arguably the essential feature of all Metaphysical poetry, implies quickness of intellect, the ability to say brilliant or sparkling things — to surprise or delight by means of unexpected thoughts or expressions. Donne's wit finds an outlet in outrageous arguments, paradoxes, puns and, above all, conceits. A paradox is a statement that on the surface seems self-contradictory but which turns out, on closer examination, to have a valid meaning that goes beyond the bounds of common sense and logic. The sonnet 'Batter my heart' is built around a series of powerful paradoxes. A conceit is a comparison, often extended, between things that at first sight seem to have little or nothing in common. A famous example is the comparison between lovers and compasses in 'A Valediction: forbidding mourning'. Those who do not like Donne's conceits tend to describe the comparisons they involve as far-fetched. Those who admire them stress the ingenuity, boldness and originality of the best examples.

Donne greatly extended the scope and subject-matter of poetic imagery. He takes his images from a very wide range of subjects. The furniture of his love poems is not limited to the assortment of stock properties traditionally employed by love poets, such as gardens, balconies, nightingales and so on. His speakers stimulate (or puzzle) the minds of loved ones with an impressively daunting array of images drawn from learned sources. Some of his most famous conceits are theological, medical or scientific, or are drawn from geographical discovery and exploration, the law or medieval philosophy. They are deployed in a witty, knowing, subtle way as, for example, in the opening line of his sonnet on death and final judgement, where the reference to 'the round earths imagin'd corners' is a clever indication that the speaker is familiar with both the old and the new astronomy. In Donne, learned images are balanced by others which are homely and realistic, drawn from the routines of daily life.

Donne introduced a new tone into English love poetry. The Elizabethan love poet tended to idealise the beloved, presenting her as a paragon of beauty and virtue to be thought and spoken of with reverence. Donne's love poetry can be impudent and insolent, sceptical and mocking, cynical and flippant. It is seldom idealistic, tender or reverential. His speakers think of the women they address as people who can respond to witty arguments and who might enjoy elaborate fooling or outrageous paradoxes. Dryden must have spoken for many puzzled readers when he declared that Donne 'perplexes the minds of the fair sex with nice speculations of philosophy when he should engage their hearts, and entertain them with the softness of love'. This comment may simply indicate that Donne had a higher opinion of the intellectual capacities of women than Dryden did. It may also mean that these two great poets held widely differing views on the nature of love poetry.

THE SUNNE RISING

Busie old foole, unruly Sunne.
Why dost thou thus,
Through windowes, and through curtaines call on us?
Must to thy motions lovers seasons run?
Sawcy pedantique wretch, goe chide   5
Late schoole boyes and sowre prentices,
Goe tell Court-huntsmen, that the King will ride,
Call countrey ants to harvest offices;
Love, all alike, no season knowes, nor clyme,
Nor houres, dayes, moneths, which are the rags of time.   10

Thy beames, so reverend, and strong
Why shouldst thou thinke?
I could eclipse and cloud them with a winke,
But that I would not lose her sight so long:
If her eyes have not blinded thine,   15
Looke, and to morrow late, tell mee,
Whether both the'Indias's of spice and Myne
Be where thou leftst them, or lie here with mee.
Aske for those Kings whom thou saw'st yesterday,
And thou shalt heare, All here in one bed lay.   20

She'is all States, and all Princes, I,
Nothing else is.
Princes doe but play us; compar'd to this,
All honor's mimique; All wealth alchimie.
Thou sunne art halfe as happy'as wee,   25
In that the world's contracted thus;
Thine age askes ease, and since thy duties bee
To warme the world, that's done in warming us.
Shine here to us, and thou art every where;
This bed thy center is, these walls, thy spheare.   30

GLOSSARY

1 *Busie old foole*: foolish old busybody

unruly: unmannerly

4 *Must … run?* must lovers plan their lives according to the movements of the sun?

5 *Sawcy*: saucy, impertinent

pedantique: over-exact, insisting too much on rules and time-tables

6 *sowre prentices*: bad-humoured apprentices

7 *Goe … ride*: King James liked to go stag-hunting in the early morning; the sun is being asked to wake those courtiers who are anxious to flatter the King by joining him

8 *countrey ants*: hard-working farmers

harvest offices: the work of harvesting

9 *all alike*: the same at all times

no season … clyme: does not depend on varying seasons or climates

10 *rags of time*: human divisions of time

11–12 *Thy beames … thinke?*: why should you imagine that your beams are so impressive in their strength?

14 *But that … long*: the speaker does not want to lose sight of his mistress even for the length of a wink

17 *the'India's … Myne*: the East Indies were famous for spice, the West Indies for goldmines

18 *or lie here with mee*: Donne's witty way of saying that his mistress is as valuable as the spices and gold of the Indies

19–20 *those Kings … bed lay*: his mistress is as great and noble as all the Kings of the world

21 *She'is … I*: his mistress is every country, while he is King of every country

22 *Nothing else is*: the lovers are enough for each other; their world consists of nothing but themselves

24 *mimique*: mimic, a poor imitation

alchimie: alchemy (brass imitating gold), thus a mere pretence

25 *Thou … wee*: since the sun is single, it is only half as happy as the lovers, each of whom enjoys the happiness of the other

29–20 *Shine here … spheare*: for the lovers, the world has contracted to a single room. The speaker imagines the bed as the earth around which the sun must revolve, and the walls of the room mark the boundaries of its revolution.

GUIDELINES

This poem is open to a few differing interpretations. On the surface, it appears that the speaker has found complete happiness, fulfilment and self-sufficiency in his relationship with his mistress: they form their own world, a world so complete as to make everything else seem irrelevant and meaningless ('Nothing else is'). Those who read the poem in the light of Donne's biography, however, tend to see the speaker as less fulfilled than he is claiming to be. Donne was an extremely ambitious man, and would have enjoyed the life at the King's court that he dismisses with such contempt in the first stanza. He compensates for his absence from this kind of life by pretending that it is of no importance compared to the kingdom he has invented for himself and the woman he loves, in which each enjoys exclusive power over the other, and to which the sun itself is a servant.

QUESTIONS

1 Why do you think the whole poem is addressed to the sun?
2 How would you describe the speaker's attitude to the sun?
3 Explain the references to time in the poem.
4 Why does the speaker refer to his mistress as 'all States and all Princes'?
5 Consider the function of the imagery in the poem.

SONG: GOE AND CATCHE A FALLING STARRE

Goe, and catche a falling starre,
    Get with child a mandrake roote,
Tell me, where all past yeares are,
    Or who cleft the Divels foot,
Teach me to heare Mermaides singing,   5
    Or to keep off envies stinging,
        And finde
        What winde
Serves to advance an honest minde.

If thou beest borne to strange sights   10
    Things invisible to see,
Ride ten thousand daies and nights,
    Till age snow white haires on thee,
Thou, when thou retorn'st, wilt tell mee
All strange wonders that befell thee,   15
        And sweare
        No where
Lives a woman true, and faire.

If thou findst one, let mee know,
    Such a Pilgrimage were sweet;   20
Yet doe not, I would not goe,
    Though at next doore wee might meet,
Though shee were true, when you met her,
And last, till you write your letter,
        Yet shee   25
        Will bee
False, ere I come, to two, or three.

1–9 *Busie Goe … minde*: the speaker lists a number of impossible tasks

2 *Busie Get … root*: make a mandrake root pregnant. The mandrake, a plant with forked roots, was believed to have human qualities

4 *Busie Who cleft the Divels foot*: the devil was said to have a cloven hoof

12 *Busie Ride … nights*: this recalls the story of a squire who engaged in a three-year countrywide search for a chaste woman, and eventually found one: a plain countrywoman, whom he could not corrupt

18 *Busie Lives a woman true, and faire*: the most unlikely of all discoveries would be a woman who was faithful as well as beautiful

20 *Busie were*: would be

21 *Busie doe not*: do not tell me

23–7 *Busie Though … or three*: the pilgrim might find a beautiful woman who was faithful when he met her. However, by the time the speaker reached her in response to this news, she would have been unfaithful to two or three men.

GUIDELINES

The theme of this witty, extravagant poem is the infidelity of women, particularly beautiful women. It is, the argument of the poem goes, as hard to find a beautiful woman who is at the same time faithful and chaste as it is to perform traditionally impossible tasks.

QUESTIONS

1 Does the speaker really believe the argument he is advancing in this poem?
2 What is the mood of the poem: is the speaker being cynical, sad, pessimistic, lighthearted or satirical for example? Or can he be serious?
3 What does the poem tell you about the kind of person the speaker is?
4 What is the significance of the reference to 'a Pilgrimage' in line 20?
5 Contrast the ideas and attitudes of this poem with those of 'The Dreame', 'The Sunne Rising', 'The Anniversarie' and the other 'Song' ('Sweetest love I do not goe').

THE ANNIVERSARIE

All Kings, and all their favorites,
   All glory of honors, beauties, wits,
The Sun it selfe, which makes times, as they passe,
Is elder by a yeare, now, than it was
When thou and I first one another saw: 5
All things, to their destruction draw,
   Only our love hath no decay;
This, no to morrow hath, nor yesterday,
Running it never runs from us away,
But truly keepes his first, last, everlasting day.   10

   Two graves must hide thine and my coarse,
   If one might, death were no divorce.
Alas, as well as other Princes, wee,
(Who Prince enough in one another bee,)
Must leave at last in death, these eyes, and eares,   15
Oft fed with true oathes, and with sweet salt teares;
   But soules where nothing dwells but love
(All other thoughts being inmates) then shall prove
This, or a love increased there above,
When bodies to their graves, soules from their graves remove.   20

   And then wee shall be throughly blest,
   But wee no more, than all the rest;
Here upon earth, we'are Kings, and none but wee
Can be such Kings, nor of such subjects bee.
Who is so safe as wee? where none can doe   25
Treason to us, except one of us two.
   True and false feares let us refraine,
Let us love nobly, and live, and adde againe
Yeares and yeares unto yeares, till we attaine
To write threescore: this is the second of our raigne.   30

GLOSSARY

title this refers to the anniversary of the lovers' first meeting. See line 5

2 *all glory of honors*: all who enjoy honours

beauties, wits: all beautiful and clever people

3 *The Sun … passe*: the sun marks the passing of time as the great people of the world passe on their journey to eternity

6 *All other … draw*: all things move towards destruction except their love

10 *Keeps … day*: their love will always be as strong as it was in the beginning

11–12 *Two graves … divorce*: we will have to be buried in separate graves when we die. If we were permitted to share a single grave, our souls would not be allowed to leave our bodies, and death would not be able to separate our bodies from our souls as it should

11 *coarse*: corpse

12 *were*: would be

divorce: separation

13–14 *Alas … bee*: see 'The Sunne Rising', note on line 21

17 *dwells*: has its permanent home

18 *inmates*: lodgers (in contrast to permanent residents)

prove: experience

19 *This*: the love they now enjoy

above: in Heaven

21 *soules … remove*: when the lovers' souls leave their bodies

21 *throughly*: thoroughly, absolutely

22 *wee … rest*: the disadvantage of being in Heaven is that the lovers will be no happier there than any of its other inhabitants

24 *nor of such subjects bee*: nor can we be subjects of such Kings (as ourselves)

27 *refraine*: control, restrain

30 *threescore*: sixty

the second … raigne: the second anniversary of our reign (as Kings of each other).

GUIDELINES

This poem should be read in conjunction with 'The Sunne Rising', where similar ideas are expressed, and where kingship is also a controlling metaphor. 'The Anniversarie' is based on an extended conceit, a set of comparisons and contrasts between the lovers and two royal persons. Each is the exclusive territory of the other and each is governed exclusively by the other. The central theme is the absolute importance of love in the lives of the lovers. While everything else is doomed to decay, their love will endure, even beyond the grave.

QUESTIONS

1 In the first stanza, Donne creates a disturbing impression of the fate of earthly and heavenly things. How does he counteract this in the same stanza?

2 Consider the significance of the contrast between lines 3–4 and lines 9–10. What point is being made?

3 Is the speaker as confident in Stanza 2 as he was in Stanza 1?

4 Does the introduction of the lovers' deaths and their graves change the mood of the poem? If so, in what way?

5 What reservations does the speaker have about death? Consider especially the last stanza.

6 Is there a touch of self-deception in the poem — an attempt to present things as better than they really are?

7 Is there evidence in the poem that the speaker does not really believe what he says at the beginning: that the love he is celebrating is independent of time? Does his attitude to this change in the course of the poem?

SONG: SWEETEST LOVE, I DO NOT GOE

Sweetest love, I do not goe,
    For weariness of thee,
Nor in hope the world can show
    A fitter Love for mee;
      But since that I   5
Must dye at last, 'tis best,
To use my selfe in jest
    Thus by fain'd deaths to dye;

Yesternight the Sunne went hence,
    And yet is here to day,   10
He hath no desire nor sense,
    Nor halfe so short a way:
      Then feare not mee,
But beleeve that I shall make
Speedier journeyes, since I take   15
    More wings and spurres than hee.

O how feeble is mans power,
    That if good fortune fall,
Cannot adde another houre,
    Nor a lost houre recall!   20
      But come bad chance,
And wee joyne to'it our strength,
And wee teach it art and length,
    It selfe o'er us to'advance.

When thou sigh'st, thou sigh'st not winde,   25
    But sigh'st my soule away,
When thou weep'st, unkindly kinde,
    My lifes blood doth decay.
      It cannot bee
That thou lov'st mee, as thou say'st,   30
If in thine my life thou waste,
    That art the best of mee.

Let not thy divining heart
    Forethinke me any ill,
Destiny may take thy part,
    And may thy feares fulfill;
      But thinke that wee
Are but turn'd aside to sleepe;
They who one another keepe
    Alive, ne'r parted bee.   40

GLOSSARY

4 *fitter*: more suitable

7 *To use my selfe in jest*: to mock myself

8 *fain'd*: pretended

11 *Nor halfe so short a way*: the sun has a longer journey ('way') than the speaker and still returns within a day

13 *Then feare not mee*: don't worry about my return

21–4 *Come bad chance … advance*: if bad luck strikes us, we do all we can to extend its effects and to teach it clever and long drawn-out ways of casting us down

25–32 *When thou sigh'st … of mee*: the idea here is that the speaker and his mistress are so intimately connected that if she sighs or weeps, some of his substance wastes away. Thus, for her to sigh or weep suggests that she does not love him

33 *divining*: foreseeing, anticipating

34 *ill*: misfortune

35–6 *Destiny … fulfill*: if you anticipate misfortune for me, fate may well bring this about.

GUIDELINES

Superficially this is a witty poem about parting, but Donne uses the temporary departure of a lover from his beloved to make a serious point: such partings will help both of them to prepare for their inevitable final parting, which will come with death. Separation is a useful rehearsal for the ultimate separation of death, and if the girl can bear separation from him calmly and nobly, she will rise above the condition of being a slave to fate.

QUESTIONS

1 Can this poem fairly be classified as a love song?

2 Consider the nature of the advice the speaker gives the girl. How do you think she might respond?

3 Discuss the poem under the heading 'A Rehearsal for Death'.

4 Consider the role of fate in the poem.

5 Analyse the speaker's arguments. Are they convincing?

A VALEDICTION: FORBIDDING MOURNING

As virtuous men passe mildly away,
And whisper to their soules, to goe,
Whilst some of their sad friends doe say,
The breath goes now, and some say, no:

So let us melt, and make no noise,   5
No teare-floods, nor sigh-tempests move,
T'were prophanation of our joyes
To tell the layetie our love.

Moving of th'earth brings harmes and feares,
Men reckon what it did and meant,   10
But trepidation of the spheares,
Though greater farre, is innocent.

Dull sublunary lovers love
(Whose soule is sense) cannot admit
Absence, because it doth remove   15
Those things which elemented it.

But we by a love, so much refin'd,
That our selves know not what it is,
Inter-assured of the mind,
Care lesse, eyes, lips, and hands to misse.   20

Our two soules therefore, which are one,
Though I must goe, endure not yet
A breach, but an expansion,
Like gold to ayery thinnesse beate.

If they be two, they are two so   25
As stiffe twin compasses are two,
Thy soule the fixt foot, makes no show
To move, but doth, if the'other doe.

And though it in the center sit,
Yet when the other far doth rome,   30
It leanes, and hearkens after it,
And grows erect, as that comes home.

Such wilt thou be to mee, who must
Like th'other foot, obliquely runne;
Thy firmness makes my circle just   35
And makes me end, where I begunne.

GLOSSARY

1–2 *As virtuous … goe*: good people are happy to die, and do not struggle against death

5–6 *So let us … move*: let us part quietly, avoiding floods of tears and windy sighs

7–8 *'Twere … our love*: our love would be brought into disrepute if we were to tell people about it who were incapable of understanding it

8 *the layetie*: unlearned, ignorant people (lay people were traditionally contrasted with the more learned clergy)

9–12 *Moving … innocent*: relatively small movements of the earth, such as earthquakes, cause damage, and make people wonder how much damage has been caused and what it signifies. On the other hand, the far greater movements of the spheres circling the earth are relatively harmless

11 *trepidation*: trembling, agitation

spheares: in ancient astronomy, which Donne uses here for poetic purposes, the spheres were concentric hollow globes moving around the earth and making music as they moved

12 *innocent*: harmless

13–16 *Dull sublunary … elemented it*: common, everyday love, being primarily sensual, does not survive the absence of the loved one, because absence removes the physical properties it depends on

13 *sublunary*: earthly

16 *which elemented it*: on which it was founded

18 *our selves … it is*: Donne often suggests that true love cannot be defined in terms of any particular feature

24 *gold … beate*: gold was beaten out fine to make gold leaf. Absence will refine their love, making it achieve the highest spiritual quality. The more the gold is hammered, the thinner it gets, becoming almost as immaterial as souls and stretching out to span continents, thus keeping the lovers united

25 *they*: the souls of the lovers

26 *stiffe*: firm

twin compasses: dividers. These were common emblems of constancy in the midst of change

35 *firmness*: constancy

makes my circle just: makes me complete a true circle. The circle was an emblem of perfection and continuity.

GUIDELINES

This is a poem of parting. In 1611, Donne's patron, Sir Robert Drury, persuaded him to accompany him on a trip to Europe, one purpose of which was to enhance his skills as a diplomat and consequently his prospects of entering the diplomatic service. His wife was deeply troubled at the thought of his departure, and asked him not to go, but to no avail. According to Donne's first biographer, the poet marked his departure with this farewell poem, and left for Europe with Drury, Lady Drury, servants, hounds and hawks. To suit his purposes on this occasion, Donne argues that continuous bodily contact is not necessary for the maintenance of the bond of love between two people (see Stanza 5).

QUESTIONS

1 Donne expresses much of his meaning in this poem through the use of metaphors, drawn from a wide variety of human activities. Examine each of these metaphors in turn, showing how they contribute to his argument.

2 Donne's poems are notable for their many conceits (comparisons between things that at first sight appear to have little in common). One of these involves the lovers as compasses. Can this comparison be justified?

3 Donne was fond of reconciling opposites in his poetry: absence and presence, material and immaterial for example. Show how 'A Valediction: Forbidding Mourning' illustrates this impulse.

4 Does Donne supply convincing reasons for leaving his wife for an extended tour?

5 Many of Donne's poems are extended arguments. Analyse each of Donne's arguments in this poem.

6 In the early twentieth century, Donne was greatly admired for his originality of thought and language. How does this poem illustrate these qualities?

THE DREAME

Deare love, for nothing lesse than thee
Would I have broke this happy dreame,
    It was a theame
For reason, much too strong for phantasie,
Therefore thou wakd'st me wisely; yet   5
My Dreame thou brok'st not, but continued'st it,
Thou art so truth, that thoughts of thee suffice,
To make dreames truths; and fables histories;
Enter these armes, for since thou thoughtst it best,
Not to dreame all my dreame, let's act the rest   10

As lightning, or a Tapers light,
Thine eyes, and not thy noise wak'd mee;
    Yet I thought thee
(For thou lovest truth) an Angell, at first sight,
But when I saw thou sawest my heart,   15
And knew'st my thoughts, beyond an Angels art,
When thou knew'st what I dreamt, when thou knew'st when
Excesse of joy would wake me, and cam'st then,
I must confesse, it could not chuse but bee
Prophane, to thinke thee any thing but thee.   20

Coming and staying show'd thee, thee,
But rising makes me doubt, that now,
    Thou art not thou.
That love is weake, where feare's as strong as hee;
'Tis not all spirit, pure, and brave,   25
If mixture it of *Feare, Shame, Honor*, have,
Perchance as torches which must ready bee,
Men light and put out, so thou deal'st with mee,
Thou cam'st to kindle, goest to come; Then I
Will dreame that hope againe, but else would die.   30

GLOSSARY

1–2 *for nothing … dreame*: I would not have wanted this dream interrupted for anybody but you

4 *phanatasie*: fantasy, imagination

7 *so truth*: so completely and absolutely the truth

7–8 *that thoughts … histories*: the thought of you is enough to turn dreams into realities, and to turn fables into true history

9–10 *Enter … rest*: the dream has involved a love-scene between the speaker and his mistress. Now that he is awake, he asks her to make the events of the dream real

11 *a Tapers light*: the light of a candle

13–14 *Yet … an Angell*: an angel is associated with truth, and her devotion to truth causes him to identify her as an angel

14 *at first sight*: when I awoke from my dream

15–16 *When I saw … art*: an angel cannot read the human mind, but God can. When he realises that she can read his thoughts, he realises that she is more God than angel

20 *Prophane*: profane, unworthy

to thinke … thee: to think that you were anybody but yourself

21 *show'd thee, thee*: showed that you were yourself

22 *doubt*: suspect

24–26 *That love … have*: Donne is saying that if fear, shame or honour are present, true love is absent

25 *pure, and brave*: unmixed and sure of itself

27–8 *as torches … put out*: a torch that has already been used ignites more quickly than an unused one

29 *to kindle*: to arouse passion

goest to come: you go only to come back again

30 *will dream … die*: the 'hope' he will dream about is a renewal of his experience of love.

GUIDELINES

What Donne describes in this poem is a common theme of the love poetry of his time. The subject matter was inherited by Donne and his contemporaries from ancient classical poetry. The speaker dreams pleasantly and happily of the joys of love with his mistress. He wakes to find her at his bedside, and they proceed to enact what he has been dreaming about. In 'The Dreame', waking and sleeping life are not distinguished from each other with absolute clarity: the girl blends into the dream, not breaking it but continuing it.

QUESTIONS

1 'To make dreames truths' is a key phrase in the poem. What is its significance? What is the relationship in the poem between 'dreams' and 'truths' (or realities)?

2 What exactly is happening in this poem? Can its details be interpreted in more than one way?

3 Donne is fond of arguing even in his love poems. Discuss some of the arguments he advances in 'The Dreame'.

4 In what respects is 'The Dreame' not a straightforward love poem?

5 Do you find 'The Dreame' a happy poem?

6 Donne is celebrated as a witty poet. How does this poem illustrate the nature of his wit?

7 On the evidence in the poem, how would you say the speaker regards its main subject, the 'Deare love' of line 1?

8 Consider how the images of the poem help to convey its meanings.

THE FLEA

Marke but this flea, and marke in this,
How little that which thou deny'st me is;
It suck'd me first, and now sucks thee,
And in this flea, our two bloods mingled bee;
Thou know'st that this cannot be said   5
A sinne, nor shame, nor losse of maidenhead,
    Yet this enjoyes before it wooe,
    And pamper'd swells with one blood made of two,
    And this, alas, is more than wee would doe.

Oh stay, three lives in one flea spare,   10
Where wee almost, yea more than maryed are.
This flea is you and I, and this
Our mariage bed, and mariage temple is;
Though parents grudge, and you, w'are met,
And cloysterd in these living walls of Jet,   15
    Though use make you apt to kill mee,
    Let not to that, selfe murder added bee,
    And sacrilege, three sinnes in killing three.

Cruell and sodaine, hast thou since
Purpled thy naile, in blood of innocence?   20
Wherein could this flea guilty bee,
Except in that drop which it suckt from thee?
Yet thou triumph'st, and saist that thou
Find'st not thy selfe, nor mee the weaker now;
    'Tis true, then learne how false, feares bee;   25
    Just so much honor, when thou yeeld'st to mee,
    Will wast, as this flea's death tooke life from thee.

5 *said*: called

6 *maidenhead*: virginity

9 *more … doe*: they don't want a pregnancy

stay … spare: refrain from killing the flea, and so spare three lives all at once (the flea's, yours and mine). Since their 'two bloods' are mingled in the flea because it bit both of them, he imagines both their lives present in its body

11 *maryed*: married

15 *cloysterd … Jet*: lodged inside the walls of the flea's black body

16 *use*: habit

17–18 *Let not … three*: don't add suicide and sacrilege to murder. She will be guilty of sacrilege if, by killing the flea, she destroys the temple in which they were married

19 *sodaine*: sudden, impulsive

since: already

20 *Purpled thy naile*: she has crushed the flea to death with her nails

21 *Wherein*: in what way

25–7 *then learne … thee*: she will lose no more of her honour by yielding to him than the flea took from her when he sucked her blood.

GUIDELINES

Flea poems were very common in European Renaissance literature. They were generally indecent. Here Donne deflects attention from the woman's body and focuses instead on the body of the flea. By sucking the speaker's blood and then that of his mistress, the flea becomes a symbol of the union he desires with her. Donne displays extraordinary ingenuity and skill in his witty exploration in the implications of a fleabite.

QUESTIONS

1 Here the flea appears in a variety of guises. List these. How appropriate are they to Donne's theme?

2 What is Donne trying to achieve in the poem?

3 Discuss 'The Flea' as an example of Donne's astonishing ingenuity and verbal dexterity.

4 Is the flea the central character of this poem?

5 Outline the argument of the poem in your own words.

6 On the evidence of the poem, what kind of woman is Donne addressing?

BATTER MY HEART

Batter my heart, three person'd God; for, you
As yet but knocke, breathe, shine, and seeke to mend;
That I may rise, and stand, o'erthrow mee, and bend
Your force, to breake, blowe, burn and make me new.
I, like an usurpt towne, to'another due,   5
Labour to'admit you, but Oh, to no end,
Reason your viceroy in mee, mee should defend,
But is captiv'd, and proves weake or untrue.
Yet dearely'I love you, and would be loved faine,
But am betroth'd unto your enemie: 10
Divorce mee, untie, or breake that knot againe,
Take mee to you, imprison mee, for I
Except you enthrall mee, never shall be free,
Nor ever chast, except you ravish mee.

GLOSSARY

1 *three person'd God*: the God of the Trinity, Father, Son and Holy Ghost

5 *like … due*: the usurped town owes its loyalty to somebody other than the one who occupies it. The speaker is the town; he owes loyalty to God, but is in the possession of God's enemy, the devil

6 *to no end*: to no purpose, without success

7 *Reason … defend*: reason should be able to defend me from evil acts or impulses. A viceroy is a monarch's representative. Donne imagines reason representing God in the human mind to help in the struggle against evil

9 *would be loved faine*: would dearly wish to be loved

10 *bethroth'd*: married

your enemie: the devil

11 *Divorce … againe*: he is asking God to divorce him from the devil by untying or breaking the bond that unites him to evil

12 *enthrall*: enslave or make prisoner.

GUIDELINES

This is one of the nineteen *Holy Sonnets* which belong to a dark period of Donne's life, after the death of his wife had profoundly affected his outlook. The loss of his wife deprived him of love and security. In this and in other *Holy Sonnets*, he looks to God for an assurance of love, but is tormented by the fear that his past sins make him undeserving of either God's love or His forgiveness.

QUESTIONS

1 How does the speaker treat God in this poem? What kind of relationship does he imagine he has with Him?

2 The poem is densely metaphorical. Examine Donne's use of metaphor as an expression of meaning. Why are the metaphors more effective than literal expression might have been?

3 By line 9, the mood and tone of the poem, as well as the key metaphors, have begun to change. Comment on this change.

4 In the final four lines, Donne brings the conflicting images of the previous ten lines together (violence and love). Is this an effective way in which to end the poem?

5 Paradox is a key figure in 'Batter my heart'. Analyse its use. What does it achieve?

6 Would you agree that the sonnet reveals a troubled mind? What are the details that suggest this idea?

AT THE ROUND EARTH'S IMAGIN'D CORNERS

At the round earth's imagin'd corners, blow
Your trumpets, Angells, and arise, arise
From death, you numberlesse infinities
Of soules, and to your scattred bodies goe,
All whom the flood did, and fire shall o'erthrow,   5
All whom warre, dearth, age, agues, tyrannies,
Despaire, law, chance, hath slaine, and you whose eyes,
Shall behold God, and never tast deaths woe.
But let them sleepe, Lord, and mee mourne a space,
For, if above all these, my sinnes abound,   10
'Tis late to aske abundance of thy grace,
When wee are there; here on this lowly ground,
Teach mee how to repent; for that's as good
As if thou'hadst seal'd my pardon, with thy blood.

GLOSSARY

1 *imagin'd corners*: The Book of Revelations refers to 'the four corners of the earth'

2 *trumpets*: St Paul tells the Corinthians that angels will play trumpets to herald the resurrection of the dead

4 *scattred bodies*: the bodies of the dead scattered about the earth as dust and bones

soules … goe: the orthodox Christian teaching is that between death and the final resurrection of the dead, human souls exist in isolation from their bodies. Donne suggests here that the soul dies with the body, and that both will be resurrected on the last day

5 *the flood*: the Book of Genesis describes the destruction of almost the entire human race in a great flood

fire: the final destruction of the world will be through fire

6 *dearth*: famine

agues: fevers

7–8 *You, whose eyes … woe*: those who survive until the last day will not have to die. Donne would like to avoid rotting away in the grave until the last day, which is why he would like the last day to come while he is still alive (lines 1–4)

8 *never … woe*: a reference to the idea that those still living on the last day will not experience the pain of death

9–12 *But let them … there*: Donne is having second thoughts. He now realises that if he were to face the Last Judgement immediately, he might not be saved because of the great number of sins he has committed

11–12 *here … repent*: he asks God to show him how to repent of his sins while he is still on earth ('this lowly ground')

14 *As if … blood*: if he can repent, he can be sure of earning the pardon that Christ's death has won for humankind.

GUIDELINES

During much of his later life, Donne showed a deep interest in the fate of those who would be alive on the Last Day, and liked to imagine that he himself might be counted as one of them. If he were, he would be able to avoid what he dreaded most: the corruption of his body and its dissolution in the grave. In one of his sermons, he numbered himself among the fortunate mortals who, by living till the Last Day, would avoid having to die, or if they did die for a brief time, would not taste the corruption of the grave. He said: 'We shall die, and be alive again, before another could consider that we were dead'. This urgent desire to be alive on the Last Day explains why he asks in this sonnet that the Last Judgement should take place now (lines 1–4) rather than at some indefinite point in the future.

QUESTIONS

1 In what ways might this sonnet be regarded as an extremely self-centred poem?

2 In the course of the sonnet, the speaker experiences a change of mind. Identify this and try to account for it.

3 Describe the state of mind emerging from the sonnet. What is the speaker's primary emotion?

4 What is the speaker's attitude to death?

5 Consider the contrast between the first eight lines of the sonnet and the final six.

6 Donne refers to 'you whose eyes, / Shall behold God, and never tast deaths woe' (lines 7–8). Show how central these lines are to the meaning of the poem.

THOU HAST MADE ME

Thou hast made me, And shall thy worke decay?
Repaire me now, for now mine end doth haste,
I runne to death, and death meets me as fast,
And all my pleasures are like yesterday;
I dare not move my dimme eyes any way,   5
Despaire behind, and death before doth cast
Such terrour, and my feebled flesh doth waste
By sinne in it, which it t'wards hell doth weigh;
Onely thou art above, and when towards thee
By thy leave I can looke, I rise againe;   10
But our old subtle foe so tempteth me,
That not one houre my selfe I can sustaine;
Thy Grace may wing me to prevent his art,
And thou like Adamant draw mine iron heart.

GLOSSARY

1 *now mine end doth haste*: my death approaches fast

5 *dimme eyes*: his eyes have been dimmed by age

8 *which … weigh*: the weight of his sins drags him towards hell

11 *our … tempteth me*: the old cunning enemy, the devil, tempts him to despair in his hour of distress

12 *not one … sustaine*: the poet cannot sustain himself for even an hour against the temptations of Satan

13 *may … art*: God's grace may draw him upwards towards Him and so frustrate the devil's tricks

like Adamant … heart: God may turn Himself into a magnet to draw the speaker's iron heart to Him. The iron heart is a hard heart, unresponsive to God.

GUIDELINES

Here the speaker is in a state of spiritual terror, looking anxiously to God to save him from despair as the devil, the clever old enemy of humankind, tempts him severely to lose hope. He is sure that God *can* save him from his despair, but not so sure that He will. Behind his despair, and feeding it, is the speaker's fear of imminent death, and the danger that he will be damned for his past sins.

QUESTIONS

1 The sonnet reveals the speaker as a helpless dependent creature. In what ways is this dependency suggested?
2 What are the speaker's main fears? Are these justified?
3 What image of God emerges from the sonnet? Is the God imagined by the speaker benevolent, punitive, to be loved or to be feared, the friend or the enemy of sinners?
4 How would you describe the mood of the poem?
5 Are the speaker's problems solved at the end?

GENERAL QUESTIONS ON JOHN DONNE

1 Donne's poems are filled with mixed emotions, ranging from playful irreverence and cynicism to profound reverence and sincerity. Examine the variety of moods displayed.

2 Examine the notion that Donne is a very original love poet.

3 What kind of audience do you think Donne addressed his poems to?

4 Consider the propositions that Donne's love poems are composed exclusively from the viewpoint of the man, and that whatever the woman does is in response to him — to his urging, pleading, arguing, bullying, weeping.

5 Discuss Donne as a witty, learned, argumentative poet.

6 Explore the idea that Donne's religious poetry reveals an insecure temperament and a profound sense of fear.

7 Much of Donne's poetry, whether secular or religious, is dominated by the need to convince whoever is being addressed. Examine this aspect of the poems.

8 Discuss Donne's treatment of death.

9 Consider some unusual and distinctive aspects of Donne's use of imagery.

10 Donne's poetry is sometimes remarkable for its witty misuse of logical arguments in support of absurd conclusions. Explore this idea.

EXAMINATION-STYLE QUESTIONS

11 Outline and discuss some features of Donne's poems which make them difficult to understand. You might refer, for example, to his learned references, his comparisons and his use of obscure sources.

12 What appeal do you think Donne's poems might have for a young, modern reader?

Poems remarkable for their
witty paradoxes.

Blends wit with
seriousness.

Critics have found Donne
difficult and over-elaborate.

Obsessed with
death.

Uses startling
effects.

Ability to surprise.

Love poems are
extremely learned.

Love poems are
often insolent, mocking
and cynical rather than
tender or adoring.

John Donne

Poetry reveals
Donne's knowledge of
science, medicine,
astronomy, geography
and theology.

Deeply interested
in religion.

Fond of logical
argument.

Balances reason
with emotion.

Imagery drawn from everyday
life, as well as from books.

ROBERT
FROST

1874–1963

BIOGRAPHY

Robert Frost was born in San Francisco in 1874. At the age of eleven, following the death of his father, Frost moved with his family to New England. He attended Dartmouth College but failed to finish his undergraduate course, taking a job at a mill instead. He started to study again in 1897 at Harvard University, but left without taking a degree. He tried shoemaking, teaching, editing a local paper and then farming. In 1895 he married Elinor White, to whom he was married for forty-three years. They had six children, one of whom died in infancy. For a number of years the family lived on a farm which Frost had inherited from his grandfather. He also supplemented his income by teaching, which he enjoyed. However in 1911 Frost sold the farm and moved to England, where he hoped to find literary success.

His first book of poems, *A Boy's Will*, was published in England in 1913. His originality was recognised by leading poet and fellow American Ezra Pound, who praised Frost for having 'the good sense to speak naturally and to paint the thing, the thing as he sees it'. W. B. Yeats, too, called the volume 'the best poetry written in America for a long time'.

Frost now began to enjoy the friendship and acceptance of the English literary society of the time. His second collection, *North of Boston* (1914), received excellent reviews.

Having returned to America in 1915, Frost and his family settled on a farm in New Hampshire. The life of a farmer appealed to him. His experience of rural life is reflected in his third collection, *Mountain Interval* (1916), in which several of his most famous lyrics appear.

His life now combined farming, family life, writing and lecturing. This was very much the pattern that would continue for the rest of his life. He was a gifted speaker, with his mixture of homespun Yankee wisdom, poetic insights and sense of humour. Invitations to speak and read his poems around the country poured in. The collection *New Hampshire* (1923) consolidated his already formidable reputation, and in 1924 he was awarded the first of four Pulitzer Prizes for Poetry which he won during his lifetime, a record number for any poet. *West-Running Brook* (1928) was followed by the *Collected Poems* in 1931. In the same year he was elected to the American Academy of Arts and Letters. Many honorary degrees and public awards followed. His other published collections were *A Further Range* (1936), *A Witness Tree* (1942), *Steeple Bush* (1947) and his last collection, *In the Clearing* (1962).

Frost's public success was not mirrored by his personal life. He himself suffered from depression. One of his daughters died at the age of twenty-nine. His wife Elinor died in 1938. His only son committed suicide in 1940. Although Frost does not refer directly to these events, it may be that the trauma of these experiences is reflected in the occasional darkness of his poems.

Robert Frost died in 1963 at the age of 89.

SOCIAL AND CULTURAL CONTEXT

Although he was a contemporary of many of the great Modernist poets of the twentieth century, such as T. S. Eliot, Ezra Pound and Wallace Stevens, Robert Frost's work differs from theirs in certain important respects. Poets of the Modernist movement were influenced by the great developments in human thought in philosophy and science that had taken place at the end of the nineteenth century, notably the work of Sigmund Freud in psychoanalysis and Charles Darwin in science. The experience of the First World War, too, altered social attitudes and structures. It no longer seemed artistically credible to write poems in the traditional metres and forms. Indeed, the central tenet of the Modernist movement, articulated by Ezra Pound, was 'make it new'.

For a time Frost was part of the literary circle in London which included Ezra Pound. However, his poetic practice was not unduly influenced by ideas current at the time. His own career took a different path. Much of the work of Modernist poets was so experimental that it could be obscure, resulting in small sales for their books. Frost, on the other hand, set out to be understood.

From the beginning, he was a traditionalist in form and metre. He avoided writing in free verse. The settings of his poems are for the most part rural, whereas the Modernists saw themselves as the poets of the metropolis. Their works allude constantly to classical literature, while Frost's poems were praised for their accessibility. He was nonetheless a learned man who wished to develop his art in an independent and ambitious way. Early in his career he had a self-confident sense of purpose. As he wrote to a friend, John Bartlett: 'To be perfectly frank with you I am one of the most notable craftsmen of my time. That will transpire presently.'

He developed a sophisticated theory of poetic language which he called the 'sound of sense'. By this he meant that language in poetry should reproduce the exact tone of meaning in human speech. He recognised that his theory was not altogether original as the Romantic poets had put forward the idea that literary language should be as close as possible to 'the language of men' as far back as the late eighteenth century. But by the end of the nineteenth century, the diction of poetry had ceased to have common currency, and Frost, like Modernist poets also, searched for a new idiom in which to write.

The story of Frost's subsequent career as a poet is interesting in the light it throws upon cultural attitudes in America. His success can be partly explained by the way he deliberately built up a public persona of himself as a typical Yankee – a plain man living in rural New England, a man for whom the hard work of farming was a real inspiration. Biographers and critics have discussed the extent to which this persona was real or invented. They point out that he was a distinguished teacher and intellectual. Nor are his poems the simple 'nature' poems that they seem to be on the surface. As he said himself: 'I'm not a nature poet. There's always something else in my poetry.' But he continued to play a role that appealed to the public as an essentially American poet rooted in rural values. The Caribbean poet, Derek Walcott describes him: 'Robert Frost: the icon of Yankee values, the smell of wood-smoke, the sparkle of dew, the reality of farm-house dung, the jocular honesty of an uncle'.

Social historians point out that in the twentieth century, the American way of life became increasingly urbanised and remote from the rustic idylls Frost's poems seem to depict. It may be that nostalgia played a part in the public acclaim of Robert Frost. Certainly in social and cultural terms he had a prominent role in American public life. During the Second World War, 50,000 copies of one of his poems were distributed to US troops stationed overseas to boost morale. Honours and awards were heaped upon him during the course of his long life. His standing in American society can be seen clearly by his participation in president John F. Kennedy's Inauguration in 1961, while in 1962 he was asked to visit Russia on a goodwill mission for the US Department of State.

His place in the canon of American literature is assured both as a poet who influenced the course of the lyric poem as written by American poets, and as a best-selling poet whose work is part of the cultural birthright of the American people.

THE TUFT OF FLOWERS

I went to turn the grass once after one
Who mowed it in the dew before the sun.

The dew was gone that made his blade so keen
Before I came to view the leveled scene.

I looked for him behind an isle of trees;   5
I listened for his whetstone on the breeze.

But he had gone his way, the grass all mown,
And I must be, as he had been—alone,

"As all must be," I said within my heart,
"Whether they work together or apart."   10

But as I said it, swift there passed me by
On noiseless wing a bewildered butterfly,

Seeking with memories grown dim o'er night
Some resting flower of yesterday's delight.

And once I marked his flight go round and round,   15
As where some flower lay withering on the ground.

And then he flew as far as eye could see,
And then on tremulous wing came back to me.

I thought of questions that have no reply,
And would have turned to toss the grass to dry;   20

But he turned first, and led my eye to look
At a tall tuft of flowers beside a brook,

A leaping tongue of bloom the scythe had spared
Beside a reedy brook the scythe had bared.

The mower in the dew had loved them thus,   25
By leaving them to flourish, not for us,

Nor yet to draw one thought of ours to him,
But from sheer morning gladness at the brim.

The butterfly and I had lit upon,
Nevertheless, a message from the dawn,   30

That made me hear the wakening birds around,
And hear his long scythe whispering to the ground,

And feel a spirit kindred to my own;
So that henceforth I worked no more alone;

But glad with him, I worked as with his aid,   35
And weary, sought at noon with him the shade;

And dreaming, as it were, held brotherly speech
With one whose thought I had not hoped to reach.

"Men work together," I told him from the heart,
"Whether they work together or apart."   40

GLOSSARY

1 *to turn the grass*: to turn the grass over so that it will dry
3 *keen*: sharp-edged
6 *whetstone*: stone used for sharpening tools
18 *tremulous*: quivering
23 *scythe*: a long curving sharp-edged blade for mowing grass

GUIDELINES

'The Tuft of Flowers' is from Robert Frost's first collection of poems, *A Boy's Will*, published in England in 1913 when he was thirty-nine years old. These are the poems that made him famous. The collection of poems was praised by reviewers, among them Ezra Pound, for their 'simplicity', but, as Frost himself remarked, 'if they are (simple) they are subtle too'.

The original gloss on the poem, provided by Frost himself in the table of contents, said that the poem was 'about fellowship'. Nature is seen to teach the poet an important lesson about human beings and their relationships with one another. The poem is in a long tradition of nature poems that see nature not only as a source of delight, but also as containing lessons that can be learned, as if nature is a text that can be read in many ways. Nature, it was suggested, can illumine human feelings and situations.

Frost takes a simple situation – the speaker goes out to turn the grass after it has been mown earlier – and from there he allows natural images to create atmosphere and symbolise human experience.

The bleakness of the scene at first is linked with the human speaker's feelings of isolation and dejection. The butterfly is personified as a creature whose role it is to lead the speaker to the flowers and thus to 'teach' him the social lesson of the poem. The image of the butterfly seems to arise naturally from the poem's setting, but it belongs also to the literary tradition of the fable in which a helpful creature points a human being in the right direction. (Butterflies had from the time of the Greeks been associated with Psyche, or the soul.) Other objects are personified, such as the flowers as messengers, for instance, so that the speaker's interpretation of the scene leads to the lesson of the final couplet, which contradicts the earlier, bleaker view of human life.

'The Tuft of Flowers' illustrates some of Frost's characteristic poetic methods in his nature lyrics. There is the figure of the speaker-poet at his solitary labour. There are the observations and loving descriptions of real situations and natural phenomena. There is also the movement from description to its metaphorical or symbolic significance, clearly indicated in this poem.

VIEWPOINTS

One of Frost's critics and biographers, William Pritchard, has suggested that this 'movement from the level of sense to spirit', as he put it, 'from the very beginning … lay at the heart of Frost's enterprise as a poet'.

Another critic, George F. Bagby, has suggested that we can read 'The Tuft of Flowers' as an allegory of Frost's vocation as a poet. He sees the poem as describing the situation of the modern poet who must find his own way of writing poems, a lonely enterprise. As the speaker finds the flowers, so the poet is asserting his realisation that he is not alone, but writing in a continuous tradition of poetry. At a public reading of his poems in 1957, Frost himself said that the poem was 'against the idea that you write poetry just to show yourself off', which would support Bagby's claim that the poem is about artistic creation.

It is up to the reader to decide whether these views are helpful or not.

QUESTIONS

1 On what evidence does the speaker base his first conclusion that all people must be alone, 'Whether they work together or apart'?

2 How is the butterfly described in the poem? What purpose is it seen to have?

3 What realisation does the speaker come to when he sees the tuft of flowers? Does it alter his attitude to the scene he has earlier described? Look carefully at the language used in this part of the poem.

4 Is this a dramatic poem? Explain your answer.

5 Comment on Frost's use of language in this poem, including the poetic techniques he uses.

6 How would you describe the attitude to nature implicit in 'The Tuft of Flowers'?

7 What do you think of the view that the poem is a metaphorical description of the act of writing poetry, as suggested in the guidelines?

8 Do you like poems that contain a 'message', as this one does?

9 If you were to include the poem in a talk entitled 'Introducing Robert Frost', what points would you make about it?

MENDING WALL

Something there is that doesn't love a wall,
That sends the frozen-ground-swell under it
And spills the upper boulders in the sun,
And makes gaps even two can pass abreast.
The work of hunters is another thing: 5
I have come after them and made repair
Where they have left not one stone on a stone,
But they would have the rabbit out of hiding,
To please the yelping dogs. The gaps I mean,
No one has seen them made or heard them made,   10
But at spring mending-time we find them there.
I let my neighbor know beyond the hill;
And on a day we meet to walk the line
And set the wall between us once again.
We keep the wall between us as we go.   15
To each the boulders that have fallen to each.
And some are loaves and some so nearly balls
We have to use a spell to make them balance:
"Stay where you are until our backs are turned!"
We wear our fingers rough with handling them.   20
Oh, just another kind of outdoor game,
One on a side. It comes to little more:
There where it is we do not need the wall:
He is all pine and I am apple orchard.
My apple trees will never get across   25
And eat the cones under his pines, I tell him.
He only says, "Good fences make good neighbors."
Spring is the mischief in me, and I wonder
If I could put a notion in his head:
"*Why* do they make good neighbors? Isn't it   30
Where there are cows? But here there are no cows.
Before I built a wall I'd ask to know
What I was walling in or walling out,
And to whom I was like to give offense.

Something there is that doesn't love a wall,   35
That wants it down." I could say "Elves" to him,
But it's not elves exactly, and I'd rather
He said it for himself. I see him there,
Bringing a stone grasped firmly by the top
In each hand, like an old-stone savage armed.   40
He moves in darkness as it seems to me,
Not of woods only and the shade of trees.
He will not go behind his father's saying,
And he likes having thought of it so well
He says again, "Good fences make good neighbors."   45

GUIDELINES

'Mending Wall' is from *North of Boston* (1914). It is one of Robert Frost's most famous poems as it established him as an authentic rural poet, familiar with the ways of farming and with the rugged landscape of New England.

Like 'The Tuft of Flowers', the poem shows a commitment to the idea of community spirit and friendship. Frost himself said in an interview that 'it contrasts two types of people'.

The two farmers mending the wall between their lands seem also to be erecting human barriers between themselves. At first they are seen to agree about the necessity of the wall. But a certain amount of tension appears as the narrator allows another point of view to surface. The wall seems to take on a life of its own, influenced perhaps by the 'something' that doesn't want it built in the first place. There are hints of elemental, even supernatural, energies that seem to comment unfavourably on human attitudes, especially those of the unresponsive neighbour. His unthinking repetition of his father's saying hints at an inability to move beyond what has always been thought and said. The rather depressing implication is that the human desire for co-operation (a theme also in 'The Tuft of Flowers') is often thwarted by people themselves.

We know from his biographers that Frost sometimes felt alienated from other people. In the sonnet 'Acquainted with the Night', he expresses these feelings vividly. In one of his prose essays, too, he wrote about the 'fear of Man – the fear that men won't understand us and we shall be cut off from them'. 'Mending Wall', in its contrasting imagery of the fantastic and the real and its theme of human separation, hints at such fears.

The poem took on a wider political significance, as a comment on East–West relations, when Robert Frost recited it to Nikita Kruschev, the leader of Russia, on a visit to the USSR in 1962. The symbolism of the 'wall' was immediately obvious.

In 'Mending Wall' we can see Frost's theory of the 'sound of sense' in the language of poetry. He believed that poems should be able to reproduce the exact tone and nuance of meaning of human speech. He defined it as 'the living part of a poem … intonation entangled somehow in the syntax, idiom and meaning of a sentence'. In this poem the effect is of someone conversing with himself, thinking aloud as it were. But it is important to note too that although the poem sounds deceptively casual, Frost uses the strict poetic metre of iambic pentameter with five main stresses within the line, although the poem does not rhyme. Frost famously said once that, for him, writing poems in so-called 'free' verse' would be 'like playing tennis with the net down'.

QUESTIONS

1 'Something there is that doesn't love a wall.' How does the poet develop this opening statement?

2 What significance can you see in the manner in which the speaker and his neighbour mend the wall? Why do you think the poet describes it in such detail?

3 What difference of opinion exists between Frost and his neighbour about the wall? Is Frost convinced by the neighbour's quotation of the proverb, for instance?

4 What impression of the poet's neighbour do we get from reading the poem? Where especially is this impression created?

5 What emotions does the poet seem to feel in this poem?

6 Would you agree that the ideas of destroying and creating are found simultaneously in the poem? Does the poem explore any other apparently contradictory ideas? Explain your view.

7 How would you describe the language used by Frost in this poem? Look in particular at the conversational effects he uses.

8 Is the saying 'Good fences make good neighbors' true, in your experience?

9 Do you find this poem realistic, depressing, enjoyable? Perhaps you would suggest another term?

10 Do you think Frost paints an interesting picture of rural life in the poem?

AFTER APPLE-PICKING

My long two-pointed ladder's sticking through a tree
Toward heaven still,
And there's a barrel that I didn't fill
Beside it, and there may be two or three
Apples I didn't pick upon some bough.   5
But I am done with apple-picking now.
Essence of winter sleep is on the night,
The scent of apples: I am drowsing off.
I cannot rub the strangeness from my sight
I got from looking through a pane of glass   10
I skimmed this morning from the drinking trough
And held against the world of hoary grass.
It melted, and I let it fall and break.
But I was well
Upon my way to sleep before it fell,   15
And I could tell
What form my dreaming was about to take.
Magnified apples appear and disappear,
Stem end and blossom end,
And every fleck of russet showing clear.   20
My instep arch not only keeps the ache,
It keeps the pressure of a ladder-round.
I feel the ladder sway as the boughs bend,
And I keep hearing from the cellar bin
The rumbling sound   25
Of load on load of apples coming in.
For I have had too much
Of apple-picking: I am overtired
Of the great harvest I myself desired.
There were ten thousand thousand fruit to touch,   30
Cherish in hand, lift down, and not let fall.

For all
That struck the earth,
No matter if not bruised or spiked with stubble,
Went surely to the cider-apple heap   35
As of no worth.
One can see what will trouble
This sleep of mine, whatever sleep it is.
Were he not gone,
The woodchuck could say whether it's like his   40
Long sleep, as I describe its coming on,
Or just some human sleep.

GLOSSARY

7 *Essence*: scent

12 *hoary*: white or greyish-white frost

20 *russet*: a reddish-brown colour

40 *woodchuck*: a North American species of marmot or burrowing rodent.
It hibernates during the winter

GUIDELINES

'After Apple-Picking' is from Robert Frost's second published book of poems, *North of Boston* (1914). Along with 'Mending Wall' and 'Birches' it was written in the autumn of 1913, while Frost and his family lived at Beaconsfield in England. The setting and imagery is undoubtedly that of the farm in New Hampshire, New England (the 'North of Boston' of the title of the collection) that Frost had temporarily left behind.

The poem evokes beautifully and lyrically the abundant apple-harvest of a New England farm. The long day's labour is over, even though the speaker may feel that he hasn't entirely finished it. He is drowsy and prepares for sleep. This gives a dream-like quality to his reveries as the poem proceeds, and leads to the central metaphors of the poem – sleep and dreaming. Images of what he has experienced during his day's work enter his mind. Reality and dream begin to merge, signalled by the image of the ice on the drinking trough as a looking glass which has transformed his way of looking at the world. Now the apples are 'magnified'. Time is confused, as in a dream. Sensuous images recreate the experience of apple-picking. There was joy in the work, as well as weariness and anxiety. The speaker has felt troubled by the loss of some of the apple harvest, perhaps even to the extent that it will affect the sleep he knows is coming on. This last image, of 'human sleep', is open to a number of interpretations.

The persona adopted in the poem is that of the farmer engaged in his hard physical toil. We know from the facts of Frost's life that farming was important to him, but we cannot ignore the fact also that he had ambitions to be a great poet. 'After Apple-Picking' may be concerned with the apple harvest, but it is also concerned with what is happening in the apple-harvester's mind as it moves back and forth over his experiences. There is a contrast between the conversational voice of the practical farmer and the more poetic images and metaphors that suggest imaginative concerns beyond those of an ordinary farmer.

QUESTIONS

1 Explore the sensuousness of the images in the poem.
2 Would you agree that there is a contrast between the poetic and the real in the language of the poem? Examine the language with this in mind.
3 How does Frost convey the dreamlike atmosphere of the poem?
4 A metaphorical reading of the poem has been suggested in the guidelines above. Do you find it helpful, or would you prefer to see the poem as a purely descriptive nature poem? Perhaps you might suggest another approach to the poem?
5 What significance does the woodchuck have in the poem, in your opinion?
6 How do you respond to the poem?
7 If you were asked to choose your three favourite poems of Robert Frost, would you include this one among them?

THE ROAD NOT TAKEN

Two roads diverged in a yellow wood,
And sorry I could not travel both
And be one traveler, long I stood
And looked down one as far as I could
To where it bent in the undergrowth;   5

Then took the other, as just as fair,
And having perhaps the better claim,
Because it was grassy and wanted wear;
Though as for that, the passing there
Had worn them really about the same,   10

And both that morning equally lay
In leaves no step had trodden black.
Oh, I kept the first for another day!
Yet knowing how way leads on to way,
I doubted if I should ever come back.   15

I shall be telling this with a sigh
Somewhere ages and ages hence:
Two roads diverged in a wood, and I—
I took the one less traveled by,
And that has made all the difference.   20

GUIDELINES

'The Road Not Taken' is from *Mountain Interval* (1916). It is said to have been inspired by Frost's friend, the poet Edward Thomas, whom he had met in England and who was subsequently killed in the First World War. Thomas was apparently in the habit of expressing regret at whatever decision he had taken.

The poem dramatises the choices we are presented with in life and their consequences. The poet uses the metaphor of two roads, one of which he had to take. He then reflects on the choice he made. Not only does he review the reasons for his decision, such as they were, but he visualises himself examining it at some time in the future.

The poem is one of Robert Frost's most popular and often-quoted poems, no doubt because it deals with a universal theme. A number of interpretations have been put forward. Is the poem concerned with choice of career in life? (We may remember that Robert Frost himself left his life as a farmer in New England to develop his gifts as a poet.) Or does the poem hint at a moral struggle that has to be confronted, in which the least popular and most difficult option is chosen? And how do we interpret the last lines of the poem?

The setting of the poem is extremely attractive, with the 'yellow wood' evoking the famous New England fall. As in many of Frost's poems, images of nature are described not merely for their own sake, but to suggest an analogy with human concerns.

QUESTIONS

1 How are the 'two roads' presented, as they appeared to the speaker?
2 Can you trace the speaker's train of thought as he makes his decision?
3 Do you think the speaker is happy with his decision? How can we tell from the tone of the poem? Look especially at the last stanza.
4 Can you speculate about the choices in Frost's life (or anyone else's) that may be symbolised in this poem?
5 What do you think the poet means by the final line: 'And that has made all the difference'?
6 Can you understand why this is a well-loved poem in America and elsewhere?

BIRCHES

When I see birches bend to left and right
Across the lines of straighter darker trees,
I like to think some boy's been swinging them.
But swinging doesn't bend them down to stay
As ice storms do. Often you must have seen them   5
Loaded with ice a sunny winter morning
After a rain. They click upon themselves
As the breeze rises, and turn many-colored
As the stir cracks and crazes their enamel.
Soon the sun's warmth makes them shed crystal shells   10
Shattering and avalanching on the snow crust—
Such heaps of broken glass to sweep away
You'd think the inner dome of heaven had fallen.
They are dragged to the withered bracken by the load,
And they seem not to break; though once they are bowed   15
So low for long, they never right themselves:
You may see their trunks arching in the woods
Years afterwards, trailing their leaves on the ground
Like girls on hands and knees that throw their hair
Before them over their heads to dry in the sun.   20
But I was going to say when Truth broke in
With all her matter of fact about the ice storm,
I should prefer to have some boy bend them
As he went out and in to fetch the cows—
Some boy too far from town to learn baseball,   25
Whose only play was what he found himself,
Summer or winter, and could play alone.
One by one he subdued his father's trees
By riding them down over and over again
Until he took the stiffness out of them,   30
And not one but hung limp, not one was left
For him to conquer. He learned all there was
To learn about not launching out too soon
And so not carrying the tree away

Clear to the ground. He always kept his poise 35
To the top branches, climbing carefully
With the same pains you use to fill a cup
Up to the brim, and even above the brim.
Then he flung outward, feet first, with a swish,
Kicking his way down through the air to the ground. 40
So was I once myself a swinger of birches.
And so I dream of going back to be.
It's when I'm weary of considerations,
And life is too much like a pathless wood
Where your face burns and tickles with the cobwebs 45
Broken across it, and one eye is weeping
From a twig's having lashed across it open.
I'd like to get away from earth awhile
And then come back to it and begin over.
May no fate willfully misunderstand me 50
And half grant what I wish and snatch me away
Not to return. Earth's the right place for love:
I don't know where it's likely to go better.
I'd like to go by climbing a birch tree,
And climb black branches up a snow-white trunk 55
Toward heaven, till the tree could bear no more,
But dipped its top and set me down again.
That would be good both going and coming back.
One could do worse than be a swinger of birches.

GLOSSARY

9 *crazes their enamel*: makes small cracks in the hard ice-coated birches

GUIDELINES

'Birches' is found in *Mountain Interval* (1916). One of Frost's most famous nature poems, it is set in New England. It is based on the children's game of swinging birches, which involves climbing birch trees until your weight brings the trunk plunging down to earth. As a child, Frost enjoyed doing this at his uncle's farm in New Hampshire. As is the usual pattern in a Frost poem, however, the act of swinging birches takes on a metaphorical significance.

The poem begins with a deceptively simple comment. When he sees birches with their boughs bent, the speaker says he likes to 'think some boy's been swinging them'. At once we are introduced to the idea both of nature and the boy who delights in it. Frost concentrates for the moment on the trees themselves, describing them after the ice-storm. He takes care to be as precise as possible, but at the same time uses highly imaginative language, images that appeal to our senses, and sound effects as well as metaphors and similes. Ironically, Frost comments on this description as 'Truth' with 'all her matter of fact'. In contrast, the boy who swings birches is depicted in ordinary everyday terms. (Nonetheless, he is a creature of Frost's imagination.)

The actual swinging of the birches is described in detail and with great care. And the lessons the poet learns can be applied to life situations. Images of conquest suggest determination. Climbing carefully to the top, and not 'launching out too soon' teaches the values of control and the joy of achievement, ending with the tremendous happiness of landing successfully on the ground.

The image of filling a cup 'Up to the brim, and even above the brim', which requires that you take considerable pains, seems to suggest a desire to reach beyond what is possible. Placed side by side with images of joyful freedom, it could be said to crystallise in a metaphorical way the two contrasting ideas mentioned earlier – those of fact and 'truth', and the imaginative expression of those facts, which is poetry itself. Poetry may begin with natural fact, but it soon learns to transcend the limitations of fact, and delight in so doing.

The speaker invites us to connect further the action of swinging birches with the writing of poems in the last section of the poem. Both offer a dream of escape from the harshness of reality. Opposing ideas of going and return reflect the tension in the poem between escaping into the world of the imagination and returning to the world of reality. Climbing a birch tree as he used to do, suggests the speaker, would be like going 'toward heaven', a movement of aspiration towards the spiritual world of the imagination, but not a complete departure from reality ('earth'). The line that could be said to comment on the entire process is: 'That would be good both going and coming back' (line 58). The words are simple, but as in many of Frost's poems there is an underlying complexity in the thought. It is as if the speaker-poet is affirming both strands of poetic endeavour, namely the engagement with the facts of the natural world and the point of departure these facts offer the poetic imagination. So the last line earns its aphoristic wisdom: 'One could do worse than be a swinger of birches'.

QUESTIONS

1 Would you agree that the language of the poem echoes the rhythms of the spoken voice? You might look at the use of colloquialisms, the pauses within the lines (caesuras) and the impression created of someone thinking aloud in a rambling way, addressing an imaginary companion. Does the poet succeed in 'Birches' in what he set out to do in his poetry, namely to echo 'the sound of sense'?

2 You might now explore the poem in terms of what may be called its 'poetic' qualities.

3 Look at the sensuousness of the images in which the birch branches and the experience of swinging birches is described, the similes and metaphors employed by the poet and the use of blank verse with its traditional iambic pentameters. Is it possible to relate these contrasting aspects of the poem to its main theme? (Refer back to previous question.)

4 In what way does the swinging of birches take on a metaphorical significance? Where in the poem does this occur? What is the first lesson a boy learns from swinging birches, for example?

5 Does the poem invite a number of further metaphorical readings as it progresses? For instance, you could take into account especially the lines where the poet refers to himself: 'So was I once myself a swinger of birches. / And so I dream of going back to be'. What might this aspiration suggest about the work of a poet?

6 Would you agree that the poem enacts the desire to escape, to move beyond the here and now of the real world to the world of the imagination? In what lines is this most evident?

7 Does the poet find this world of the imagination ultimately satisfying, or does he express reservations about it? Explain.

8 One critic has said that 'Birches' is 'not only a poem about trees but also a celebration of spiritual thirst'. Can you see how the poem might be interpreted in this way?

9 Discuss the view that the form and language of 'Birches' mirrors the poet's awareness of the tension between the human desire to withdraw from the world and the longing to remain a part of it.

10 Robert Frost once said that poetry 'begins in delight and ends in wisdom'. Does this remark help you to appreciate the theme and mood of 'Birches'?

11 '"Birches" is a poem likely to appeal to young people'. Do you agree with this view?

"OUT, OUT—"

The buzz saw snarled and rattled in the yard
And made dust and dropped stove-length sticks of wood,
Sweet-scented stuff when the breeze drew across it.
And from there those that lifted eyes could count
Five mountain ranges one behind the other   5
Under the sunset far into Vermont.
And the saw snarled and rattled, snarled and rattled,
As it ran light, or had to bear a load.
And nothing happened: day was all but done.
Call it a day, I wish they might have said   10
To please the boy by giving him the half hour
That a boy counts so much when saved from work.
His sister stood beside them in her apron
To tell them "Supper." At the word, the saw,
As if to prove saws knew what supper meant,   15
Leaped out of the boy's hand, or seemed to leap—
He must have given the hand. However it was,
Neither refused the meeting. But the hand!
The boy's first outcry was a rueful laugh,
As he swung toward them holding up the hand,   20
Half in appeal, but half as if to keep
The life from spilling. Then the boy saw all—
Since he was old enough to know, big boy
Doing a man's work, though a child at heart—
He saw all spoiled. "Don't let him cut my hand off—   25
The doctor, when he comes. Don't let him, sister!"
So. But the hand was gone already.
The doctor put him in the dark of ether.
He lay and puffed his lips out with his breath.
And then—the watcher at his pulse took fright.   30
No one believed. They listened at his heart.
Little—less—nothing!—and that ended it.
No more to build on there. And they, since they
Were not the one dead, turned to their affairs.

GUIDELINES

'Out, Out—' is from the collection *Mountain Interval* (1916). One of Robert Frost's most affecting poems, it is based on a true story. In 1910 the child of one of Frost's neighbours in Vermont, New England, died as a result of an accident on his father's farm. The local newspaper, *The Littleton Courier*, reported the incident like this:

> *Raymond Tracy Fitzgerald, one of the twin sons of Michael G. and Margaret Fitzgerald of Bethlehem, died at his home Thursday afternoon, March 24, as a result of an accident by which one of his hands was badly hurt in a sawing machine. The young man was assisting in sawing up some wood in his own dooryard with a sawing machine and accidentally hit the loose pulley, causing the saw to descend upon his hand, cutting and lacerating it very badly. Raymond was taken into the house and a physician was immediately summoned, but he died very suddenly from the effects of shock, which produced heart failure.*

Frost's narrative poem dramatises the incident reported above. The scene is set in the yard of the New England farm. From the beginning, the saw seems to be almost like another character in the drama, personified by 'snarled', with ominous implications. Without direct comment, the poem conveys a great deal about the hardworking and possibly even harsh conditions in which the boy lives and ultimately dies, adding to the sense of impending doom as the poem proceeds.

Critics have paid attention to the strangeness of the image of the saw as an animate object seemingly looking on the boy's hand as its 'supper'. And the line that follows almost goes so far as to suggest that the boy willed his death, or at least did nothing to prevent it.

But it is the depiction of the boy's death itself that has attracted most comment. The boy knows he is facing death: 'He saw all spoiled'. The word 'spoiled' suggests simply that the boy's future is spoiled, as of course it is. Frost's biographer Jay Parini interprets 'spoiled' as referring to the family dynamic that is now altered for ever:

The boy has subliminally come to understand that within the framework of a subsistence economy there is small room for a boy who cannot pull his weight. Circumstances are such that an extra 'hand' is essential for survival.

Such a reading, although harsh, fits in with the tone of the concluding lines of the poem.

The boy's death is described with no expression of grief or consolatory comment. But it is the reaction of those who are still living that takes us aback: 'And they, since they / Were not the one dead, turned to their affairs'.

QUESTIONS

1 Would you agree that there is a sense of foreboding in the poem from the beginning? How is this sense created?

2 What impression of rural life is given in the poem? How did you respond to it?

3 Are there any particular lines in the poem that puzzle or disturb you? Can you say why?

4 What might the poet be suggesting in the line beginning 'Then the boy saw all …'?

5 Examine the last two lines of the poem. Do you think this is an appropriate way to respond to a tragic death such as this? Do you find the effect chilling, callous, resigned, accepting, realistic? Perhaps your response could be described in an entirely different way? You might link your response with the impression of rural life you get from reading the entire poem.

6 Would you agree that this is a dramatic poem? Take into account the setting, characters, climax and ending, as well as the poem's title.

7 Do you like this poem?

SPRING POOLS

These pools that, though in forests, still reflect
The total sky almost without defect,
And like the flowers beside them, chill and shiver,
Will like the flowers beside them soon be gone,
And yet not out by any brook or river,   5
But up by roots to bring dark foliage on.

The trees that have it in their pent-up buds
To darken nature and be summer woods—
Let them think twice before they use their powers
To blot out and drink up and sweep away   10
These flowery waters and these watery flowers
From snow that melted only yesterday.

GUIDELINES

The lyric 'Spring Pools' is the opening poem in the volume *West-Running Brook* (1928). The poem describes the natural phenomenon of how leaves and flowers are 'brought on' by the act of sucking up spring pools through the roots of trees.

The images in the first stanza create an impression of peace and tranquillity, but there is an underlying bleakness in the language that suggests change and death. Ironically, it is nature itself that brings about destruction. The roots of the trees, themselves images of growth, will destroy the pools.

The theme of natural process and organic change continues in the second stanza. The tone is regretful and sombre as the poet, perhaps rather helplessly, urges the trees to 'think twice' before destroying the pools. There is dark irony in the fact that Frost presents spring, a time of renewal, as also a time of decay.

As in most poems by Robert Frost, metaphorical readings have been suggested. Nature has often been used as an emblem of human life, a tradition with which Frost was familiar. We saw in 'The Tuft of Flowers' how Frost sees in nature a lesson that can be learned. Whereas in that poem nature is seen as benign and the lessons it offers hopeful, in this poem there is a much less optimistic mood. The cycle of birth and death depicted in the poem may symbolise the cyclic nature of human life, with words such as 'dark' and 'darken' underlining the shadow of death.

Frost's biographer, Jay Parini, suggests that 'Spring Pools' is about writing. He points to the fact that water, for Frost, often signified a source of poetic inspiration. The image of the pools that reflect the sky becomes a metaphor for the power of the artist to reflect the world in all its beauty. But this world, Parini goes on to say, must be transformed by the poet's imagination before he can make of it a new work of art – the work of the artist involves a certain destructiveness as well as creativity. Such work is both beautiful and frightening at the same time. We can see how this reading has a great deal to recommend it when we consider how often Frost has contemplated the power of the imagination – in 'After Apple-Picking' and in 'Birches', for example.

You may notice how the two stanzas of the poem are patterned in exactly the same way, mirroring each other as the pools mirror the sky. Each has six lines with the first two lines rhyming, the other four lines having alternate rhymes. The continuity of nature is echoed in the many run-on lines that carry the images like a chain from beginning to end. Repetition of words and whole phrases also reinforces the theme of continuity. For these reasons and others Parini has referred to the poem as one of Frost's most intricately made poems.

QUESTIONS

1 How is the beauty of the spring pools suggested in the early lines of the poem?

2 What irony is there in the manner in which their beauty will be soon destroyed?

3 Would you agree that the poem recognises the inexorable process of nature while at the same time lamenting that it must be so?

4 How would you describe the mood or atmosphere of the poem?

5 Would you agree with the view expressed in the guidelines above that 'Spring Pools' is an intricately made poem?

6 In your view, is the poem purely concerned with nature, or does it have a relevance to human life?

7 Compare the attitude to nature implied in this poem with those in 'The Tuft of Flowers' and 'Design'.

ACQUAINTED WITH THE NIGHT

I have been one acquainted with the night.
I have walked out in rain—and back in rain.
I have outwalked the furthest city light.

I have looked down the saddest city lane.
I have passed by the watchman on his beat   5
And dropped my eyes, unwilling to explain.

I have stood still and stopped the sound of feet
When far away an interrupted cry
Came over houses from another street,

But not to call me back or say good-by;   10
And further still at an unearthly height
One luminary clock against the sky

Proclaimed the time was neither wrong nor right.
I have been one acquainted with the night.

GLOSSARY

12 *luminary clock*: a clock that gives out light (possibly the moon)

GUIDELINES

This short lyric, a sonnet, is from *West-Running Brook* (1928). The poem is unusual among Frost's work in that it is set in the city rather than in rural surroundings. It depicts the dark, alienating side of urban existence. The speaker in the poem experiences a sense of deep depression and loneliness as he walks through the city streets.

The title of the poem and the first line set up a rich association of ideas for the reader. It seems clear that the 'night' is not meant purely literally but also reflects the 'dark night of the soul' that the speaker has experienced. Nature itself seems to echo his sadness and despair. There is a suggestion of hidden violence in the city. But what strikes the reader most perhaps is the sense of isolation that the poem expresses. It may be that the 'luminary clock' he sees (possibly the moon or an actual lit-up clock) symbolises, in a general way, the passage of time. Its message, 'the time was neither wrong nor right', is slightly mysterious. Is it saying that time is indifferent to those who live in the isolation of the city? That right or wrong is irrelevant in urban life? It may also echo Hamlet's expression of despair in Shakespeare's play: 'The time is out of joint'.

The poem is a sonnet of fourteen lines, but it is not divided into the traditional octave and sestet or three quatrains and a couplet. Instead there are four tercets (three-line stanzas) and a couplet with the rhyming pattern *aba bcb cdc ded aa*. Apart from the rhyming couplet, this rhyme pattern corresponds to what is called *terza rima*. The Italian poet Dante, who invented the form, wrote in his *Inferno* about a descent into hell. Frost would have had this in mind as he chose the form in which to express his own sense of despair.

Critics have pointed out that 'Acquainted with the Night' shows Robert Frost's awareness of the themes and poetic technique of modernist poets of the early twentieth century, such as T. S. Eliot and Ezra Pound, for whom the city was an image of alienation. Certainly the poem offers a contrast in the work of a poet whose social vision seems so optimistic, as expressed in 'The Tuft of Flowers' or 'Mending Wall'.

It may be that in this poem Robert Frost reveals some of his darkest fears about living – fears that were reflected in his frequent bouts of depression and psychosomatic illness during his lifetime. One of Frost's critics, Lionel Trilling, caused quite a stir when he once referred to Frost as 'a tragic poet whose work conceived of a terrifying universe'. Poems such as 'Acquainted with the Night', 'Design' and 'Provide, Provide' would bear out this perception of Frost's vision.

QUESTIONS

1 What do you think the poet suggests when he says that he has been 'acquainted with the night'? How do the images that follow develop this opening statement?

2 Would you agree that the sound of the poem echoes the poet's emotions? Look, for instance, at the rhymes used, the rhythm within the lines, the repetitions and the onomatopoeic effects of the long vowel sounds.

3 How is the indifference of the city suggested in the imagery of the poem?

4 What insight does the poem give us into Robert Frost as a person, in your opinion?

5 Do you find this poem different in tone from other poems by Frost on your course?

6 How did you respond to the theme and mood of the poem?

DESIGN

I found a dimpled spider, fat and white,
On a white heal-all, holding up a moth
Like a white piece of rigid satin cloth—
Assorted characters of death and blight
Mixed ready to begin the morning right,   5
Like the ingredients of a witches' broth—
A snow-drop spider, a flower like a froth,
And dead wings carried like a paper kite.

What had that flower to do with being white,
The wayside blue and innocent heal-all?   10
What brought the kindred spider to that height,
Then steered the white moth thither in the night?
What but design of darkness to appall?—
If design govern in a thing so small.

GLOSSARY

1 *dimpled spider*: the spider has a small dent on its body, rather like a dimple
2 *heal-all*: a type of flower, once used for medicinal purposes
3 *rigid satin cloth*: satin is often used to line coffins
4 *blight*: disease

GUIDELINES

The sonnet 'Design' was included in the volume *A Further Range* (1936). However, it had been written much earlier, around 1911–12.

Since the time of the medieval philosopher Thomas Aquinas, one of the arguments often put forward for the existence of a benevolent deity is the 'argument from design'. Aquinas had argued that God had made each detail in nature with some particular function and purpose in mind. In this sonnet Frost speculates on the possibility that nature is not only an impersonal force that offers no guidance in human affairs, but that the very force which drives it may in fact be evil.

The poem moves naturally from a description of a scene to a meditation on its significance. In the octave the speaker describes how he finds a spider holding up a moth he has captured. At first the scene seems innocent, as the repetition of 'white' suggests, but the images become more menacing as the poem proceeds, with connotations of deceit and death. All of these specimens of nature, the spider, the moth, and even the heal-all, play their part in nature's destructiveness.

As in most sonnets, there is a change of focus in the sestet. The situation described in the octave is now commented upon. The tone becomes angry as the speaker questions the motives of the plant which helped the spider kill the moth. The answer given for this is that it was nature's design all along to bring about this chain of events. It is a 'design of darkness', Frost suggests: in other words, evil. But if the last line is read as a statement, as it could be, it may imply that the question of 'design' in nature does not really arise at all. If there is no design, it follows logically that there may be no designer. This is the final disturbing vision of the poem.

'Design' speculates about a problem that has interested philosophers for centuries, namely how to account for the presence of evil in the world. Frost takes an ironic approach to the theme. The title is heavily ironic in view of the discovery the speaker makes at the end. Throughout the sonnet, words that suggest goodness turn out to be evil. For example, the innocent heal-all is obviously not innocent, the 'white' spider, flower and moth are part of the powers of 'darkness', and the apparent design in nature turns out to be illusory.

QUESTIONS

1 Explore the imagery of the octave, paying special attention to Frost's use of the colour white and the connotations of his similes.

2 Having considered the imagery, how would you describe the tone of the octave?

3 What emotions are conveyed in the sestet? How are both octave and sestet linked together?

4 Structurally, a sonnet is often said to move from 'sight to insight' — that is, from description to contemplation. In what way might this be true of 'Design'?

5 What vision of nature is suggested by this poem? How does it compare with that expressed in 'The Tuft of Flowers' and 'Spring Pools'?

6 The critic James Dickey has said that the best of Frost's poetry has to do with 'darkness, confusion, panic, terror'. Do you think this comment is relevant to a poem like 'Design'?

7 Do you think 'Design' is a well-made poem?

PROVIDE, PROVIDE

The witch that came (the withered hag)
To wash the steps with pail and rag
Was once the beauty Abishag,

The picture pride of Hollywood.
Too many fall from great and good   5
For you to doubt the likelihood.

Die early and avoid the fate.
Or if predestined to die late,
Make up your mind to die in state.

Make the whole stock exchange your own!   10
If need be occupy a throne,
Where nobody can call *you* crone.

Some have relied on what they knew,
Others on being simply true.
What worked for them might work for you.   15

No memory of having starred
Atones for later disregard
Or keeps the end from being hard.

Better to go down dignified
With boughten friendship at your side   20
Than none at all. Provide, provide!

1 *hag*: ugly old woman

3 *Abishag*: a biblical allusion. Abishag was a beautiful Shunammite girl who came to attend the dying King David (*1 Kings 1.3*)

12 *crone*: withered old woman

20 *boughten*: a regional word meaning something shop-bought, as against something naturally acquired

GUIDELINES

'Provide, Provide' was written in 1933 and appeared in the collection *A Further Range* (1936). Frost himself said that the central character of the poem, the witch who came to wash the steps, was based on a real woman whom he had seen cleaning the steps of a university building. The Caribbean poet Derek Walcott has speculated that the poem had its origin in Frost's childhood experience of poverty. When his father died at the age of thirty-four, Frost's mother had exactly $8 to pay for her husband's funeral. Understandably, this would have created an anxiety in him about money throughout his life.

It has also been suggested that Frost's vehement opposition to the New Deal policies of Franklin D. Roosevelt in 1930s' America sparked off a cynical reaction in him which finds expression here. Frost was opposed to the new social welfare policies, preferring the more conservative policies of self-sufficiency and individualism. Whatever the possible personal background to the poem, its stark phrases and bitter tone are unlike anything else in Frost's work.

The language of the poem is straightforward and direct, as if Frost is addressing a public audience. The moral is clear: the old woman who is reduced to menial work may once have been young and successful. Like many of the great and beautiful, she failed to provide for herself financially. The poet has some mock-advice, to 'Die early', but if we can't do that then we ought at least try to be self-sufficient. He counsels his readers to recognise the value of both money and power. Memories of past glories simply aren't enough. Better to finish our days surrounded by paid friendship ('boughten') rather than by none at all.

The imperative tone adds an urgency to the poem, as does the four-beat (tetrameter) rhyming triplets that give it a strong forward thrust. Frost himself referred to this metre as having 'plenty of tune'.

'Provide, Provide' has been called 'an immortal masterpiece'. With unsentimental honesty it faces the fact that old age brings with it a diminishing of beauty and success. It accepts that much of our experience of love, power and friendship is illusory. It offers us advice on how to live out our lives in some dignity. Although it is impersonal (no 'I' figure appears), it reveals a great deal about Frost himself. It raises questions about Frost's personal happiness at a time when he was at the height of his fame in America. The critic Frank Lentricchia suggests that Frost is talking directly to himself in the poem:

> Hollywood's poet, talking contemptuously to and at himself, looking down the road at a possible fate that he would not be able to say he hadn't chosen, were it to turn out to be his – because he had made the decision to commit himself to fame's course.

From this point of view, the poem is even more honest and revealing. Although he enjoyed giving performances of his poems and speaking in public, Frost may have felt ambivalent about his experience of being famous. Lentricchia's comment throws some light, in retrospect, on a poem such as 'The Road Not Taken', which dramatises such a decision-making process.

QUESTIONS

1 What advice does the poet give to people who wish to avoid the 'fate' of people like Abishag? In what tone is the advice given?
2 How would you describe the tone of the poem?
3 Would you agree that the view of life expressed in 'Provide, Provide' is darkly cynical? How do you respond to it personally?
4 What do you think of Frost's advice?
5 What sort of person does this poem reveal Frost to be? Do you think you would like him?
6 The critic Randolph Jarrell described this poem as 'an immortal masterpiece'. What qualities of the poem might have led him to this conclusion?
7 The poem is unlike most of Frost's other poems. Would you include it in a personal selection of Frost's poems for an anthology?

GENERAL QUESTIONS

1. Robert Frost accepted the view of the poet and critic Ezra Pound that his poems were 'simple' but added 'if they are they are subtle too'. Do you think Frost's assessment is true of the poems that are on your course?

2. The critic James Dickey has said that the best of Frost's poetry has to do with 'darkness, confusion, panic, terror'. Another critic, Lionel Trilling, spoke of him as a 'terrifying poet'. How do you respond to these views?

3. W. H. Auden described the characteristic voice of Frost's poems as 'always that of the speaking voice, quiet and sensible'. Examine this statement in the light of your reading of Frost's poems.

4. 'Many of Robert Frost's poems begin with straightforward description and move towards meditation and commentary.' Discuss this view.

5. 'It begins in delight and ends in wisdom' is how Frost himself described the process of composing a poem. How far might this reflect the imaginative structure of a typical Frost lyric?

6. 'In his poems Robert Frost sees the beauty of nature, but there is also an awareness of its menace.' Do you agree with this view?

7. 'Robert Frost seldom describes nature merely for its own sake. He uses it also as analogy for human and even artistic concerns.' Discuss.

8. Frost himself said of his poetry that it provided a 'momentary stay against confusion'. To what extent might this statement illuminate the feelings behind the poems on your course?

9. Can you suggest what the qualities of his poetry were that made Robert Frost one of the most popular and best-selling poets of twentieth-century America?

10. Robert Frost: a personal response.

EXAMINATION-STYLE QUESTIONS

11. Write an introduction to a short collection of poetry chosen from the poems of Robert Frost on your course.

Guidelines

You are of course free to choose whatever poems you like to answer this question. Some possible areas for discussion include:

- Frost's themes, such as nature and what we can learn from it about human experience etc.
- what his poems reveal about him as a person his poetic 'voice'
- his use of language, in particular his use of metaphor

- his choice of traditional forms in which to write
- the emotions underlying his best poems.

Always support the points you make with relevant quotation or reference.

12 Write a response to the view that Robert Frost's poems reflect the poet's own life and reveal his personality.

Possible points include:
- his poems are almost always set in the rural surroundings of New England that he lived in and loved
- his poetic 'voice' reveals his personality, his love of nature, his interest in its deeper significance etc.
- many of his poems deal with particular times and emotions he experienced e.g. childhood, decision-making, depression, cynicism of old age etc.
- he reveals that he is aware of the darker side of human existence as well as its beauty.

Remember to support your points with relevant quotation or reference.

13 Robert Frost was one of the most popular and best-selling of American poets in the twentieth century. Can you suggest why?

Possible points include:
- his choice of themes, while personally expressed, have a universal appeal (illustrate with examples)
- his use of language is attractive and accessible, his images and phrases are memorable etc.
- the imagery of his poems is rooted in the American landscape and experience
- his poems reveal his personality to the reader
- his poems appeal to the reader both intellectually and emotionally
- the reader can always gain some insight or learn some lesson from his poems.

You must support the points you make with relevant quotation or reference to the poems on your course.

Language of poems is
accessible and memorable.

Writes about nature, but not
merely for its own sake.

Poems reveal Frost's
personality.

Writes about artistic
creation and the power of
the imagination.

Rural settings of poems are
attractive to readers.

Robert Frost

Uses traditional metres
and rhythms.

Poems can often be read
metaphorically.

Poems show awareness of the
darker side of life.

Said that 'poetry begins in
delight and ends in wisdom'.

Voice in poems described as
'always that of a speaking voice,
quiet and sensible'.

PHILIP LARKIN

1922–85

BIOGRAPHY

Philip Larkin was born in Coventry in August 1922 into a middle-class family. He was the second child of Sydney and Eva Larkin. The family name is common in Ireland and it was often assumed that the poet had Irish ancestry. Larkin himself has no interest in family history but his father established that their branch of the family was English and had lived in the same part of the Midlands for generations.

Sydney Larkin was an accountant and, at the time of his son's birth, he was Treasurer of Coventry Corporation. He was well-read, agnostic in outlook and outspoken in his convictions. Eva, Larkin's mother, was intelligent but she was also nervous and timid and her husband ruled the household. There were constant tensions between Larkin's parents and this coloured his childhood, which he described as 'a forgotten boredom'. From an early age Larkin was ungainly and short-sighted. He was also shy and self-consciousness, so much so that, at age four, he developed a stammer.

By all accounts, the family home was a cold, lonely place. Because his sister, Kitty, was nine years older, Larkin felt like an only child. As he got older, his mother grew more anxious and nervous, his father more domineering and scornful, especially to Kitty, although he did communicate his love of literature and music to his son. Reviewing his parents' relationship in the 1950s, Larkin wrote: 'Certainly the marriage left me with two convictions: that human beings should not live together, and that children should be taken from their parents at an early age'. He also said that although he liked his parents, 'they were rather awkward people and not very good at being happy. And these things rub off.'

Larkin's father was an admirer of Hitler and German efficiency and he brought the teenage Philip on holiday to Germany in the 1930s. Later, Larkin said that these trips 'sowed the seed of my hatred of abroad'. In Germany, his natural shyness was intensified by his inability to speak the language and he was embarrassed by his father's enthusiasm for the National Socialists. As Larkin grew to manhood, he rejected all interest in politics although his outlook on life was decidedly conservative. From his father he inherited a 'total disbelief in Christianity'.

Larkin attended the local grammar school as his father despised the notion of elitist, private education. The school had a high academic standard and Larkin did well without excelling or wanting to excel. He made a number of close friends, one of whom, James Sutton, encouraged him to write and introduced him to jazz. In his final year, Larkin worked earnestly and wrote in a serious way. He was a regular contributor to the school magazine and acted as its assistant editor. Impressed by the improvement in his work, his English teacher suggested that he should study English at university. He took the entrance examination for St John's College, Oxford, in March 1940 and began his studies in autumn of that year. He read the poetry of W. H. Auden and his first poem, published as an undergraduate, reflects Auden's influence.

Philip Larkin spent three years at Oxford, from 1940 to 1943. Although the war curbed the activities of the students, Larkin enjoyed undergraduate life, adopting the pose of a dandy and listening to recordings of American jazz. It would be hard to overstate his love of jazz. He was intensely excited by it and many of his closest friends were fellow enthusiasts, including the young writer Kingsley Amis. Although dismissive of the set courses, Larkin read widely. Auden remained central to his view of literature and he admired Lawrence, Yeats (though he revised his opinion later) and Dylan Thomas. Above all, however, Larkin valued those writers who wrote without affectation and whose work remained close to ordinary, everyday life. Thomas Hardy embodied all that Larkin looked for in a poet.

Because of his poor eyesight, Larkin was not called up to the army. Fortunately none of his friends or close relatives was killed so Larkin was largely unaffected by the war and disinterested in its progress. In some respects Larkin was a flamboyant character at Oxford, but he still remained shy and self-conscious, especially with girls. The example of his father's unflattering opinion of women did little to help him overcome his awkwardness around members of the opposite sex.

With his friend and fellow writer, Kingsley Amis, Larkin developed a strong dislike of pomposity and a scathing, private disregard for 'respectability' that was to last a lifetime, although his public persona was polite and conformist.

As Larkin approached the end of his time in Oxford, he was sunk in depression. His writing was not progressing; the war had interrupted his friendships and his vexed relationships with women continued. Moreover, he had no idea of a career and seemed indecisive and passive as the time came for him to choose, a pattern that was to repeat itself at other, critical junctures in his life.

Much to his surprise and delight, Larkin got a First in his final exams. More surprisingly, returning to his parents' house from Oxford, his writing began to flow. Then he saw an advertisement for a librarian in a small town in the Midlands and decided to apply for it. His application was successful and he began work on 1 December, 1944. Although his letters reveal his initial dislike and contempt for the job, he soon began to enjoy the life of a librarian and found time for his writing. In 1945, his first collection of poetry, *The North Ship*, was published, by the small Fortune Press, which also published his novel *Jill* in 1946. This book describes, in fictional terms, Larkin's life as a student. Both the novel and the collection of poems met with muted responses. In 1947, Faber published Larkin's second novel, *A Girl in Winter*. It received favourable reviews and Larkin believed that he had begun his writer's life in earnest. In fact, he was to write no more fiction and produced only a small body of published work over his lifetime. However, he maintained a voluminous correspondence with his many friends. In his letters he presented different aspects of his personality to each of the correspondents. The letters, along with his diaries, reveal a complex personality and constitute an impressive and fascinating body of work.

During his time in Shropshire, Philip Larkin met and fell in love with a young girl, Ruth Bowman. To her, Larkin was witty, kind, outrageous and brilliant. To him, she was someone in whom he could confide and be himself. In 1948, when Larkin was 25 and struggling to come to terms with his father's death and his duty to his mother, he became engaged to Ruth, then aged 21. However, the omens were not good. In the first poems he wrote after they became lovers, Larkin dwelt on death. Furthermore, the prospect of marriage and the example of his parents' life together terrified Larkin, who was not prepared to give up his freedom or risk losing time for his writing. There was also the matter of his fear and stated dislike of children, for which he achieved a degree of notoriety. As with all the relationships in his life, Larkin failed to act decisively and the affair dragged on for two years before Ruth ended it.

Thereafter, Philip Larkin never married, though he was involved in two long-term relationships. One was with Monica Jones, a lecturer in the English Department at the University of Leicester, where Larkin worked for a short time. The other was with Maeve Brennan, a colleague of Larkin's whom he met in 1955 at the University of Hull.

In the summer of 1946, Larkin applied to and got a job in the library of University College, Leicester. The publication and success of *A Girl in Winter* brought him into contact with members of the academic staff and thus he met Monica Jones. But Larkin felt stifled by his life in Leicester and in 1950 he came to Belfast to work in the Library at Queen's University. Belfast freed Larkin from the pressures of personal relationships and family obligations. He enjoyed university life and conversation and he prepared his first major poetry collection, *The Less Deceived*, published by fledging publishing house The Marvell Press. In later years Larkin recalled that Belfast provided him with the best conditions for writing. He was surrounded by interesting and stimulating company; he had comfortable accommodation provided by the university; and he formed a number of romantic attachments that did not threaten him or impede his writing.

One of these attachments was for Winifred Arnott, a student and later a colleague of Larkin's at the library in Queen's. Her decision to marry and the departure of several close friends unsettled him. In 1955, he applied for the post of Librarian in the University of Hull. Larkin's quiet air of authority, his eloquence and the incisiveness of his mind impressed the interview board. They duly appointed him. During his time in Hull, the library underwent a transformation, growing from a staff of eleven to over one hundred. And while Larkin often spoke of his 'boring job', he took a professional pride in his stewardship of the library and was admired and respected within his profession. He personally oversaw the building of the new library in Hull and contributed many ideas to its design and decoration.

As Larkin established himself as a librarian, he won increasing recognition as a writer. *The Less Deceived* was highly successful, selling over 6,000 copies in the first years of publication and receiving favourable reviews. Selections of his poems appeared in all the major anthologies published in the late 1950s and early 1960s and he recorded a number of programmes for the BBC. He regularly reviewed poetry for *The Guardian* newspaper and became the jazz correspondent for the *Daily Telegraph*.

In a spirit of growing confidence, Larkin moved into a new flat in Hull in 1956 (and lived there until 1974.) Here he preserved his solitude, rarely inviting guests and keeping his work separate from his life as a writer. The intention was to create a space for his writing but the space often remained empty and he wrote less poetry than he had hoped to write. And all the while there was the conflict between his feelings for Maeve Brennan ('The woman I want to marry') and his loyalty to Monica Jones ('The woman I should marry') and the ambivalence of his attitude towards love and marriage.

Larkin's literary reputation was ensured with the publication of the collections *The Whitsun Weddings* (1964) and *High Windows* (1974), both of which were acclaimed as contemporary masterpieces. Awards and honours were heaped upon him, including a CBE in 1975. Following the publication of *The Whitsun Weddings*, he was invited to make a television programme for the BBC on his life and work, a project that gave him much delight and he made recordings of his poems. The Oxford University Press invited him to edit a new *Oxford Book of Modern Verse*, to replace the anthology edited by Yeats in 1936. (On its publication in 1973 it proved to be every bit as controversial as the original.) Larkin also served as a committee member for various poetry organisations using his administrative know-how to good effect. The student unrest of the 1960s brought out Larkin's reactionary prejudices. Students, trade unionists and immigrants were the targets of his acerbic wit.

As Philip Larkin grew older, he became somewhat reclusive. He disliked publicity, and enjoyed living in Hull, a long way from the centre of literary life in London. He liked to depict himself as a disgruntled, misanthropist, but friends testify to his humour and good companionship. In the last ten years of his life, Larkin wrote very little poetry. He believed that his inspiration had deserted him.The onset of deafness restricted his social activities, and deepened his frequent bouts of melancholy. His love-hate relationship with his family lasted right up to his mother's death in 1977, at the age of 91. In a letter he remarked that 'To escape from home is a life's work'. The economic cutbacks of the 1970s meant that the library in Hull was forced to curtail its services. To Larkin it seemed that everything was falling apart. By the age of fifty he had the mien of an old man and was gripped by bouts of remorse of feelings of failure. He described his situation in the opening verse of 'Aubade':

I work all day, and get half-drunk at night.
Waking at four to soundless dark, I stare.
In time the curtain edges will grow light.

Till then I see what's really there:
    Unresting death, a whole day nearer now,
Making all thought impossible but how
And where and when I shall myself die.

Dispirited and melancholic, he turned to his closest friends and colleagues for support. The end of his days was marked by a sense of failure. He believed that he had set out to perfect his work and was left with only a failed life. Not even the offer to succeed John Betjeman as poet laureate, which he declined, cheered him. In June 1985, he was diagnosed as having cancer. After surgery and a short remission, he died in December, aged 63. His final words were 'I am going to the inevitable'. On his death, he was acclaimed as England's finest post-war poet, whose work transformed the contradictions, frustrations, fears and indignities of ordinary life into eloquent poetry.

SOCIAL AND CULTURAL CONTEXT

T. S. Eliot was the dominant figure in English poetry for the first third of the twentieth century. Eliot was a Modernist poet. Modernism arose out of the developments in psychoanalysis in the early part of the century and out of the crisis caused by the experience of the First World War. Psychoanalysis called into question our common-sense understanding of the world and the way we perceive it, while the war called standards of morality into question. To many, it seemed that the world was absurdly meaningless. In all areas of life, old forms had failed and new ones needed to be invented. Thus, as a movement, Modernism rejected traditional practices in favour of new techniques and experiments. Melody and harmony were abandoned in music, perspective and pictorial form rejected in art and linear narrative and argument were rejected in literature and replaced by new experimental forms. The result was an exciting kind of poetry, often fragmentary and random in its organisation – a poetry that was neither popular nor easily accessible.

As Europe went into recession in the late 1920s and Fascism rose in many countries, the experimentation of Modernism seemed indulgent to a generation of younger writers. Many of them were committed Socialists. Their concern was to give expression to their political and social awareness and to speak to and for the poor and the working class within society. W. H. Auden became the leading figure in English poetry in the 1930s. For Auden, to be a writer was to be a citizen and to write was to put your insights at the service of your fellow citizens, to give them strength to withstand their enemies. In some respects, Auden's view of poetry was shared by Larkin, who believed that poetry should help us to 'enjoy and endure'. However, Larkin was not interested in the political awareness that shaped Auden's work. For him, poetry was concerned with private, individual experience:

> *I write about experiences, often quite simple, everyday experiences which somehow acquire some sort of special meaning for me, and I write poems about them to preserve them. You see, I want to express the experience in a poem so that it remains preserved, unchanging; and I then hope that other people will come upon this experience, pickled as it were in verse, and it will mean something to them, sound some chord in their own recollection, perhaps, or show them something familiar in a new light.*

The first coherent development in poetry after the Second World War was The Movement – a loose grouping of poets who strove for clarity in their work and who used traditional forms in reaction against Modernism. The manifesto of The Movement was Robert Conquest's introduction to *New Lines*, an anthology he edited in 1956 in which he described the poets' refusal to abandon a rational structure and comprehensible language, even when the verse is most highly charged with sensuous or emotional intent.

For his part, Larkin rejected the example of T. S. Eliot in favour of the example of Thomas Hardy. Indeed, Larkin's work expresses nostalgia for the England evoked by Hardy, and Larkin admired the style of Hardy's writing, which is narrative, direct and personal. From Hardy's example, Larkin sought to explore the dilemmas of ordinary individuals in a language that was close to everyday speech and English in tone and manner. In a review of Hardy's collected poems, Larkin declared that it was the best body of poetic work the twentieth century so far had to show. Of course, this is not to say that Larkin's work does not reflect elements of the Modernist style or is simply an imitation of Hardy. Many of his own poems are complex and subtle, rich in symbolism and straining to go beyond the ordinary. In the words of the critic James Booth, Larkin strains language 'to the limits of grammatical tolerance'. However, it is true that Philip Larkin had little time for the experimentalism of Modernism or for poetry that was intellectually obscure. He admired poetry that was accessible and written with a keen sense of formality, using traditional verse patterns. He thought that life, as it was lived by ordinary people, should and could provide the subject of poetry. He wanted his poems to address a non-academic audience in the language of the everyday. Compared to the poetry of Ezra Pound or T. S. Eliot, Larkin succeeds in his ambitions.

Compared to the work of Modernist poets, Larkin makes few references to other poems or poets in his writing. Modernism was open to European and American influences and to the influence of the past. Larkin, however, disliked the idea that poems come from other poems. He believed that poems should arise from personal experience. (Of course, in discussing influence in poetry, everything is a matter of degree, for Larkin's poetry hints at other poets and poems, from Shakespeare to Keats, and his themes of death and transience are found in every major poet.) In Larkin's eyes, Modernism had destroyed the quality of delight that should accompany poetry: 'This is my essential criticism of modernism … it helps us neither to enjoy nor to endure'.

Larkin's life and career coincided with remarkable changes in English society. He lived through the Second World War and the economic depression of the 1950s. He was a librarian in Hull during the rapid expansion of the university system in England and the changes in attitude and culture brought about by the affluence of the 1960s. Student unrest in the late 1960s and early 1970s won no sympathy from him. Nor was he sympathetic to the increasingly multiracial nature of British society. His cure for unemployment was to stop unemployment benefit. As he grew older, he expressed alarmingly reactionary views in his private correspondence. In his final collection, *High Windows* (1974), there is a coarseness in some of the poems that is striking. He admired the leadership of Margaret Thatcher, though, ironically, it was the financial policies pursued by her government which led to the cutbacks in the university. These cutbacks undid many of Larkin's professional achievements.

These changes are almost totally absent from Larkin's poems. Whatever insights are won in his poetry arise from the observation of his own life and the ordinary lives around him. Perhaps it is only in the rueful tone of some poems in *High Windows*, where the persona of the poems envies the young their freedom, do we see the poetry reflecting public events.

WEDDING-WIND

The wind blew all my wedding-day,
And my wedding-night was the night of the high wind;
And a stable-door was banging, again and again,
That he must go and shut it, leaving me
Stupid in candlelight, hearing rain,   5
Seeing my face in the twisted candlestick,
Yet seeing nothing. When he came back
He said the horses were restless, and I was sad
That any man or beast that night should lack
The happiness I had.   10

       Now in the day
All's ravelled under the sun by the wind's blowing.
He has gone to look at the floods, and I
Carry a chipped pail to the chicken-run,
Set it down, and stare. All is the wind   15
Hunting through clouds and forests; thrashing
My apron and the hanging cloths on the line.
Can it be borne, this bodying-forth by wind
Of joy my actions turn on, like a thread
Carrying beads? Shall I be let to sleep   20
Now this perpetual morning shares my bed?
Can even death dry up
These new delighted lakes, conclude
Our kneeling as cattle by all-generous waters?

GLOSSARY

5 *Stupid*: in this context, drowsy or not fully awake, or stunned through lack of sleep

12 *ravelled* made clear. It also means to untangle and to entangle

14 *pail*: a bucket

18 *borne*: sustained, tolerated, endured. The word also derives its force from its association with childbearing and birth

18 *bodying-forth*: to give expression or form to something

GUIDELINES

'Wedding-Wind' was written in September 1946. It appeared in *The Less Deceived* (1955). It was written during Larkin's engagement to Ruth Bowman. 'Wedding-Wind' is one of the few poems by Larkin which celebrates, in an unqualified way, passionate love. It is also one of the few poems in which the persona of the poem can be totally divorced from the poet himself.

In the poem the wind is a symbol of passion and change. The images of the wind and the wind-changed world suggest the powerful forces affecting the young bride.

In the first stanza, the bride tells us that her wedding night was the night of the 'high wind'. In Larkin's work, the word 'high' is associated with experiences which are elevated and elevating and which have a spiritual resonance. The joy of the bride on her wedding night makes her sympathetic to all creatures, 'man or beast', who lack the happiness that she possesses.

The second stanza speaks of the day after the wedding. Now everything is bright and joyful. The wind continues to move through the world of 'clouds and forests', 'thrashing / My apron and the hanging clothes on the line'. Here, as elsewhere in the poem, the meaning advances by means of suggestion and indirect statement. The verb 'thrashing', for example, suggests the forceful nature of the energy which affects the young bride and the violent strength of human passion.

The stanza concludes with three questions. Surrendering herself to the images of the wind, the bride asks:

> *Can it be borne, this bodying-forth by wind*
> *Of joy my actions turn on, like a thread*
> *Carrying beads?*

The bride wonders if she can bear the joy of love, embodied in the wind, a joy that informs everything in her life. However, paraphrasing the lines in this way fails to convey the richness of the language and imagery, which opens out in many directions. For example, the verbs 'borne' and 'bodying-forth' suggest pregnancy and birth and links the wind to human passion, joy and generation. (See also the images of fruitfulness and generation in the concluding stanza of 'The Whitsun Weddings'.) The image of the beads suggests prayer and associates love with the sacred, as well as suggesting a necklace or a gift of love.

The second question, 'Shall I be let to sleep / Now this perpetual morning shares my bed?', suggests the radiance of the bride's new-found love and sexual passion, which are as bright as the 'perpetual morning'.

The bride is a farmer's wife. She knows that wind dries water but, such is the intensity of her love, she wonders if the waters of 'these new delighted lakes' of love will ever be dried? She questions whether death itself will force them to stop drinking from the generous waters of love:

> Can even death dry up
> These new delighted lakes, conclude
> Our kneeling as cattle by all-generous waters?

In all of Larkin's poetry, this ending is unique in celebrating the possibility of love and joy outliving death. The concluding lines have the rhythm and syntax of liturgy, turning the poem into a hymn of praise to human love. The phrase 'all-generous waters' is one of the poet's most memorable. Indeed, the language throughout the poem is dignified and uplifting. Larkin skilfully uses long vowels, alliteration and repetition to give a sense of dignified eloquence to the simple vocabulary of the bride. Note, too, how in the last line of the poem, the bride speaks of 'Our kneeling', using the first person plural form of the pronoun for the first time in the poem.

Andrew Motion, Larkin's biographer, suggests that 'Wedding-Wind' was intended to ease the door open through which Larkin could contemplate marriage. Yet, Larkin scribbled in his notebook during the period in which the poem was written: 'At 1.45 p.m. let me remember that the only married state I know (i.e. that of my parents) is bloody hell. Never must it be forgotten.'

QUESTIONS

1 The bride describes her wedding night as the night of 'the high wind'. What is the meaning of the adjective 'high' in the context of the poem?
2 Why does the bride say that she felt 'stupid in candlelight' when her husband went to shut the banging stable door?
3 What effect does the joy of love have on the young woman?
4 What changes in the world and in the bride are described in the second stanza?
5 There are a number of interesting choices of word in the second stanza. Comment on the range of meaning in the following: 'thrashing'; 'borne'; 'bodying-forth'. Taken together, what do the words suggest?

6 The poem concludes with three questions. Consider the first of these, 'Can it be borne ... Carrying beads'. Paraphrase the meaning of these lines, and suggest some of the ways in which the language and imagery open out beyond one single meaning.

7 The waters of love are described as 'all-generous'. What possibility is contemplated by the bride in the final lines of the poem?

8 The language of the poem is simple. How does Larkin manage to give it eloquence and dignity?

9 Clearly the imagery of wind, storm and flood has a symbolic purpose in the poem. What complex of ideas and emotions does it express?

10 The poem has been described as a hymn to human love. Is this an apt description? Where else in Larkin's poetry is love presented in a positive light?

AT GRASS

The eye can hardly pick them out
From the cold shade they shelter in,
Till wind distresses tail and mane;
Then one crops grass, and moves about
 – The other seeming to look on –   5
And stands anonymous again.

Yet fifteen years ago, perhaps
Two dozen distances sufficed
To fable them: faint afternoons
Of Cups and Stakes and Handicaps,   10
Whereby their names were artificed
To inlay faded, classic Junes –

Silks at the start: against the sky
Numbers and parasols: outside,
Squadrons of empty cars, and heat,   15
And littered grass: then the long cry
Hanging unhushed till it subside
To stop-press columns on the street.

Do memories plague their ears like flies?
They shake their heads. Dusk brims the shadows.   20
Summer by summer all stole away,
The starting-gates, the crowds and cries –
All but the unmolesting meadows.
Almanacked, their names live; they

Have slipped their names, and stand at ease,   25
Or gallop for what must be joy,
And not a fieldglass sees them home,
Or curious stop-watch prophesies:
Only the groom, and the groom's boy,
With bridles in the evening come.   30

GLOSSARY

3 *distresses*: ruffles or upsets. The word may suggest the nervousness of thoroughbred horses

4 *crops*: grazes or eats the grass

8 *Two dozen distances*: two dozen races or the distance of the race itself. (A distance' is a point 240 yards back from the winning post.)

9 *fable*: to make famous in the lore of racing

10 *Cups and Stakes and Handicaps*: types of horse races

11 *their names were artificed / To inlay classic Junes*: Larkin takes a noun (artifice') and turns it into a verb. The formal, registered names of the horses were made fancy ('artificed') to decorate or ornament (inlay') the important ('classic') races of the season. These races were held in June and have now 'faded' from memory

13 *Silks*: the colourful garments worn by jockeys

23 *unmolesting*: the implied contrast is between the meadows and the crowds who swarm around the winning horse at the end of an important race

24 *Almanacked*: here, as in many of his poems, Larkin plays with words. He transforms the noun 'almanack' into a verb. An almanack is an annual calendar, giving information of particular topics. In this case, the verb means 'recorded in the racing records'

25 *slipped*: to be let loose from. Larkin plays with the idea of horses being freed from their bridles. The horses are freed from their racing names and the obligation to race

28 *stop-watch prophesies*: the prospects of young race horses are determined by the times they register on the stop watch

GUIDELINES

Larkin wrote this poem in 1950. It appeared in *The Less Deceived* (1955).

The idea for 'At Grass' came to Larkin after he attended the cinema and saw a documentary on a retired racehorse. The film made a deep impression on the poet.

The poem begins in a quiet, undramatic manner and captures the visual quality of the documentary that inspired the poem. However, the vocabulary hints at themes beyond the level of description. The phrase 'the cold shade' suggests death, and sets up an expectation that this meditation on the retired horses will involve an apprehension of death. The first line, 'The eye can hardly pick them out', suggests that the horses are becoming indistinct as, in the words of one critic, 'their fame recedes and their death approaches'.

In the second stanza, we get an idea of Larkin's richly-layered poetic method. Picking up on the idea of distance – the distance of the horses from the poet and the distance of the horses from their former lives – the poet thinks of the distances the horses ran to bring them into racing history. The final two lines of the stanza suggest the formal, registered names of the racehorses, as well as the inscription of the winning horse's name on racing trophies. The lines also contain the suggestion that horse racing, itself, is a kind of rich ornamentation or inlay to social life.

In Stanza Three Larkin uses a cinematic effect to evoke the fashion, wealth, hope, expectation and media interest that surrounds horse-racing in England. The opening of Stanza Four is whimsical. The horses shake their head in answer to the question posed in the first line: 'Do memories plague their ears like flies? / They shake their heads'. The lines bring into focus a major theme of the poem. However much human beings use horses for their sporting purposes, the horses themselves remain outside any understanding of that world. The racing names live on in the records of racing annuals, but the horses themselves 'have slipped their names' and have returned to 'the unmolesting meadows'. The fourth and fifth stanzas imply that the horses, now in the twilight of their lives, are free of the unwelcome attention of humans.

The ending of the poem is beautifully achieved. The horses' names and their fame will live long after they have died. The thought of the final line of stanza four is left incomplete: 'Almanacked, their names live; they … [will die]'. But before death comes, there is the freedom of the days at grass. Now the horses gallop 'for what must be joy', away from the watchful eyes of racegoers. The final two lines take on an emotional resonance through the mellow-sounding phrases and the alliteration. The poetic effect is heightened by the inversion of the word order. The effect is to create a fine sense of closure, as the groom and the groom's boy come to take in the horses:

Only the groom, and the groom's boy,
With bridles in the evening come.

The ending suggests the final homecoming of horses whose lives have been safely and successfully concluded.

Larkin's biographer, Andrew Motion relates 'At Grass' to the personal crisis through which the poet was living. Larkin had yet to come to terms with the death of his father. His relationship with Ruth Bowman was coming to an end, and his relationship with his mother was beset by guilt and frustration. In these circumstances, the situation of the horses was to be envied.

QUESTIONS

1 The opening stanza of the poem is quiet and undramatic. What words or phrases hint at themes beyond the level of description?

2 The first stanza suggests the distance of the horses from the observer. The concept of distance runs through the poem. What other types of distances are explored in 'At Grass'?

3 In Stanza Three the world of racing is suggested in a series of cinematic images. What kind of world emerges from these images?

4 The phrase 'unmolesting meadows' is a startling one. What does it contribute to the reader's understanding of the poem's themes?

5 The final stanza is rich and complex. Explain how the images, language and rhythm suggest both freedom and the approach of death.

6 Some critics read 'At Grass' as expressing Larkin's nostalgia for an England that is disappearing. Others read it as expressing Larkin's personal sense of loss at the ending of his engagement to Ruth Bowman. Can you find evidence in the poem to support either of these readings?

7 What, in your opinion, are the main themes of 'At Grass'? What other poems by Larkin share these themes?

CHURCH GOING

Once I am sure there's nothing going on
I step inside, letting the door thud shut.
Another church: matting, seats, and stone,
And little books; sprawlings of flowers, cut
For Sunday, brownish now; some brass and stuff   5
Up at the holy end; the small neat organ;
And a tense, musty, unignorable silence,
Brewed God knows how long. Hatless, I take off
My cycle-clips in awkward reverence,

Move forward, run my hand around the font.   10
From where I stand, the roof looks almost new –
Cleaned, or restored? Someone would know: I don't.
Mounting the lectern, I peruse a few
Hectoring large-scale verses, and pronounce
'Here endeth' much more loudly than I'd meant.   15
The echoes snigger briefly. Back at the door
I sign the book, donate an Irish sixpence,
Reflect the place was not worth stopping for.

Yet stop I did: in fact I often do,
And always end much at a loss like this,   20
Wondering what to look for; wondering, too,
When churches fall completely out of use
What we shall turn them into, if we shall keep
A few cathedrals chronically on show,
Their parchment, plate and pyx in locked cases,   25
And let the rest rent-free to rain and sheep.
Shall we avoid them as unlucky places?

Or, after dark, will dubious women come
To make their children touch a particular stone;
Pick simples for a cancer; or on some   30
Advised night see walking a dead one?

Power of some sort or other will go on
In games, in riddles, seemingly at random;
But superstition, like belief, must die,
And what remains when disbelief has gone?   35
Grass, weedy pavement, brambles, buttress, sky,

A shape less recognisable each week,
A purpose more obscure. I wonder who
Will be the last, the very last, to seek
This place for what it was; one of the crew   40
That tap and jot and know what rood-lofts were?
Some ruin-bibber, randy for antique,
Or Christmas-addict, counting on a whiff
Of gown-and-bands and organ-pipes and myrrh?
Or will he be my representative,   45

Bored, uninformed, knowing the ghostly silt
Dispersed, yet tending to this cross of ground
Through the suburb scrub because it held unspilt
So long and equably what since is found
Only in separation – marriage, and birth,   50
And death, and thoughts of these – for which was built
This special shell? For, though I've no idea
What this accoutred frowsty barn is worth,
It pleases me to stand in silence here;

A serious house on serious earth it is,   55
In whose blent air all our compulsions meet,
Are recognised, and robed as destinies.
And that much never can be obsolete,
Since someone will forever be surprising
A hunger in himself to be more serious,   60
And gravitating with it to this ground,
Which, he once heard, was proper to grow wise in,
If only that so many dead lie round.

GLOSSARY

4 *sprawling*: arrangements of flowers which spread out in an irregular way

9 *cycle-clips*: metal clips which prevent the legs of trousers from flapping or catching in the chain of the bicycle

13 *the lectern*: a stand with a sloping surface for holding a book or Bible from which the readings from scripture are read during a church service

14 *Hectoring*: intimidating or bullying

15 *'Here endeth'*: the phrase which concludes each reading during services in the Anglican Church

17 *an Irish sixpence*: the poem is set in Northern Ireland, so the 'Irish' sixpence is considered foreign currency and next to worthless

24 *chronically*: constantly

25 *parchment*: Larkin uses 'parchment' to refer to all the sacred books kept in a church

25 *plate*: the gold and silver vessels used in church services

25 *pyx*: container or vessel in which the consecrated host is kept

28 *dubious*: uncertain but also suspicious or untrustworthy

30 *simples*: herb used for medicinal purposes.

31 *Advised night*: a night chosen deliberately

36 *buttress*: a stone support on the outside walls of the church

41 *rood-loft*: rood means a cross, especially the cross above the altar in a church. A rood-loft is a gallery built above the altar

42 *Ruin-bibber*: Larkin coined this word for people who love to drink in the atmosphere of ruins.

44 *myrrh*: the scent or fragrance in incense

44 *gown-and-bands*: a band is a large white collar, often with extensions, which hangs down over the gown. Gown and bands are worn by the clergy and/or by members of the church choir

46 *the ghostly silt*: this is a fine example of Larkin's ingenuity in his use of words. The phrase may be read as meaning, 'The deposit ('silt') of belief in spiritual ('ghostly') matters

53 *this accoutred frowsty barn*: accoutred means 'decorated with all the appropriate trappings'. Frowsty means musty or stale-smelling

56 *compulsions*: impulses, deep-seated desires

61 *gravitating*: moving towards a centre of influence, as if drawn by a force. The word combines the meaning of being attracted to the serious earth of the Church, as well as the suggestion of weighty and solemn matters, and a reminder of the graves of the dead who lie round

GUIDELINES

This poem was written in 1954 and appeared in the collection *The Less Deceived* (1955). In 'Church Going' Larkin develops a style (and a poetic persona) that he was to use with great effect in several of his most important poems. The style is self-mocking, conversational and rich in detail.

The title 'Church Going' is a pun, describing a visit to a church and the practice of attending religious services, but also suggesting that religion is on the way out. The poem arose out of a real experience in which Larkin, on a cycling expedition, stopped to look inside a church.

The speaker of the poem, the Larkin persona, begins by presenting himself as an interloper, anxious to show no disrespect but uninformed. In Stanza Two, as 'the echoes snigger briefly', the speaker appears as a faintly ridiculous figure, glad to be on his way. Like an ill-informed tourist, the speaker leaves the church noting that 'the place was not worth stopping for' and admitting to feeling 'at a loss'. And it is in pursuit of an explanation for this feeling that the poem opens out in a rich, imaginative way.

In the course of the third stanza, the poem moves from the private 'I' to the communal 'We' and there is a corresponding shift from a descriptive to a reflective mode. The speaker considers a number of questions: what will happen when churches 'fall completely out of use'? (The speaker presumes that religion will die and churches fall into disuse. The questions project the successive stages in the process.) Will churches be avoided 'as unlucky places?' Will Christianity ('belief') be followed by superstition ('disbelief')? Will abandoned churches attract people who want to harness, in some superstitious way, the power that attended churches? And when superstition dies, will the purpose of churches become obscure? What will follow after that? The tone of Stanzas Three and Four is vaguely mocking and unconcerned for the future of churches.

In the fifth stanza, the speaker considers who will be the very last person to seek the church where he stands for 'what it was'. The tone of the stanza is sneering and dismissive, as the speaker considers the possible, future visitors. However, just as suddenly as the satire surfaces, it disappears, and the speaker returns to the implied question of Stanza Two; 'Why did I stop at this church?' And the answer and the tone of the stanza becomes deeper.

The speaker now suggests that he is attracted to churches because they recognise and give meaning to the three most fundamental and vital experiences or necessities in our lives: love, procreation and death. The church is a space where these profound experiences may be contemplated in an appropriate way. And, as the stanza comes to an end, the voice of the speaker takes on a more confident tone, losing the awkwardness of the first stanza: 'It pleases me to stand in silence here'.

This statement sets up the mood of the last stanza. The speaker now breaks completely with the scepticism of the earlier stanzas and speaks in a tone of elevated seriousness. The poem becomes solemn, and resonant with the recognition of the deepest needs of human beings. Churches will attract individuals in the future for everyone has 'A hunger in himself to be more serious' (including the poet?). That seriousness will bring them to churches because of the needs churches once served, and because the dead lie buried round. The final stanza is written in a style that is weighty, dignified and quite removed from the earlier colloquialisms of the poem. Although churches may fall into ruin, and traditional church-going become a thing of the past, the speaker sees that human beings will always hunger after seriousness and hunger to contemplate the mysteries of birth, love and death – the stages in human life which churches have recognised and made holy.

Andrew Motion says that the speaker in the poem 'speaks as someone without faith who is trying to recover the comfort that it used to give'. This comfort is not the usual one of love or other human beings. The speaker is alone and drawn to a place where 'so many dead lie around'.

QUESTIONS

1 Comment on the appropriateness of the title of the poem.

2 Examine Stanzas One and Two. How does the speaker present himself in these stanzas? Is his attitude disrespectful? Is there, as some critics suggest, an ambivalence in his attitude?

3 What are the questions which the speaker addresses in Stanzas Three to Five? The questions amount to a projected history of churches. Do you share the speaker's vision of the future of churches?

4 The poem takes on a savage tone in the fifth stanza. At whom is the speaker's contempt directed? Does the poem supply a reasonable explanation of this anger?

5 The final two stanzas return to the question of why the speaker stopped at the church. What reason does the speaker give for gravitating to church grounds?

6 The final stanza achieves an impressive, elevated tone. What contributes to this tone?

7 What truth or insight into human nature does the poem announce? Is 'Church Going', in any sense, a religious poem?

8 The voice of the poem clearly changes. Does this make the poem more or less interesting?

9 '"Church Going" represents a highly selective, distilled, and disciplined use of language.' Comment on this view of the poem.

10 Read the opening stanza of the poem in minute detail. Examine each word. Note the precise nature of the descriptions; the observed details; the change in tone and attitude conveyed by a single word or detail. Note the use of colloquial phrases. Note the use of enjambment; the complex rhyme scheme; the syllable count. Now write a note on Larkin's poetic method in the stanza.

11 'Church Going' and 'The Whitsun Weddings' are linked both in terms of style and the persona of the poem. From the evidence of 'Church Going' describe this persona.

AN ARUNDEL TOMB

Side by side, their faces blurred,
The earl and countess lie in stone,
Their proper habits vaguely shown
As jointed armour, stiffened pleat,
And that faint hint of the absurd –   5
The little dogs under their feet.

Such plainness of the pre-baroque
Hardly involves the eye, until
It meets his left-hand gauntlet, still
Clasped empty in the other; and   10
One sees, with a sharp tender shock,
His hand withdrawn, holding her hand.

They would not think to lie so long.
Such faithfulness in effigy
Was just a detail friends would see: 15
A sculpture's sweet commissioned grace
Thrown off in helping to prolong
The Latin names around the base.

They would not guess how early in
Their supine stationary voyage   20
The air would change to soundless damage,
Turn the old tenantry away;
How soon succeeding eyes begin
To look, not read. Rigidly they

Persisted, linked, through lengths and breadths   25
Of time. Snow fell, undated. Light
Each summer thronged the glass. A bright
Litter of birdcalls strewed the same
Bone-riddled ground. And up the paths
The endless altered people came,   30

Washing at their identity.
Now, helpless in the hollow of
An unarmorial age, a trough
Of smoke in slow suspended skeins
Above their scrap of history,   35
Only an attitude remains:

Time has transfigured them into
Untruth. The stone fidelity
They hardly meant has come to be
Their final blazon, and to prove   40
Our almost-instinct almost true:
What will survive of us is love.

GLOSSARY

title *Arundel*: a town in West Sussex. The tomb in Chichester Cathedral is a monument
to the Earl of Arundel and his wife

7 *pre-Baroque*: Baroque is a style of art and architecture that flourished in the
seventeenth century. It is characterised by elaborate ornamentation. Pre-Baroque
suggests a style of art that is plain and free from ornamentation

9 *gauntlet*: the glove in a suit of armour

14 effigy: a sculpted likeness or a portrait used in a monument

16 *grace*: goodwill or kindness or elegance

20 *supine*: the word describes the pose of the sculptured earl and countess who lie
on their backs with their faces upwards

22 *tenantry*: the tenants of an estate

33 *unarmorial age*: the post-medieval period, or an age that has no concern for social
distinctions based upon the status of a family. 'Armorial' relates to heraldry i.e.
coats of arms and genealogies

34 *skeins*: the usual meaning is a length of thread or yarn. It also can refer to a lock
of hair, or here, wisps of smoke

40 *blazon*: coat of arms or symbol. It also has the meaning of a public statement
or proclamation

GUIDELINES

The poem was written in 1956 following a holiday visit to Chichester Cathedral in the company of Monica Jones. Larkin had spent time nursing his mother who had been seriously ill, and he had worries about his own state of health. The poem is a meditation on transience, death and the survival of love. 'An Arundel Tomb' appeared in *The Whitsun Weddings* (1964).

The poem is a meditation on the notion of the permanence of love and the strong hope and desire that humans have that love will remain – a hope which Larkin refers to as 'Our almost-instinct'. The Arundel tomb, featuring sculptured effigies of the Earl of Arundel and his wife, is a reminder of the inevitability of death and yet, in the clasped hands of the reclining figures, the tomb stands as a monument to enduring, faithful love.

In 'An Arundel Tomb' there is a clear conflict between the emotional force of the poem, which wants to proclaim 'What will survive of us is love' and the intellectual honesty, which denies the truth of this sentiment and declares: 'Time has transfigured them into untruth'. It is a familiar tension in Larkin's work.

The meditation on the tomb, and on the passing of time, is both aware of and alert to the ironic transformation which the tomb has undergone. The poem recognises that the contemporary meaning of the tomb is at odds with the original purpose that the monument was intended to serve. The tomb now expresses a meaning that neither the earl and countess nor the sculptor could have envisaged.

Now the couple serve as an emblem of faithful, tender love, an English version of Romeo and Juliet. The lesson that the speaker takes from this is that we, too, are subject to time. We have little control over the meaning of our lives after we have gone. And while the tomb stands as an emblem of love's survival, the individual identities of the earl and his countess have been washed away. What remains of them is the sculptured pose.

The poem points out an illusion of art – the illusion that art can preserve meaning and hold back time. But this is not so. The original intention of the tomb was to keep alive the names of the dead, to honour important people. Yet what remains is the gesture of affection and tenderness, the hands clasped in each other's, although we have no way of knowing if the couple were the devoted lovers suggested by this gesture. A deeper irony is that, unknown to Larkin when he wrote the poem, the gesture upon which the poem depends is a late addition. It was added to the effigies some four hundred years after the burial of the earl and the countess during restoration work in the cathedral in the 1840s.

It is possible to read a poem as a meditation on falsehood. The gesture of affection is simply a lie and the poem reveals Larkin's doubts about the possibility of a long-lasting relationship. Read in this way, the last two lines indicate Larkin's belief that no living couple could ever be truly happy and remain permanently in love.

Andrew Motion provides an interesting insight into Larkin's attitude to his own achievement in 'An Arundel Tomb'. He tells us that:

> *At the end of the manuscript draft of 'An Arundel Tomb' Larkin wrote, 'Love isn't stronger than death just because statues hold hands for 600 years'. It is a remark which reinforced, privately, the sense of futility that hovers around the poem's conclusion in words like 'helpless', 'scrap', 'attitude', 'Untruth' and 'almost' (and it typifies his habit of writing cynical graffiti on his own most monumental lines.)*

QUESTIONS

1 What is the tone of the opening stanza: detached, disinterested, amused, superior? Perhaps you could suggest another term.
2 '…a sharp tender shock …' (line 11). This is a key moment in the poem. How does the phrase succeed in drawing attention to itself? How does Larkin convey the tenderness of the gesture in the language of the final line of Stanza Two? Select other examples of lines where there is a successful blending of sound and sense.
3 The gesture of fidelity is now what gives meaning to the monument. What does the speaker suggest, in Stanza Three, was the original significance of the gesture of the earl holding the hand of his wife?
4 How, throughout the poem, and in particular in the fourth and fifth stanzas, does the poet convey the idea that the monument serves less and less as a commemoration of two individuals?
5 What purpose does the monument now serve?
6 What is the effect of the verb 'begin' in line 23? What potential difficulties are there in reading Stanza Four in terms of grammar and syntax?
7 There is a brilliant evocation of the passage of time, beginning in the last line of Stanza Five and continuing into the first line of Stanza Seven. Examine each of the images in this passage and comment on their effectiveness. How does the rhythm of these lines form part of their meaning?
8 'The endless altered people.' In what way are the people altered? There is clearly a pun on the words alter/altar. Explain it.

9 The lives and feelings of earl and the countess are gone. Now, all that remains is 'a trough of smoke ... above their scrap of history'. What, do you think, is the speaker's attitude towards the loss of their identity?

10 The final stanza begins with the grave and dignified statement: 'Time has transfigured them into untruth'. What is the untruth? Is the untruth of the monument a beautiful untruth? Does it fill a need in us? Is the poem suggesting here that art is a form of self-delusion?

11 Read 'Wedding-Wind' and 'An Arundel Tomb' again. What views of love and marriage emerge from the two poems? What differences are there between them?

THE WHITSUN WEDDINGS

That Whitsun, I was late getting away:
    Not till about
One-twenty on the sunlit Saturday
Did my three-quarters-empty train pull out,
All windows down, all cushions hot, all sense   5
Of being in a hurry gone. We ran
Behind the backs of houses, crossed a street
Of blinding windscreens, smelt the fish-dock; thence
The river's level drifting breadth began,
Where sky and Lincolnshire and water meet.   10

All afternoon, through the tall heat that slept
    For miles inland,
A slow and stopping curve southwards we kept.
Wide farms went by, short-shadowed cattle, and
Canals with floatings of industrial froth;   15
A hothouse flashed uniquely: hedges dipped
And rose: and now and then a smell of grass
Displaced the reek of buttoned carriage-cloth
Until the next town, new and nondescript,
Approached with acres of dismantled cars.   20

At first, I didn't notice what a noise
    The weddings made
Each station that we stopped at: sun destroys
The interest of what's happening in the shade,
And down the long cool platforms whoops and skirls   25
I took for porters larking with the mails,
And went on reading. Once we started, though,
We passed them, grinning and pomaded, girls
In parodies of fashion, heels and veils,
All posed irresolutely, watching us go,   30

As if out on the end of an event
    Waving goodbye

To something that survived it. Struck, I leant
More promptly out next time, more curiously,
And saw it all again in different terms: 35
The fathers with broad belts under their suits
And seamy foreheads; mothers loud and fat;
An uncle shouting smut; and then the perms,
The nylon gloves and jewellery-substitutes,
The lemons, mauves, and olive-ochres that   40

Marked off the girls unreally from the rest.
        Yes, from cafés
And banquet-halls up yards, and bunting-dressed
Coach-party annexes, the wedding-days
Were coming to an end. All down the line   45
Fresh couples climbed aboard: the rest stood round;
The last confetti and advice were thrown,
And, as we moved, each face seemed to define
Just what it saw departing: children frowned
At something dull; fathers had never known   50

Success so huge and wholly farcical;
        The women shared
The secret like a happy funeral;
While girls, gripping their handbags tighter, stared
At a religious wounding. Free at last,   55
And loaded with the sum of all they saw,
We hurried towards London, shuffling gouts of steam.
Now fields were building-plots, and poplars cast
Long shadows over major roads, and for
Some fifty minutes, that in time would seem   60

Just long enough to settle hats and say
        I nearly died,
A dozen marriages got under way.
They watched the landscape, sitting side by side
 – An Odeon went past, a cooling tower,   65
And someone running up to bowl – and none
Thought of the others they would never meet
Or how their lives would all contain this hour.

I thought of London spread out in the sun,
Its postal districts packed like squares of wheat: 70

There we were aimed. And as we raced across
    Bright knots of rail
Past standing Pullmans, walls of blackened moss
Came close, and it was nearly done, this frail
Travelling coincidence; and what it held   75
Stood ready to be loosed with all the power
That being changed can give. We slowed again,
And as the tightened brakes took hold, there swelled
A sense of falling, like an arrow-shower
Sent out of sight, somewhere becoming rain.   80

GLOSSARY

title *Whitsun*: Pentecost Sunday, the seventh Sunday after Easter. This feast celebrates the descent of the Holy Spirit upon the Apostles. Traditionally, Whitsun was regarded as lucky time to celebrate a wedding

19 *nondescript*: bland, characterless

25 *skirls*: high-pitched shrieks, shrill cries (like those made by the bagpipes)

26 *larking*: having fun, playing the fool

28 *pomaded*: perfumed

30 *irresolutely*: in a hesitant or uncertain manner

37 *seamy*: lined or wrinkled (it can also mean greasy or even disreputable)

38–39 *the perms / The nylon gloves and jewellery-substitutes*: a perm was a popular hairstyle in the 1950s. Nylon goods were an inexpensive alternative to many other fabrics. The list is an unflattering description of working-class taste in fashion

55 *a religious wounding*: the phrase refers to the bleeding that sometimes follows the breaking of the hymen when sexual intercourse takes place for the first time. The 'wound' is a religious one in that it arises from the consummation of the marriage. The girls are 'staring' into the future, and thinking about their own weddings. The marriage may also involve different kinds of wounding, which may be inferred from the poem as a whole

57 *gouts of steam*: drops or splashes of steam

65 *An Odeon*: the name of a cinema

73 *Pullmans*: a Pullman is a luxurious railway carriage, often with sleeping accommodation, named after its designer

GUIDELINES

'The Whitsun Weddings' was written over a two-year period and completed in October 1958. It appeared in *The Whitsun Weddings* (1964). Larkin claimed that there was nothing of him in the poem. His biographer, Andrew Motion, suggests that 'there is everything of him in it – the yearning for love as well as the standing off'.

The poem was inspired by a journey Larkin took from Hull to London on Whit Saturday, 1955. Larkin said that he caught:

> *A very slow train that stopped at every station and I hadn't realised that, of course, this was the train that all the wedding couples would get on and go to London for their honeymoon; it was an eye-opener to me. Every part was different but the same somehow. They all looked different but they were all doing the same things and sort of feeling the same things. I suppose the train stopped at about four, five, six stations between Hull and London and there was a sense of gathering momentum. Every time you stopped fresh emotion climbed aboard. And finally between Peterborough and London, when you hurtle on, you felt the whole thing was being aimed like a bullet – at the heart of thing, you know. All this fresh, open life. Incredible experience. I've never forgotten it.*

For most of the poem, the speaker is a detached observer. He notes the towns and countryside as the train speeds past, and also the wedding parties gathered on the station platforms at each stop. For the first five stanzas, the tone of the poem is amused to the point of disdain but, as the poem moves to consider the significance of the marriages whose beginnings the speaker has just witnessed, the tone becomes elevated and hopeful. The poem is one of the longest that Larkin ever wrote. Its length, and the ten-line stanza form, allows the speaker to capture both the journey and also the movement and development of his responses to what he observes. Read aloud, the poem has a leisurely colloquial feel, but Larkin achieves this effect without deviating from the rhyme or metre of the poem.

'The Whitsun Weddings' contains many paradoxes: the romantic ending which is preceded by a catalogue of ordinary, downbeat sights and sounds; a tone that is, in the words of Andrew Motion, 'both awestruck and sharply conscious of absurdity'; a poem rich in concrete details, which seems to reach for transcendence; a point-of-view which appears to dismiss the wedding parties as it celebrates what they represent. In many respects, this is the quintessential Larkin poem, in which the poet satisfies the preconditions of his sceptical, almost brutal, intellect before surrendering himself to the imaginative possibilities of what the poem has recorded.

The persona of the poem appears to sneer at the working-class culture he observes. However, a pivotal moment in 'The Whitsun Weddings' occurs in the sixth stanza when the speaker moves from observer to participant, sharing in the honeymoon journey of the couples, just as they share in each other's. The 'frail coincidence' of travelling on the same train is worked by the poet into something more substantial, something full of possibility, in the optimistic, regenerative images of the final stanza.

This final stanza is inspired by what Larkin called, in 'An Arundel Tomb', the 'almost-instinct' that love will survive. The physical sensation of being pitched forward by the braking train is transformed by Larkin into the image of the arrow-shower. It is a complex, compact and rewarding image. The ceremony of watching the couples embark on their wedding journey, of launching them or aiming them towards a future which includes human generation, is conveyed in the image of the arrow-shower 'somewhere becoming rain'. The couples on the train are the arrows aimed at London, mingling with the rain to make germinate the future. The image contains a suggestion of strength, of something launched with great force, and also the idea of dispersal and gentle falling at the flight's end. The couples will disperse to their separate destinies, in postal districts that are crowded but fruitful.

Characteristically, Larkin was dismissive of his own achievement in 'The Whitsun Weddings', remarking that the poem was 'just the transcription of a very happy afternoon. I didn't change a thing, it was just there to be written down.'

QUESTIONS

1 From the tone and imagery of the first two stanzas, what is the observer's view of the urban landscape through which he passes?
2 Would you agree with the view that the observer is cruelly mocking in his description of the weddings parties (which begins in Stanza Three and continues into Stanza Six)? What comments are particularly telling?
3 What view of working-class English life emerges in the poem?
4 Larkin keenly observes the feelings that the marriages call out in the wedding guests. What feelings are evident in their actions? Are the responses connected in any way to human sexuality?
5 What is the change of tone and perspective evident in the sixth stanza? Pinpoint the moment of change.

6 The final two stanzas move from description to meditation. What role does the observer take on himself in relation to the newly married couples on the train? From the evidence of 'The Whitsun Wedding', what is the poet's role in relation to ordinary lives?

7 The tone and language of the final stanzas is more elevated and excited than in the earlier stanzas. Where is the excitement and elevation most evident?

8 The final movement of the poem is dominated by the rich, complex and rewarding image of the arrow-shower. Discuss the image in terms of the various elements which it brings together: a sense of beauty; a sense of energy and dispersal; generation; a sense of lives being launched; a sense of hope.

9 'The Whitsun Weddings' is noted for its method of detail collecting and its observation of ordinary life. Comment on what you consider to be three of the most impressive and significant details of the poem. Would you agree with the opinion that, despite the method of collecting details, of social life, 'The Whitsun Weddings' is a poem that strives to go beyond the ordinary?

10 There are many changes of tone and changes in the stance of the poet/observer. Select what you consider to be three of the most important points of change in the poem. Describe how the transition from one viewpoint to another is achieved and explain the significance of each of the changes.

11 Reviewing the poem, trace both the emotional and the philosophical journey made by the speaker in the course of 'The Whitsun Weddings'.

12 Discuss the view that 'The Whitsun Weddings' is, ultimately, a celebration of marriage and a celebration of the hope and commitment to the future that it embodies.

MCMXIV

Those long uneven lines
Standing as patiently
As if they were stretched outside
The Oval or Villa Park,
The crowns of hats, the sun   5
On moustached archaic faces
Grinning as if it were all
An August Bank Holiday lark;

And the shut shops, the bleached
Established names on the sunblinds,   10
The farthings and sovereigns,
And dark-clothed children at play
Called after kings and queens,
The tin advertisements
For cocoa and twist, and the pubs   15
Wide open all day;

And the countryside not caring:
The place-names all hazed over
With flowering grasses, and fields
Shadowing Domesday lines   20
Under wheat's restless silence;
The differently-dressed servants
With tiny rooms in huge houses,
The dust behind limousines;

Never such innocence,   25
Never before or since,
As changed itself to past
Without a word – the men
Leaving the gardens tidy,
The thousands of marriages   30
Lasting a little while longer:
Never such innocence again.

title *MCMXIV*: the title of the poem is '1914'. The year is written in Roman numerals, as it might appear on a monument. Indeed the poem might be described as a monument to life in England on the eve of the First World War

4 *The Oval or Villa* Park: a reference to the English love of sport. The Oval is the home of English cricket. Villa Park is the ground of the soccer team, Aston Villa. Larkin was a lover of all things English

6 *archaic*: from an earlier period, old-fashioned

11 *The farthings and sovereigns*: British coins in use in 1914. A farthing was one quarter of the old British penny and was the least valuable coin in circulation. A sovereign was the most valuable coin, worth a pound

15 *twist*: a roll of tobacco

20 *Domesday lines*: lines of death. Domesday is an older spelling of Doomsday, the Day of Judgement. The word refers back to the Domesday Book made under orders of William the Conqueror in 1086, in which the division and ownership of the land of England was registered and recorded. The register was considered as authoritative as The Last Judgement. The word is a reminder of the millions of young men who registered to fight in the First World War and who were sent to their doom

GUIDELINES

This poem was completed in May 1960 and published in *The Whitsun Weddings* (1964). In the first stanza of 'MCMXIV', the emphasis is on the men waiting to enlist in the army. There is a mingled awe and horror in Larkin's tone as he contemplates 'those long uneven lines'. The 'archaic' faces of the men belong to the past, to a different world. In the contemporary world, it is impossible to envisage lines of young men queuing so eagerly and patiently to enlist to fight in war, as if it were 'An August Bank Holiday lark'. However, the innocence of the men is not mocked. 'MCMXIV' is animated by the same gravitas evident in the treatment of the miners' death in 'The Explosion'. The men are 'grinning', a description with darker undertones calling to mind skeletal images of the dead, so that the image of the men is overshadowed by the poet's knowledge of what lay in store for them.

In Stanzas Two and Three, the poem evokes a wistful view of England on the eve of war. The town of Stanza Two is on holiday; the pubs 'Wide open all day'. The names on the shops are established names, suggesting a stable society. The same effect is achieved by the reference to farthings and sovereigns, coins in use for centuries but no longer current. In the next stanza, the reference to

Domesday lines establishes a continuity between the England of 1914 and the England of William the Conqueror. In a century of rapid change and discontinuity, it is easy to understand the appeal of such order.

However, the idyll of Stanza Two is not maintained in Stanza Three. The 'wheat's restless silence' which shadows 'the Domesday lines' is a chilling reminder of the battlefields where 'the long uneven lines' of men from the first stanza will die. As with the use of the word 'grinning' in Stanza One, the image is poised between past and future, between delight and horror. The poem shows us the countryside emptied of the men who stand in lines, men who signed up for a 'lark', with no way of foreseeing that the war would drag on with unimaginable loss of life.

The final stanza makes an emotional appeal to the readers' sympathy in evoking the innocence of the men 'leaving the gardens tidy' as they set out to war. The domestic detail works more powerfully than any rhetorical denunciation of war. The same emotional effect is achieved by the understatement of: 'The thousands of marriages / Lasting a little longer'. The final line of the poem, 'Never such innocence again', echoes the opening line of the final stanza.

Interestingly, the poem is written as one sentence without a main verb. This creates an impression of timelessness, of a world divorced from historical change. It also suggests that the past is not over and, perhaps, it suggests that the line of men waiting to die represents a truth that is timeless. Some critics read the poem as an ironic view of innocence, the irony made gentle by Larkin's respect for those who died in the war. Here, as in 'An Arundel Tomb', Larkin is interested in the way in which the past is interpreted from the viewpoint of the present; in the way that the meaning of lives and events is changed over time. To borrow a phrase from 'An Arundel Tomb', time has transfigured the England of 1914 into untruth, into what the critic John Saunders calls 'a seductively false and unrepresentative image of reality'.

QUESTIONS

1 The title of the poem is written in Roman numerals. Why, in your opinion, has Larkin chosen to do this? What effect does it achieve?

2 In the first stanza, the men wait to enlist in the army. How are 'the long uneven lines' of men portrayed? In what sense are their faces 'archaic'? Is there any irony in Larkin's depiction of the men?

3 Examine the images of Stanza Two. How is the continuity and joy of the social world conveyed?

4 Read through all the images used to evoke the past in the first two stanzas. Where is there evidence that the evocation of the past also contains intimations of a darker future? What words strike the darker note in the poem?

5 Look at the final lines of Stanza Three. Would you agree that these lines paint a less idyllic picture of England on the eve of the war than the earlier images in the poem? Explain your answer.

6 The final stanza makes a direct appeal to the emotions of the reader. Does the repetition and the domestic imagery constitute a satisfying ending to the poem?

7 In your view, is the reader intended to accept the pre-war England, which the poem evokes, as real, or does the poem present us with a mythic England? (Compare the presentation of England in this poem with its presentation in 'The Whitsun Weddings'.)

8 'Every comment about the past is also a comment about the present.' Is this statement true of 'MCMXIV'?

9 'MCMXIV' is written as one sentence, without a main verb. What effect does this achieve? How does the absence of a main verb support the theme of the poem?

10 Innocence and the loss of innocence are clearly the major concerns of the poem. Whose innocence is celebrated/lamented – the men who died, the nation, the poet?

11 How would you describe the dominant mood of the poem?

AMBULANCES

Closed like confessionals, they thread
Loud noons of cities, giving back
None of the glances they absorb.
Light glossy grey, arms on a plaque,
They come to rest at any kerb: 5
All streets in time are visited.

Then children strewn on steps or road,
Or women coming from the shops
Past smells of different dinners, see
A wild white face that overtops   10
Red stretcher-blankets momently
As it is carried in and stowed,

And sense the solving emptiness
That lies just under all we do,
And for a second get it whole,   15
So permanent and blank and true.
The fastened doors recede. *Poor soul,*
They whisper at their own distress;

For borne away in deadened air
May go the sudden shut of loss   20
Round something nearly at an end,
And what cohered in it across
The years, the unique random blend
Of families and fashions, there

At last begin to loosen. Far   25
From the exchange of love to lie
Unreachable inside a room
The traffic parts to let go by
Brings closer what is left to come,
And dulls to distance all we are.   30

GLOSSARY

1 *confessionals*: the small enclosed stall in a church where the priest sits to hear confessions

4 *plaque*: the medical crest on the side of the ambulance

13 *solving*: unbinding, dissolving. An interesting choice of adjective. It may also suggest that the emptiness is the final answer to life's question

22 *cohered*: came together, connected

25–30 *At last…all we are*: the final sentence of the poem is difficult to read. In the ambulance, the logical connection of language begins to unravel. The critic, James Booth, suggests this reading of it: 'To lie far from the exchange of love, unreachable inside a room [which] the traffic parts to let go by, brings closer what is left to come, and dulls to distance all we are'

GUIDELINES

The poem was written in 1961 and appeared in *The Whitsun Weddings* (1964). Larkin said of his poetry, 'Everything I write, I think, has the consciousness of approaching death in the background'. This statement is certainly true of 'Ambulances'.

'Ambulances' is a stark poem. It maintains that life is governed by the 'permanent and blank and true' fact of death. The ambulances of the title are a reminder of the way in which death visits everyone; a reminder that death underlies everything we do. And so the poem closes speaking of 'all we are'.

The poem is carefully structured and formed. It works like a sonnet, with the first three stanzas presenting the subject of the poem in concrete terms, while the final two stanzas consider the deeper significance of what has been described.

The poem is rich in words that carry multiple connotations. The word 'confessionals', in the first line, for example, suggests the closed secret world of the ambulance, as well as the soul preparing itself before God, while the verb 'visited', which concludes the first stanza, suggests a ghostly visitation, turning the ambulance into a harbinger of death. The fact that the ambulances may come to rest at any kerb and that 'All streets in time are visited' captures both the randomness of suffering and dying, and the inevitability of death.

The 'wild white face that overtops / Red stretcher-blankets' becomes the 'it' of line 12, a piece of cargo that is stowed and transported. There is a brutality in this line that conveys the mercilessness of dying. The children and women, who witness the scene, sense 'the solving emptiness / that underlies all we do'. The phrase 'solving emptiness' conveys the idea of solving life's riddle, but the solution is a dread emptiness. The word 'solving' draws in the meaning of related words: 'resolving', 'dissolving' and 'absolving'.

The final two stanzas give expression to the meaning that the spectators sense. In the ambulance, the threads of life, the 'blend / Of families and fashions', begin to unravel, and the speeding ambulance brings its cargo towards its sure extinction and away from all that it was. The end of the poem, in its movement from 'it' (the person put into the ambulance) to the 'we' of the final line, collapses the distance not only between life and death, but also between those inside the locked room of the ambulance and those who see it pass by. At the end of this journey poem, both Larkin and the readers have an uncomfortable sense of being co-travellers in the journey of the dying person in the ambulance.

The language of the poem is complex, as in the phrase 'the sudden shut of loss' (line 20). Here, Larkin has transformed a verb into a noun, so the reader must tease out its meaning. And 'shut' has many connotations, in the context of the poem. It suggests the closing of the ambulance door, which may shut or stop the loss of life which has already gathered around the victim. Equally, the ambulance door shuts the spectators off from the drama of dying and carries it away elsewhere. In doing so, the ambulance seals the loss of life within its locked room, confining it to something nearly at an end. And, perhaps, Larkin is hinting at the human capacity for detachment and self-preservation. We want death to be shut away. Here, as in other moments of intensity in his poems, Larkin strains at the limits of language and grammar.

QUESTIONS

1 Consider Larkin's use of the words 'confessionals' and 'visited' in Stanza One. In what way do they open out the meaning of the stanza?

2 In Stanza Two, the victim is described as 'it'. What is the effect of this usage?

3 The phrase 'the solving emptiness' is a striking one. How do you interpret it?

4 The women and children who witness the victim being taken away in the ambulance sense a truth about life. What is it, and what is their response to it?

5 'In stanzas Four and Five, the poem suggests that death undoes the life that has been led and reduces it to nothing.' Is this a fair assessment of these stanzas? Explain your answer.

6 The critic James Booth, writing about the intricacy of thought in Stanzas Four and Five, suggests that Larkin takes the thought to the limits of grammar. Do you think the poem gains from this strategy?

7 What does the poem reveal about Larkin's philosophical attitude to life?

8 Do you think Larkin's use of the ambulance as a symbol is successful?

9 As in many of Larkin's poems, there are changes in diction from a colloquial to a poetic register. Select examples of each from 'Ambulances'. What is the effect of Larkin's blending of these two forms of language in the poem?

10 The critic Andrew Gibson says of Larkin's poetry that it teeters on the edge – that Larkin is fascinated by impoverishment, loss, nullity. Is this assessment true of 'Ambulances'?

11 Read through the selection of Larkin's poetry in this anthology. What constants do you find in the poet's attitude to death?

THE TREES

The trees are coming into leaf
Like something almost being said;
The recent buds relax and spread,
Their greenness is a kind of grief.

Is it that they are born again   5
And we grow old? No, they die too.
Their yearly trick of looking new
Is written down in rings of grain.

Yet still the unresting castles thresh
In fullgrown thickness every May.   10
Last year is dead, they seem to say,
Begin afresh, afresh, afresh.

GUIDELINES

'The Trees' was written in 1967 and appeared in the collection *High Windows* (1971). The poem is a meditation of the theme of transience. It was written during a period in which Larkin's personal relationships were vexed and complicated and his mother began to show the first signs of Alzheimer's Disease.

'The Trees', along with 'Cut Grass', deals with the classical theme of time and the decay it brings. The language of the poem is eloquent and harmonious. The careful phrasing and the use of long vowel sounds gives a sombre tone to the poem. In 'The Trees', spring is given a qualified welcome. The new leaves suggest a perpetual cycle of rejuvenation. No such renewal and rejuvenation occurs in the human life, so the sight of the new buds is 'a kind of grief' to humans.

In the second stanza there is a realisation that the trees will die too, and the appearance of renewing themselves is 'a trick'. Despite this realisation, the burgeoning trees offer an encouragement to humans for fresh starts and new beginnings. Unusually for Larkin, having established the inevitably of death, the poem goes back to the attractive but false idea of renewal and concludes with the remarkably vibrant final line: 'Begin afresh, afresh, afresh'. This line expresses an irresistible longing for life and may represent an act of self-persuasion.

In the final stanza Larkin allows himself to express a sense of awe. This allowance was short-lived. Larkin distrusted what he described in a letter as his 'astonished delight at the renewal of the natural world'. In his manuscript, he wrote the words 'bloody awful tripe' after the date (2 June 1967) of the poem.

QUESTIONS

1 The poem turns on a contrast between the trees and human beings. Why is the appearance of the leaves on the trees described as a kind of grief by the poet?

2 The argument of the poem advances in an ordered way. Trace the thought through the statements of Stanza One, the question and answer of Stanza Two; and the qualification and tentative conclusion of Stanza Three.

3 Comment on the phrase 'unresting castles' (line 9) to describe the trees.

4 Against the logic of the poem, the burgeoning trees, in the final stanza, are taken as an encouragement to begin afresh. The repetition of 'afresh' gives an emphatic affirmation of the will to live. From your reading of Larkin's poetry, are there similar moments of affirmation in his poems?

5 '"The Trees" can be read as an exercise in self-persuasion.' Give your view of this reading of the poem.

6 The poem is eloquent and harmonious throughout. Examine the phrasing, the vowels and the rhymes to discover how the harmony is created.

7 In his notebook, Larkin scrawled the judgement 'bloody awful tripe' at the end of the poem. Do you think this is a fair assessment of 'The Trees'?

THE EXPLOSION

On the day of the explosion
Shadows pointed towards the pithead:
In the sun the slagheap slept.

Down the lane came men in pitboots
Coughing oath-edged talk and pipe-smoke,   5
Shouldering off the freshened silence.

One chased after rabbits; lost them;
Came back with a nest of lark's eggs;
Showed them; lodged them in the grasses.

So they passed in beards and moleskins,   10
Fathers, brothers, nicknames, laughter,
Through the tall gates standing open.

At noon, there came a tremor; cows
Stopped chewing for a second; sun,
Scarfed as in a heat-haze, dimmed.   15

The dead go on before us, they
Are sitting in God's house in comfort,
We shall see them face to face –

Plain as lettering in the chapels
It was said, and for a second   20
Wives saw men of the explosion

Larger than in life they managed –
Gold as on a coin, or walking
Somehow from the sun towards them,

One showing the eggs unbroken.   25

GLOSSARY

2 *pithead*: the top of the mine shaft and the various buildings around it

3 *slagheap*: the hill or mound made of the waste material from coal mining

10 *moleskins*: a hard-wearing cotton used for work clothes. Miners wore moleskin trousers to work.

16–18 *The dead … face-to-face*: the verse is taken from a prayer from the funeral service. These words formed part of the vision of the wives

GUIDELINES

The poem was written over Christmas in 1969. It appeared in *High Windows* (1971). The poem presents an account of a mine explosion in which many miners lost their lives. It was reported that, at the moment of the explosion, the wives of the miners had visions of their husbands. The source of the poem was a television documentary on the mining industry that Larkin watched with his mother. It may also have been influenced by his rereading of the work of D. H. Lawrence.

The poem is unusual in that there is no 'I' persona to supply the customary Larkin perspective on the events described. Instead, 'The Explosion' is a poem of observation and takes its tone from the event itself.

The first stanza paints a quiet scene, but there are hints of the disaster to come in the references to shadows and the sleeping slagheap. In the second stanza, the miners are portrayed as rough and ready as they make their way to the pithead. In Stanza Three, a miner, hurrying after the rabbit and returning with a nest of lark's eggs, alerts us the vitality in these men, and their closeness to nature. The fourth stanza suggests the close-knit community of the pit workers: fathers and sons, and friends and companions, laughing together as they pass through 'the tall gates standing open'. The image of the gates suggest the entry into death's kingdom. The long vowel sound of this stanza create an elegiac tone, as if the poet wishes to rouse our sympathy for these innocent men marching towards their death, without a care or an intimation of what is to come.

In Stanza Five, the explosion is registered on the surface by a mere tremor. This stanza suggests that, much as we might wish it otherwise, sudden death does not stop the flow of life. However, the poem seeks to register the deaths of these men, and the vision of the wives is used to give the poem a remarkably uplifting ending, in the final, floating, line with its suggestion of Easter eggs and resurrection: 'One showing the eggs unbroken'.

In 'The Explosion', Larkin is back to the 'almost-instinct' of 'An Arundel Tomb', that what will survive of us is love. The poem does not declare that the men are transformed by death, but that they are transformed in the visions of their wives. This final, optimistic image contains a suggestion of continuity and generation. The poem, without stating anything directly, offers a testament to the power of love to withstand tragedy and death.

QUESTIONS

1 Unlike the most celebrated of Larkin's poems 'The Explosion' does not have the customary Larkin narrator to comment and reflect on the action. In reading the poem, can you see why he may have chosen to dispense with his usual poetic persona?

2 From as early as the first stanza, the poem hints at the disaster to come. How is this done? Where else, in the first four stanzas, are there intimations of disaster?

3 Between Stanzas Two and Four, Larkin deftly sketches the community of pit workers. What do we learn of the men and their relationship to each other?

4 One miner discovers a nest of lark's eggs. He lodges them in the grasses. Why does he do this? What is the point of this detail in relation to the impending disaster and the theme of the poem?

5 The sixth stanza consists of an extract from the funeral service. Is the tone and rhythm of this stanza in keeping with the rest of the poem?

6 How does the poem deal with the reported visions of the wives of the explosion? What is the poem's attitude to death and suffering?

7 The final four stanzas are difficult to read, both in terms of syntax and grammar. Attempt a paraphrase of the stanzas, supplying missing words where needed. What, in your view, is lost or gained in paraphrasing the lines?

8 The poem ends with an image of unbroken eggs. This image contains a suggestion of both continuity and generation. What does this line contribute to your understanding of the theme of the poem?

9 What similarities in theme and attitude can you find between this poem and 'Wedding Wind', 'The Whitsun Weddings', 'MCMXIV', 'Ambulances' and 'An Arundel Tomb' in relation to marriage and death?

CUT GRASS

Cut grass lies frail:
Brief is the breath
Mown stalks exhale,
Long, long the death

It dies in the white hours 5
Of young-leafed June
With chestnut flowers,
With hedges snowlike strewn,

White lilac bowed,
Lost lanes of Queen Anne's lace, 10
And that high-builded cloud
Moving at summer's pace.

GLOSSARY

10 *Queen Anne's Lace*: a wild flower with clusters of white flowers and a purplish centre. It is a species of wild carrot, though it is sometimes known as Cow Parsley

GUIDELINES

This short lyric, on the theme of transience, was composed in 1971 and appeared in *High Windows* (1971). The poem comes from the final third of Larkin's life, when he expressed dissatisfaction with life in England in virulent terms in his private correspondence.

'Cut Grass' deals with a classical theme in a classical manner. The theme is announced without delay. 'Brief is the breath' and 'Long, long the death' sum up Larkin's attitude to life. The cut grass dies its death in mid-summer in a world that is in full bloom. But each of the flowers mentioned in the poem will last only a short time and, then, they, too, will die. The flowers teach us the brevity of life. This lesson is a common one in classical literature, especially in the work of the Latin poet Ovid. In Ovid the flowers teach us the fragile nature of beauty and the relentless approach of death. There is no religious consolation in 'Cut Grass', nor does the poem advise us to live life passionately, knowing that our time is short, as Ovid does in his poetry.

The language of 'Cut Grass' is sweet and simple and the general sweetness is heightened by the use of long, vowel sounds, as if the poet wants to linger over the beauty that is fading.

Interestingly, 'Cut Grass' was written during a period when Larkin was expressing his most bitter right-wing views about the state of England, complaining of socialism and the influx of black citizens into England. Not surprisingly, then, in his private correspondence, Larkin was dismissive or distrustful of the poem's lyrical impulse, describing it as 'pointless crap'.

QUESTIONS

1 As with 'The Trees', this is a beautifully phrased and executed poem. Write a short note on the pattern of sound and phrasing in the poem. How do the sound patterns contribute to the tone of the poem?

2 The grass dies in high summer, surrounded by a beauty that will also fade and die. Yet the poem offers no consolation. What does this suggest about Larkin's frame of mind at the time of writing?

3 Compare this poem to 'The Trees'. Which of the poems do you prefer?

4 Larkin, writing about the poem, declared that the logical sense of the poem ceases at line six, and the rest of the poem consists of no more than a succession of images. Is Larkin being fair to his own work in making this judgement?

GENERAL QUESTIONS ON PHILIP LARKIN

1 What attitude to love emerges from the poetry of Philip Larkin? Support the points you make by reference to the poems by Larkin that you have studied.

2 'Loneliness and isolation are striking features of Larkin's poetry.' Do you agree with this statement? Support the points you make by reference to the poems on your course.

3 'Although Larkin's poetry is not religious, the poems do convey a sense of the spiritual.' Give your view of this statement, supporting the points you make by reference to the poems by Larkin on your course.

4 If you were asked to give a public reading of a small selection of the poetry of Philip Larkin, which poems would you choose to read? Give reasons for your choice, supporting them by reference to the poems on your course.

5 'We enjoy the poetry of Philip Larkin for its ideas and its language.' Using the above as your title, write an essay on Larkin's poetry. Support the points you make by reference to the poems by Larkin on your course.

6 In many of Larkin's poems, there are passages in which the thought is hard to paraphrase. Do you regard these difficulties as a failure of

technique or an enrichment of meaning? Support your view by reference to the poems by Larkin on your course.

7 Would you agree with Philip Larkin when he described each of his poems as representing 'a composite and complex experience'? Support the points you make by reference to the poems by Larkin on your course.

EXAMINATION-STYLE QUESTIONS

8 From your reading of his poetry, what kind of person do you imagine Philip Larkin to have been? Support the points you make by reference to the poems by Larkin on your course.

Guidelines
Your answer might consider some or all of the following:
- the ambiguity towards love
- the self-mocking quality in some of the poems
- the mixture of formal and colloquial language
- the way the poems move from description to meditation
- the sense of the spiritual in many of the poems
- the consciousness of death in the background
- the sense of loneliness in some of the poems.

9 You have been asked to introduce the poetry of Philip Larkin to your fellow students. Write the speech you would make, referring to a representative selection of Larkin's poems.

Guidelines
- the thematic range of Larkin's poetry: poems which explore love; poems which express a nostalgia for an older England; poems which are dominated by death
- Larkin's skill as a poet   ■ the traditional form of many of the poems
- the occasional difficulty in interpreting lines in the poems
- the tone of the poems   ■ the character of the poet
- the philosophy of life which emerges from the poetry.

10 *Philip Larkin: a Personal Response.*
Using this title, give your view of the poetry of Philip Larkin. Your answer might address some or all of the following:
- the themes of love and death   ■ Larkin's portrait of England
- the Larkin persona   ■ the effect of reading the poetry
- the mixing of the colloquial and the formal.

Love-hate relationship
with his family.

In later years, beset by feelings
of remorse and failure.

The attraction and
the fear of love.

Distrustful of his talent and
dismissive of his achievements
and insights.

Self-mocking observer
present in many of
the poems.

Poems contain intricate
thoughts in carefully
crafted stanzas.

Mix of formal and
colloquial language.

Themes of love,
loneliness and transience.

The language of his
poems can test the limits
of grammar.

Philip Larkin

Consciousness of
death in the background of
all he wrote.

Believed that ordinary
life should and could provide
the subject of poetry, yet his
poetry often goes beyond
the ordinary.

There is an imaginative
opening out in many
of the poems.

Poetry expresses affection
for the English way of life.

Poetry of rich detail
and complex imagery.

Social rather than
political observations.

Though not religious,
the poetry conveys a sense
of the spiritual.

Movement from
description to meditation
in the poetry.

DEREK MAHON

B. 1941

BIOGRAPHY

Derek Mahon was born on 23 November, 1941 in Belfast and brought up in the suburb of Glengormley. His father was an engine-inspector in the Belfast shipyard of Harland and Wolff, where both his grandfathers had also been employed, while his mother worked for a time in York St Flax Spinning Company. As he himself has said, his parents thus 'embodied the two principal industries in Northern Ireland, ship-building and linen'.

Although Mahon's own background was working-class Protestant, Mahon played as a child with Catholic children, Glengormley being a mixed neighbourhood. He describes himself in one of his poems as having been 'A strange child with a taste for verse'. He went to secondary school at the Royal Belfast Academical Institution. The poet Michael Longley was a contemporary of his at the school and remembers him as already being an accomplished poet at this time.

Like Longley, Mahon went on to study at Trinity College, Dublin. He studied modern languages there, specialising in French, but also began to work seriously at the craft of poetry. Mahon was part of a group of other gifted young poets studying at TCD at the time: Eavan Boland, Brendan Kennelly and Michael

Longley. For the first time Mahon felt that there was a poetry-writing community that he could be part of, as well as a thriving literary scene in Dublin.

After taking his BA in Trinity College, Mahon studied at the Sorbonne in Paris. He worked as a teacher in the USA, Canada and Ireland before becoming a journalist and writer in London. He was theatre critic for *The Listener* for a time, poetry editor for *The New Statesman*, and features editor of *Vogue* magazine. He was also involved in adapting Irish novels for television, among them Jennifer Johnston's *How Many Miles to Babylon?*, as well as radio adaptations and features. He was writer-in-residence at New University of Ulster 1978–79, and at TCD in 1988. He has been a regular contributor of literary journalism and book reviews to *The Irish Times*.

For several years in the 1990s Mahon lived in New York where he taught at New York University. Having by this time divorced his wife Doreen Douglas, whom he married in 1972, much of his work from New York was addressed to his two children, Rory and Katie, with whom he was no longer living. By 1996 he had returned to live in Dublin.

Poems 1962–78 brings together most of the poems from his first three collections, *Night Crossing* (1968), *Lives* (1972) and *The Snow Party* (1975). *Courtyards in Delft* appeared in 1981, *The Hunt by Night* in 1983, and *Antarctica* in 1985. *Selected Poems* (1991) was the winner of the *Irish Times*-Aer Lingus Irish Literature Prize for Poetry in 1992.

Derek Mahon has also edited some poetry anthologies and published several verse translations, including Moliere's *School for Wives*, the poems of Philippe Jaccottet from the French and a version of *The Bacchae* by the Greek Euripides.

A member of Aosdána and a fellow of the Royal Society of Literature, he has received numerous awards, among them the American Ireland Literary Award and the C. K. Scott-Moncrieff prize for translation.

In 1999 he published his *Collected Poems*, with updated versions of many of the poems he has written during the course of his distinguished career. His latest collection is *Harbour Lights* (2005).

SOCIAL AND CULTURAL CONTEXT

Derek Mahon once said in an interview that he considers himself to be a European poet who happens to be Irish, and who also just happens to have been born in Belfast. Each of the three strands of his chosen cultural identity has its place in the development of his work.

As a poet from Northern Ireland his work responds in a complex way to the society into which he was born. He is acutely aware of his roots, as the poem 'Grandfather' suggests, revealing a certain admiration for traits that have been associated with the Northern Irish character, such as a certain rebelliousness and self-reliance. On the other hand, in a poem such as 'Ecclesiastes' he rejects the bigoted attitudes of the churchmen of his native Belfast – a rejection that is tinged with admission of the attractions of that way of life. He has never sought to engage with the political problems or the conflict in Northern Ireland. He once said that he felt that poets in Ulster are 'supposed to write about the Troubles; a lot of people expect us to act as if it were part of our job – it's not, unless we choose to make it so'.

And yet it is true to say that Mahon does not flinch from confronting the issue of violence, even if in a rather oblique way. The lesson of history is an important theme in his poems, and his attitude to the questions that have caused much grief in Ireland can be seen from his statement that 'whatever we mean by the "Irish situation", the shipyards of Belfast are no less a part of it than a country town in the Gaeltacht'.

Mahon's education at Trinity College Dublin widened his cultural experience. In the 1960s students at Trinity College were predominantly Protestant since Catholics were forbidden to attend. Mahon, however, met several Southern Irish Catholic students at the university, among them the Kerry poet Brendan Kennelly and the Dublin poet Eavan Boland. Having lived in Dublin while attending college and for some time afterward, Mahon became familiar with life in the south of Ireland, which he may not have done had he remained in Belfast. An abiding love for the landscape of the west of Ireland is shown in his poems about Inis Oirr, Achill and Donegal.

Mahon's assimilation of French literature at university led to his translations of classical French texts and modern French poetry. As a student in Paris, Mahon met the Irish dramatist Samuel Beckett , who, like himself, had been educated at Trinity. Like Beckett, Mahon's self-induced exile enabled him to write of his native country as an observer rather than as a participant in the Irish cultural scene. Many of his poems reflect also an interest in European art. He is conscious of the complex link between poetry and painting that is so important in his work.

His imagery is frequently concerned with the effects of light and shade, as an artist would be.

Derek Mahon has lived in the USA and some of his poems describe the American landscape and way of life. Although he has returned to Ireland, his poetic vision continues to be truly international. His themes are universal. His frame of reference and allusions contain many diverse cultural echoes. He has expressed the view that for him poetry is primarily an artistic activity rather than an expression of a particular cultural identity: 'for me, poetry is about shape and sound. It's about taking the formless and making it interesting; creating art out of formlessness.'

GRANDFATHER

They brought him in on a stretcher from the world,
Wounded but humorous; and he soon recovered.
Boiler-rooms, row upon row of gantries rolled
Away to reveal the landscape of a childhood
Only he can recapture. Even on cold   5
Mornings he is up at six with a block of wood
Or a box of nails, discreetly up to no good
Or banging round the house like a four-year-old—

Never there when you call. But after dark
You hear his great boots thumping in the hall   10
And in he comes, as cute as they come. Each night
His shrewd eyes bolt the door and set the clock
Against the future, then his light goes out.
Nothing escapes him; he escapes us all.

GLOSSARY

3 *gantries*: overhead platform for a travelling crane used in shipbuilding

GUIDELINES

'Grandfather' is from the collection *Night Crossing* (1968).

Derek Mahon's grandfather was a boiler-maker in Harland and Wolff, the ship-builders in Belfast where the *Titanic* was built. In this sonnet the poet paints an interesting portrait of the old man.

In the first eight lines, the octet, we see the old man as an outsider, isolated from the real world but living his own rich life. Images of his working life recede as he seems to recapture the freedom of childhood. Mahon's wry humour evokes a picture of a harmless old man.

The sestet offers a slightly different perspective on the grandfather, however. The colloquial phrase 'as cute as they come' suggests that his actions are far from aimless. Perhaps he has found a way to avoid confronting the problems of real life. Certainly we are left with an impression of an old man who has stubbornly refused to adapt to the conventions of 'normal' elderly behaviour.

QUESTIONS

1 What do the first two lines of the poem convey to you about the grandfather? Is this initial impression borne out by the rest of the poem?

2 Why do you think the poet refers to his grandfather's working life? Is this significant in the poem, in your view?

3 Look at the colloquial phrases 'up to no good', 'as cute as they come', and the similes and metaphors used to describe the old man. What do they contribute to our sense of the sort of person he is?

4 Is there another view of the grandfather suggested in the sestet? Look in particular at the last three lines.

5 Which of these words best describes the grandfather, as he is presented in the poem: mysterious, eccentric, innocent, doddering, rebellious, clever? Perhaps you would suggest another word?

6 How would you describe Mahon's attitude to his grandfather?

7 Using poetic means, Mahon has given us a vivid picture of his grandfather. Write a short descriptive portrait of the most interesting person you know.

DAY TRIP TO DONEGAL

We reached the sea in early afternoon,
Climbed stiffly out; there were things to be done,
Clothes to be picked up, friends to be seen.
As ever, the nearby hills were a deeper green
Than anywhere in the world, and the grave   5
Grey of the sea the grimmer in that enclave.

Down at the pier the boats gave up their catch,
A writhing glimmer of fish; they fetch
Ten times as much in the city as here,
And still the fish come in year after year—   10
Herring and mackerel, flopping about the deck
In attitudes of agony and heartbreak.

We left at eight, drove back the way we came,
The sea receding down each muddy lane.
Around midnight we changed-down into suburbs   15
Sunk in a sleep no gale-force wind disturbs.
The time of year had left its mark
On frosty pavements glistening in the dark.

Give me a ring, goodnight, and so to bed …
That night the slow sea washed against my head,   20
Performing its immeasurable erosions—
Spilling into the skull, marbling the stones
That spine the very harbour wall,
Muttering its threat to villages of landfall.

At dawn I was alone far out at sea   25
Without skill or reassurance — nobody
To show me how, no promise of rescue—
Cursing my constant failure to take due
Forethought for this; contriving vain
Overtures to the vindictive wind and rain.   30

6 *enclave*: a piece of territory entirely enclosed within foreign territory

8 *writhing*: twisting

21 *erosions*: eating away, wearing down

30 *Overtures*: offers or proposals, especially in negotiations

30 *vindictive*: revengeful

GUIDELINES

'Day Trip to Donegal' is from the collection *Night Crossing* (1968).

In this poem we can see Derek Mahon's love of the sea and his perception of it as a mysterious, creative force. It begins as a straightforward narrative with details of preparation for the trip, but the language used, with words such as 'grave', 'grey' and 'grimmer', hints at a darker vision, as do the striking visual images of almost-human fish on the decks of boats.

Although the title of the poem suggests an account of the actual trip, the speaker seems more interested in the return, probably to his home town of Belfast (though it is not named). Donegal seems to recede from his consciousness. The implication is that there is an essential difference in life as experienced in the suburbs and life as it is experienced close to nature in Donegal. The change is not merely physical but also psychological.

The last two stanzas plunge us into the terrifying world of the subconscious. In the speaker's dream the sea has appeared again, but different as is the case in dreams. We can almost hear the sound of the sea and feel its power in these lines. The dream experience becomes even more nightmarish as the speaker sees himself as lost, cut adrift from everyone and everything. What is being described here goes beyond physical fear. It is as if being 'far out at sea' has become a metaphor for alienation, both psychological and spiritual.

The atmosphere created in the final lines of the poem is utterly intense. The threat posed by the sea, the wind and the rain, all elements of nature, may symbolise the wilderness of the subconscious or the imagination. It is a realm over which we can have no control, but it is central to the work of a poet. Or it may suggest the deepest human fears of loss and ultimate death which we must face alone. The imagery here recalls a long tradition in mythology and literature of representing the sea and wind as animate presences that are malevolent and powerful and will not easily be appeased, no more than the human sense of nameless dread can easily be overcome.

QUESTIONS

1 What expectations does the title of the poem set up? Are these expectations realised?

2 How would you describe the tone of the first two stanzas? How is it conveyed?

3 Why do you think the poet describes the fish in such detail?

4 Was the poet's trip to Donegal as ordinary and uneventful as it seemed? How did it affect him in his later dreams?

5 In what terms does the poet describe the sea? Would you agree that the imagery here is sensuous, almost frightening in its intensity? Look carefully at words such as 'spilling', 'marbling' and 'muttering'.

6 Would you agree that the sense of danger and isolation intensifies in the last stanza? How is this reflected in the language used?

7 How would you account for the sense of fear and disorientation experienced by the speaker?

8 Look carefully at the sound patterns – the full end-rhymes, half-rhymes, alliteration, assonance and consonance – and say what they contribute to the overall impact made by the poem.

9 Discuss 'Day Trip to Donegal' as a nature poem.

10 What does the poem reveal to us about the personality of the speaker?

ECCLESIASTES

God, you could grow to love it, God-fearing, God-
    chosen purist little puritan that,
for all your wiles and smiles, you are (the
    dank churches, the empty streets,
the shipyard silence, the tied-up swings) and   5
    shelter your cold heart from the heat
of the world, from woman-inquisition, from the
    bright eyes of children. Yes you could
wear black, drink water, nourish a fierce zeal
    with locusts and wild honey, and not   10
feel called upon to understand and forgive
    but only to speak with a bleak
afflatus, and love the January rains when they
    darken the dark doors and sink hard
into the Antrim hills, the bog meadows, the heaped   15
    graves of your fathers. Bury that red
bandana, stick and guitar; this is your
    country, close one eye and be king.
Your people await you, their heavy washing
    flaps for you in the housing estates—   20
a credulous people. God, you could do it, God
    help you, stand on a corner stiff
with rhetoric, promising nothing under the sun.

2 *purist*: someone who insists on purity in language or art

2 *puritan*: a person of strict moral conduct

3 *wiles*: coaxing, pleasant ways

5 *tied-up swings*: in Northern Ireland it was formerly the custom to close playgrounds on Sundays

7 *woman-inquisition*: questioning by a woman

9 *zeal*: intense, sometimes fanatical, enthusiasm for a cause

10 *locusts and wild honey*: in Matthew chapter 3, John the Baptist is said to have survived in the desert by eating locusts and wild honey

13 *afflatus*: divine inspiration

17 *bandana*: silk or cotton handkerchief, worn on the head

18 *close one eye and be king*: the phrase echoes the words written by Erasmus: 'In the kingdom of the blind the one-eyed man is king'

20 *credulous*: gullible

23 *rhetoric*: art of using language so as to persuade others

GUIDELINES

'Ecclesiastes', originally published in 1968, is from the collection *Lives* (1975).

Northern Ireland, particularly in pre-Troubles time (before the late 1960s), had a great number of independent Protestant preachers who would travel around preaching the Bible. 'Ecclesiastes' vividly evokes their way of life and attitudes.

The first thing we notice about the poem is its tone. You can hear the poet's passion as he addresses himself with a mixture of honesty and contempt. He acknowledges the hidden attractions of a strict ('puritan') way of life, even as he focuses on its dreariness in images that evoke a gloomy Presbyterian Sunday in his native Belfast. The advantages are that you might avoid the problems of the world or real human relationships with women or children.

The tone becomes even fiercer as the poet describes what his life as a preacher would be like. He would live simply, like the Biblical prophets, driven by religious fervour. But this brand of religion would not require him to preach love or understanding. It is rather a harsh interpretation of God's word, associated with rain and darkness. This is the tradition within which these preachers worked.

A few evocative images conjure up a completely contrasting way of life, that of the romantic 'hippies' of the 1960s and 1970s. The speaker exhorts himself to leave this way of life and take his place among the preachers in his own country. With heavy irony the poet suggests that this is the way to gain power, preaching religious intolerance to a gullible people.

'Ecclesiastes' expresses Mahon's complex emotional relationship with his native city, Belfast, and with the religious tradition of Protestant Ulster. By constantly repeating the word 'God', the poem forces the reader to look at the vision of God that is put forward in this society. But because much of the irony and the pity is directed at himself, the poem stops short of being a condemnation of a whole way of life.

QUESTIONS

1 What exactly are the attractions of the preacher's way of life? Why might they appeal to the poet?

2 Do you think that he is also aware of the inadequacies of their way of life? How is this inadequacy suggested?

3 Would you agree that the poem satirises a certain kind of religious fanaticism? Look carefully at the religious references and the harsh adjectives used throughout.

4 How would you describe the tone of the poem? Is it consistent throughout, for instance?

5 What picture of the Protestant people of Ulster is created for the reader of 'Ecclesiastes'? How did you respond to it?

6 What do you think Mahon's feelings about his own people are, as expressed in the poem?

7 Would you agree that the form of the poem, with its language, organisation, rhythm and sound patterns, contributes greatly to the forcefulness of its effect? Look in particular at the accumulation of images, the imperative mood of the verbs and the use of run-on lines that carry the poem forward to the implications of the last line.

8 If you were to choose the poem as one of your favourite poems by Derek Mahon, what case would you make for your choice?

AFTER THE TITANIC

They said I got away in a boat
And humbled me at the inquiry. I tell you
    I sank as far that night as any
Hero. As I sat shivering on the dark water
    I turned to ice to hear my costly   5
Life go thundering down in a pandemonium of
    Prams, pianos, sideboards, winches,
Boilers bursting and shredded ragtime. Now I hide
    In a lonely house behind the sea
Where the tide leaves broken toys and hat-boxes   10
    Silently at my door. The showers of
April, flowers of May mean nothing to me, nor the
    Late light of June, when my gardener
Describes to strangers how the old man stays in bed
    On seaward mornings after nights of   15
Wind, takes his cocaine and will see no-one. Then it is
    I drown again with all those dim
Lost faces I never understood. My poor soul
    Screams out in the starlight, heart
Breaks loose and rolls down like a stone.   20
    Include me in your lamentations.

GLOSSARY

6 *pandemonium*: chaos, confusion

7 *winches*: machinery used to lift heavy goods

8 *ragtime*: the popular jazz music that was played by the ship's orchestra as it
was sinking

21 *lamentations*: mourning. There is also a book of the Old Testament called
'The Lamentations of Jeremiah'

GUIDELINES

This poem comes from the collection *Lives* (1975).

In April 1912 The *SS Titanic* struck an iceberg off the coast of Newfoundland and sank with the loss of almost 1,500 lives. After the tragedy, an inquiry was held into the disaster. Among those questioned was Bruce Ismay, the President of White Star Line (the ship's owners), one of the few male passengers who had managed to escape in the lifeboats. In this dramatic monologue, Derek Mahon gives a voice to Bruce Ismay. The poem was in fact originally entitled 'Bruce Ismay's Soliloquy'.

The *Titanic* had been built in Belfast, at the Harland and Wolff shipyard. Perhaps the fact that Mahon's own grandfather was a boiler-maker for the ship (the poem contains a reference to boilers bursting) inspired the poet to reconstruct the events and enter imaginatively into the mind of the speaker.

Even though he distances himself from the verdict of the inquiry, Bruce Ismay wants to convince himself (and his listeners) that he, too, was a victim of the tragedy. In vivid images he evokes the atmosphere of chaos as the ship was sinking. Then he describes how he lives his life in the aftermath of the disaster. Feeling ashamed and guilty, he hides away from the world. Ironically, he has chosen to live by the sea, where the detritus left by the tide seems further to accuse him.

The metaphors and similes in the last few lines convey feelings of utter desolation. He suffers emotionally and physically. Although we can detect a note of self-pity here, the speaker seeks to justify why he too should be included in any 'lamentations' or expressions of grief for those who suffered.

QUESTIONS

1 Why do you think the speaker of this poem feels compelled to give his side of the story?

2 What might he mean when he says 'I turned to ice to hear my costly / Life go thundering down ...'? Does what he says later help to explain it further?

3 Does he paint a vivid picture of the disaster, in your view?

4 Do you find it strange that he has chosen to live out his days beside the sea? Why might he have made this decision?

5 From the list of phrases that follow, choose one that is closest to your own reading of the poem and explain your choice:
a) This man is trying to justify his own cowardly actions.
b) This speaker feels genuinely sorry for what he has done.
c) This speaker has suffered greatly — it would have been better for him to have drowned like the others.

6 What does the speaker of the poem reveal about his personality? Do you find him a sympathetic character?

7 Examine the sound effects of the poem (alliteration, onomatopoeia, assonance). What do they contribute to its overall impact?

8 Would you agree that the dramatic monologue succeeds in conveying several points of view at once? Explain your view.

9 The poem evokes the disaster and its aftermath in an imaginative way. The speaker also refers to the inquiry. Using the language of information, write an account of the inquiry. (You need not base your account on historical facts only.)

10 Do you like this poem? Give reasons for your opinion.

We hunted the mad bastard
through bog, moorland, rock, to the star-lit west
And gunned him down in a blind yard
Between ten sleeping lorries
And an electricity generator.   5

Let us hear no idle talk
Of the moon in the Yellow River;
The air blows softer since his departure.

Since his tide-burial during school hours
Our children have known no bad dreams.   10
Their cries echo lightly along the coast.

This is as it should be.
They will thank us for it when they grow up
To a world with method in it.

GLOSSARY

7 *the moon in the Yellow River*: this is possibly a reference to a play by Denis Johnston, *The Moon in the Yellow River*, which deals with violence in Civil War times. In the play, there is a particularly brutal episode in which the perpetrator of a plan to destroy a hydro-electrical power plant is shot by one of his former comrades, a supporter of the Irish Free State. One of the characters in the play refers to the Chinese poet Lo Pi who wished to embrace the moon in the Yellow river. This is interpreted as a metaphor for wishing to do the impossible, ideal thing

GUIDELINES

This poem is from the collection *Lives* (1975).

'As it Should Be' is another poem in which Derek Mahon gives a voice to a persona who expresses a distinct point of view. We enter into the mind of the speaker as he outlines his chilling justification of violence. Although the poem makes no direct reference to any particular conflict, the reference to the 'moon in the Yellow River' suggests a connection with the violence of the Irish Civil War, and, by extension, the conflict in Northern Ireland.

From the beginning the speaker assumes an authority to kill that suggests official sanction for his actions. Possibly this is a hint that the speaker is identified with the Irish Free State character in Johnston's play. The enemy is dehumanised as he is 'hunted' like an animal. The manner of his death is described in chillingly factual terms. There is no expression of pity or remorse. It is as if the world is a better place without this human being. The speaker firmly rejects any possibility of idealism that may have been associated with his enemy's political views. In fact he sees his violent death, ironically, as easing the fears of violence in the community.

We hear the voice of fanaticism most clearly in the final stanza. This is 'as it should be', with no room for self-doubt or moral agonising. The world, according to the speaker, will now have 'method in it', which casts an even more damning, ironic perspective on what he has described.

Although the poem is short, it conveys a great deal about the psychology of the fanatic, whether he has the support of the State or not. The poet allows the speaker to reveal the irony of his position, without direct authorial comment. The issues touched on may have their basis in historical events, but the picture of the speaker as it emerges is surely universally applicable in any conflict.

QUESTIONS

1 How does the speaker of 'As It Should Be' justify the violent actions of himself and his companions?

2 How would you describe the tone of the poem? Look carefully at the use of the plural 'we' and the language and images the poet chooses when describing the events.

3 Is there another ironic voice of which we are aware, however? How does this affect our interpretation of the poem?

4 How did you respond to this poem?

5 'Ecclesiastes' and 'After the Titanic' are two other poems in which Derek Mahon enters the mindset of other characters. Which of the three poems succeeds best in doing so, in your view?

A DISUSED SHED IN CO. WEXFORD

'Let them not forget us, the weak souls among the asphodels.'
Seferis, *Mythistorema*

(for J. G. Farrell)

Even now there are places where a thought might grow—
Peruvian mines, worked out and abandoned
To a slow clock of condensation,
An echo trapped for ever, and a flutter
Of wild-flowers in the lift-shaft,   5
Indian compound where the wind dances
And a door bangs with diminished confidence,
Lime crevices behind rippling rain-barrels,
Dog corners for bone burials;
And in a disused shed in Co. Wexford,   10

Deep in the grounds of a burnt-out hotel,
Among the bathtubs and the washbasins
A thousand mushrooms crowd to a keyhole.
This is the one star in their firmament
Or frames a star within a star.   15
What should they do there but desire?
So many days beyond the rhododendrons
With the world waltzing in its bowl of cloud,
They have learnt patience and silence
Listening to the rooks querulous in the high wood.   20

They have been waiting for us in a foetor
Of vegetable sweat since civil war days,
Since the gravel-crunching, interminable departure
Of the expropriated mycologist,
He never came back, and light since then   25
Is a keyhole rusting gently after rain.
Spiders have spun, flies dusted to mildew
And once a day, perhaps, they have heard something—

A trickle of masonry, a shout from the blue
Or a lorry changing gear at the end of the lane. 30

There have been deaths, the pale flesh flaking
Into the earth that nourished it;
And nightmares, born of these and the grim
Dominion of stale air and rank moisture.
Those nearest the door grow strong— 35
'Elbow room! Elbow room!'
The rest, dim in a twilight of crumbling
Utensils and broken pitchers, groaning
For their deliverance, have been so long
Expectant that there is left only the posture. 40

A half century, without visitors, in the dark—
Poor preparation for the cracking lock
And creak of hinges; magi, moonmen,
Powdery prisoners of the old regime,
Web-throated, stalked like triffids, racked by drought 45
And insomnia, only the ghost of a scream
At the flash-bulb firing-squad we wake them with
Shows there is life yet in their feverish forms.
Grown beyond nature now, soft food for worms,
They lift frail heads in gravity and good faith. 50

They are begging us, you see, in their wordless way,
To do something, to speak on their behalf
Or at least not to close the door again.
Lost people of Treblinka and Pompeii!
'Save us, save us,' they seem to say, 55
'Let the god not abandon us
Who have come so far in darkness and in pain.
We too had our lives to live.
You with your light meter and relaxed itinerary,
Let not our naïve labours have been in vain!' 60

epigraph *asphodels*: lily-like plants, associated with the dead in Greek mythology. The epigraph is taken from *Mythistorema* by the Greek poet George Seferis (1900–1971). These short poems deal with the myth of Odysseus in modern form. Their themes are often political

6 *compound*: an enclosure round a house or factory

14 *firmament*: sky

20 querulous: complaining

21 *foetor*: a strong, offensive smell

24 *expropriated*: dispossessed.

24 *mycologist*: someone who studies fungi

27 *mildew*: a disease on plants

43 *magi*: here, probably sorcerers

43 *moonmen*: like men from the moon because they have been without the light of the sun. The shape of the mushrooms also suggests the round moon

45 *triffids*: monstrous stinging plants invented by the writer John Wyndham in his science-fiction novel *The Day of the Triffids* (1951)

54 *Treblinka*: a Polish concentration camp in which Jews were incarcerated and killed during the Second World War

54 *Pompeii*: scene of the eruption of the volcano Vesuvius in AD 79

59 *light meter*: device for measuring light (in camera)

59 *itinerary*: plan of a journey

GUIDELINES

This poem, from *The Snow Party* (1985), has been called Derek Mahon's masterpiece. Its impact depends upon our awareness of the symbolic significance the poet gives to the mushrooms in the old shed that he came across in Co. Wexford. Lonely and abandoned, the mushrooms come to stand for the lost lives of those who have suffered through violence and neglect. The Irish location of the poem links the suffering of the Irish people throughout history with the suffering of other peoples at other times.

The epigraph, 'Let them not forget us, the weak souls among the asphodels', is echoed throughout the poem itself in the plea for remembrance.

The poem is dedicated to J. G. Farrell, author of the novel *The Troubles* (1970). The subject-matter of the novel may throw some light on the implications of the poem. *The Troubles* is a historical novel, set in Ireland in the

1920s. It evokes the fate of the Anglo-Irish Ascendancy class by describing the gradual ruin of a hotel, which is burnt down by Irish Republicans during the Irish Civil War. This was a time when the Anglo-Irish community felt abandoned politically and emotionally by the British to whom they owed their allegiance. Mahon has set his poem in a shed in the grounds of a burnt-out hotel, echoing Farrell's novel. Although the poem is not restricted to the theme of the novel, it is interesting that Mahon wrote it as the Protestant people of Ulster (his own people) began to express their sense of abandonment by the British government during the conflict in Northern Ireland in the 1970s.

From the beginning there is a strong sense of place in the poem, which the language allows us imaginatively to enter. Places of emptiness rather eerily become places where meaning is possible. This insight prepares us for the vision of the mushrooms in the disused shed. The mushrooms themselves and their setting are described in a series of precise and rich images. At times they are presented literally as mushrooms, but their symbolic function is soon made clear. Linked explicitly with 'civil war days', their decaying world seems to represent the Anglo-Irish who were displaced and ultimately abandoned. Sensuous language evokes suffering and fear. The mushrooms, too, are perceived as symbolic of suffering people within a larger frame of historical reference that includes the fate of the Jewish people in Nazi Germany. Like many oppressed people, all they can do is wait for their deliverance.

In the last two stanzas the focus changes to the moment of discovery on the part of the poet/speaker and his companions. (The plural 'we' is used throughout.) Sound effects and vivid metaphors capture the mysteriousness of the mushrooms and their possible symbolic echoes. The poet continues to attribute human qualities to them as he describes their reactions to his entry into the shed. As he takes his photograph, it is as if he is part of a 'firing-squad' rather than a rescuer. These lines and those that follow are full of rich metaphors that may remind us of the many scenes of mass suffering that have been captured by the world's media in photographs, films and on television. The final lines assume a certain responsibility to the mushrooms by giving them a voice in which they may speak. They even seem to acknowledge the power of poetry itself (is there a pun on the word 'meter' here?) in speaking on behalf of those who are powerless.

QUESTIONS

1 Would you agree that the imagery of the first stanza suggests desolation and abandonment? Do you find the effect melancholy or eerie?

2 What human qualities are ascribed to the mushrooms in the second and third stanzas? How is their plight suggested?

3 How does the language of the poem reflect the passing of time in the second and third stanzas?

4 Is it significant that the mushrooms have been waiting since 'civil war days', having been abandoned by the mycologist who never came back? What link does this reference create with the places and peoples mentioned in the first stanza?

5 How would you describe the tone and atmosphere of the fourth stanza? Look carefully at the language the poet uses. Do the mushrooms take on an even more poignant weight as metaphors of suffering and loss at this stage in the poem?

6 What echoes of historical suffering are found in the fourth stanza?

7 The moment of entry by the humans, presented in terms of an invasion, provokes a reaction of passive terror in the mushrooms. How does the poet dramatise this?

8 Would you agree that the images in which the mushrooms are presented in the fifth stanza are imaginative, almost surreal? Discuss the contribution made by the sound-effects (alliteration and onomatopoeia) in building the images.

9 In the final stanza the full symbolism of the mushrooms is made apparent. What exactly do they represent? In considering this, take into account not only the explicit historical references of the poem but also the potential contemporary implications for the Protestant people of Ulster.

10 Look carefully at how the six stanzas are formed. Why do you think the poet chose the longer line-lengths and ten-line stanzas for his theme?

11 You have chosen to speak about this poem in a talk entitled 'Introducing Derek Mahon'. Write out the talk you would give.

12 Write a short essay giving your response (positive or negative) to the statement: 'This poem is one of the finest poems of the 1970s.'

THE CHINESE RESTAURANT IN PORTRUSH

Before the first visitor comes the spring
Softening the sharp air of the coast
In time for the first 'invasion'.
Today the place is as it might have been,
Gentle and almost hospitable. A girl   5
Strides past the Northern Counties Hotel,
Light-footed, swinging a book-bag,
And the doors that were shut all winter
Against the north wind and the sea mists
Lie open to the street, where one   10
By one the gulls go window-shopping
And an old wolfhound dozes in the sun.

While I sit with my paper and prawn chow mein
Under a framed photograph of Hong Kong
The proprietor of the Chinese restaurant   15
Stands at the door as if the world were young,
Watching the first yacht hoist a sail
— An ideogram on sea-cloud — and the light
Of heaven upon the mountains of Donegal;
And whistles a little tune, dreaming of home.   20

GLOSSARY

title *Portrush*: a seaside resort in Co. Antrim

13 *chow mein*: a Chinese dish

18 *ideogram*: in Chinese writing, a written character or symbol that stands not for a word or sound but for the thing itself

GUIDELINES

'The Chinese Restaurant in Portrush' is collected in the volume *Poems 1962–1978*.

Derek Mahon rarely deals with the Northern Ireland conflict in his poems, but we cannot ignore the implications of the title. Portrush, a seaside town in north Co. Antrim, has been a predominantly Protestant Unionist area of Northern Ireland. This lyrical depiction of the resort as a peaceful, welcoming place must be set against a backdrop of violence and intransigence in the North of Ireland at the time of writing.

The poem celebrates Portrush while also acknowledging, with some regret, an undercurrent of defensiveness. Lively visual images – the girl, the gulls, the dog – bring the place to life for the reader. When we meet the figures of the poet and the owner of the Chinese restaurant, the scene is one of pleasure and relaxation. The lines that follow have the clarity of a painting. The poet seems to enter imaginatively into the mind of the proprietor of the restaurant and describes what he sees from that particular perspective, looking out to sea. There is a certain poignancy when we recall that he is far away from home.

By positioning the place-names throughout the poem in such close proximity to each other, the poem makes us aware of how one place can be viewed from another. By ending with the word 'home', too, we become aware that the idea of visiting, of movement from one place to another, is central to the poem, as is the concept of home itself.

QUESTIONS

1 What atmosphere is created by the images in the first stanza? Take into account the description of the weather, the girl, the gulls and the dog.

2 What do you think the poet is suggesting when he says 'Today the place is as it might have been'? What feelings may lie behind this?

3 What does the phrase 'as if the world were young' suggest to you?

4 Discuss the significance of the notions of place, visitors and home.

5 Would you agree that the visual images in the second stanza have the clarity and vividness of a painting? What features combine to create this impression?

6 '"A Chinese Restaurant in Portrush" celebrates the ordinary experiences of life amidst an awareness of their vulnerability to change'. Discuss this view of the poem.

RATHLIN

A long time since the last scream cut short—
Then an unnatural silence; and then
A natural silence, slowly broken
By the shearwater, by the sporadic
Conversation of crickets, the bleak   5
Reminder of a metaphysical wind.
Ages of this, till the report
Of an outboard motor at the pier
Shatters the dream-time, and we land
As if we were the first visitors here.   10

The whole island a sanctuary where amazed
Oneiric species whistle and chatter,
Evacuating rock-face and cliff-top.
Cerulean distance, an oceanic haze—
Nothing but sea-smoke to the ice-cap   15
And the odd somnolent freighter.
Bombs doze in the housing estates
But here they are through with history—
Custodians of a lone light which repeats
One simple statement to the turbulent sea.   20

A long time since the unspeakable violence—
Since Somhairle Buí, powerless on the mainland,
Heard the screams of the Rathlin women
Borne to him, seconds later, upon the wind.
Only the cry of the shearwater   25
And the roar of the outboard motor
Disturb the singular peace. Spray-blind,
We leave here the infancy of the race,
Unsure among the pitching surfaces
Whether the future lies before us or behind.   30

GLOSSARY

title *Rathlin*: an island off the coast of Co. Antrim.

  4 *shearwater*: an oceanic bird that skims the water

  4 *sporadic*: occasional

12 *oneiric*: relating to dreams

14 *Cerulean*: dark blue or sea-green

16 *somnolent*: sleepy

16 *freighter*: a cargo-carrying boat

22 *Somhairle Buí*: Sorley Boy , chieftain of the MacDonnell clan of Antrim, whose castle was situated at Dunanyie, near Ballycastle.

GUIDELINES

Rathlin Island was the scene of a cruel massacre that took place in the year 1557. Sir Henry Sydney, then vice-treasurer of Ireland, took part in a raid on the island of Rathlin. He and his soldiers managed to land without being discovered, taking the inhabitants by surprise. They then proceeded to destroy all the crops and cattle, before massacring in cold blood all the men, women and children on the island. Their screams were said to have been heard on the mainland by Somhairle Buí at his castle.

In the poem there is an awareness of the island's violent history that throws an ironic light on contemporary violence in Northern Ireland. The historical massacre is recalled, but for a long time the only sounds have been the sounds of nature. The arrival of the 'visitors' seems to disturb the silence of the place. Everything on the island is seen as if in a dream. It is a world of its own, almost like the garden of Eden.

But the poem does not retain its dream-like atmosphere for long. A link between the violent history of Rathlin and the contemporary bombs that 'doze' on the housing estates is made. The phrase 'through with history' has complex implications that readers will have to tease out for themselves. Does the phrase suggest that Rathlin represents some post-historical place in which history has no relevance? As 'custodians of a lone light' (literally, the lighthouse), metaphorically speaking, the island and its inhabitants can be seen as representing the light of the imagination, the 'dream-time' which offers escape and simplicity, whereas the notion of history must encompass the reality of ongoing violence.

The final lines of the poem must also leave us with some questions. Does the poet suggest that the violence once known on Rathlin awaits them in the future, or does he suggest that the peacefulness he experienced on the island is what the future holds? Or might the ambiguity here reflect his own uncertainty, just as the journey has made them 'spray-blind'?

QUESTIONS

1 The poem speaks of the singular peace on the island of Rathlin. How does the language used help to convey this sense of peace?

2 What other perspective on the island is suggested? Do the contrasting images of violence, past as well as present, contribute to the atmosphere presented throughout the poem?

3 Would you agree that the poem is remarkable for the vividness and sensuousness of its natural imagery?

4 How would you explain the line 'But here they are through with history'? Is this idea echoed elsewhere in the poem?

5 The phrase 'dream-time' occurs in the first stanza. How is the notion of dreams elaborated upon in the poem?

6 What effect has the visit to the island had upon the speaker of the poem? Look carefully at the last two lines.

7 Compare the poem with 'Day trip to Donegal' as a description of nature. Which poem do you prefer, and why?

8 Would you agree that Derek Mahon has a remarkable sense of place in his poems? Refer to the poems 'Kinsale' and 'The Chinese Restaurant in Portrush' as well as 'Rathlin'.

ANTARCTICA

(for Richard Ryan)

'I am just going outside and may be some time.'
The others nod, pretending not to know.
At the heart of the ridiculous, the sublime.

He leaves them reading and begins to climb,
Goading his ghost into the howling snow;   5
He is just going outside and may be some time.

The tent recedes beneath its crust of rime
And frostbite is replaced by vertigo:
At the heart of the ridiculous, the sublime.

Need we consider it some sort of crime,   10
This numb self-sacrifice of the weakest? No,
He is just going outside and may be some time—

In fact, for ever. Solitary enzyme,
Though the night yield no glimmer there will glow,
At the heart of the ridiculous, the sublime.   15

He takes leave of the earthly pantomime
Quietly, knowing it is time to go.
'I am just going outside and may be some time.'
At the heart of the ridiculous, the sublime.

Antarctica: the Antarctic is the South polar region

for Richard Ryan: Richard Ryan is an Irish diplomat and poet

3 *sublime*: noble, awe-inspiring

5 *goading*: urging on

7 *rime*: frost

8 *frostbite*: damage to body tissue exposed to freezing temperatures

8 *vertigo*: dizziness, tendency to lose balance

13 *enzyme*: an enzyme is a protein that causes a living organism to change but is not changed itself

GUIDELINES

This poem comes from the collection *Antarctica* (1985). It is dedicated to the poet Richard Ryan.

In 1912 the explorer Captain Scott led an expedition to the South Pole, but he and his men perished in the attempt. In the diary found after his death, Scott describes how one of the men, Captain Oates, sacrificed himself in order to save food for the others by crawling out into a blizzard, saying only 'I am just going out and may be some time'. The words have become famous as examples of understatement and a certain kind of heroism.

Derek Mahon dramatises the incident in a villanelle that matches beautifully the dignity of Oates's last grim resolve. Oates's words open the poem and form one of the two refrains used in the poem. In exploring the implications of these words, Mahon is writing from a modern perspective where extreme heroic gestures have become more rare and even slightly suspect. We can see how he might suggest that the words are ridiculous in their failure to register even the smallest amount of emotion and their glaring understatement. As we know, 'some time' means, in fact, for ever.

On the other hand, the poet acknowledges the 'sublime' aspect of the event too – the nobility and unselfishness with which Oates acted. As Oates climbs to his death, he is depicted in images of suffering and endurance that lend dignity to his famous words.

The poem then questions present-day attitudes to such sacrifices. Oates is finally depicted, metaphorically, as a 'solitary enzyme' that will glow in the night. He knew the right thing to do and when to do it. The refrain, ending finally with the word 'sublime', now appears as a tribute.

The form of the poem is a villanelle. It is said to have a singing line. There is a sequence of tercets (three lines), with rhyming scheme aba, aba, aba in each. Each tercet ends in a refrain, and there are only two refrains alternating throughout the poem. The set of tercets is rounded off with a quatrain in which the two refrains at last come together, one capping the other. A villanelle is a highly stylised, formal poem that has become associated with meditations on death or grief.

QUESTIONS

1 Why do you think the words 'I am just going out and may be some time' could be seen as ridiculous? Why are they also sublime?

2 What picture of the members of the expedition do you get from reading this poem?

3 What sort of person was Oates, as suggested in the poem?

4 What do you think the poet is suggesting when he asks 'Need we consider it some sort of crime / This numb self-sacrifice of the weakest?'

5 Does the poem celebrate heroism, or does it have an ironic attitude to it?

6 What attitude to life and death is suggested by 'Antarctica'?

7 What is your own response to the issues raised in the poem?

KINSALE

The kind of rain we knew is a thing of the past—
deep-delving, dark, deliberate you would say,
browsing on spire and bogland; but today
our sky-blue slates are steaming in the sun,
our yachts tinkling and dancing in the bay   5
like race-horses. We contemplate at last
shining windows, a future forbidden to no-one.

GUIDELINES

This poem comes from the collection *Antarctica* (1985).

It is difficult to read this poem without remembering the battle which took place in Kinsale in 1601, in which the Irish, led by Red Hugh O'Donnell and Hugh O'Neill, were defeated by the army of Elizabeth 1 – a decisive victory that altered the course of Irish history.

Kinsale these days is a thriving, fashionable town, well known for sailing activities and tourism. The contrast between past and present is depicted in the imagery Mahon uses to describe it. Images of darkness and sorrow are followed by images of light and movement. The effect is celebratory and carefree. The race-horses and the yachts suggest prosperity and optimism that is open to all. Is this the new Ireland, free from the shackles of the past, the burden of history? Might there also be an ironic comment on the desire of the nouveau riche to leave aside the old ways of life, the church and the land?

QUESTIONS

1 Look carefully at the poet's use of contrast in this short lyric.
2 Might the rain and the sun have a metaphorical significance? Can you say what associations they might carry?
3 Would you agree that the sound patterns of the poem create a musical effect?
4 What is the tone of the poem? Take into account the images of yachts and race-horses as well as of spires and bogland.
5 Does the historical significance of Kinsale have any bearing on the theme of the poem, in your view?
6 Derek Mahon has himself cited the work of the painter Raoul Dufy as an influence on his poetry, and on 'Kinsale' in particular. Dufy has painted watercolours and gouaches depicting harbour scenes, yachts and race-courses. You might like to find some illustrations of Dufy's work and comment on any connections you see between both artists — the painter and the poet.

GENERAL QUESTIONS ON DEREK MAHON

The following questions may help you to focus on different aspects of Derek Mahon's work.

1. Discuss the importance of history in the poems of Derek Mahon.
2. 'A sense of alienation and distance pervades the poetry of Derek Mahon.' Discuss this view in relation to the poems on your course.
3. 'In his poems Derek Mahon is interested in giving a voice to those who are marginalised, no matter how unpalatable their views are.' To what extent is this true of the poems that are on your course?
4. 'Images of the sea and the shoreline, of light and dark, give a painterly quality to the work of Derek Mahon.' Discuss this view.
5. 'As a poet Derek Mahon sees the imaginative potential in ordinary, concrete things.' Discuss this view of Mahon's poetry.
6. 'Although he rarely deals directly with the Troubles in Northern Ireland, Mahon is acutely aware of the effects of fanaticism and violence on society.' Do you agree with this point of view?
7. 'In his poems Derek Mahon has a keen sense of place.' Discuss.
8. Derek Mahon has been described as a poet of 'great richness, elegance, and technical brilliance'. Do you agree with this opinion of Derek Mahon's work?
9. Write a review of the poetry of Derek Mahon for a serious journal.
10. If you were asked to interview Derek Mahon about his work, what questions would you like to ask him?

EXAMINATION-STYLE QUESTIONS

11. Why read the poetry of Derek Mahon?

Write out the text of a talk you would give in response to the above title. Support the points you make by reference to the poetry of Derek Mahon on your course.

In your talk, you might include the following reasons why we might read Mahon's poetry:

- his themes are interesting and varied e.g. explorations of history, individual experiences, personal narrative
- he is capable of writing from many different perspectives, even unpopular ones
- his use of language is precise and vivid, his metaphors and images carefully chosen, his use of sound musical and evocative

- he has a keen sense of place to which the reader can respond well
- he raises important questions, directly or indirectly, about political issues and attitudes

Note: you must support your points by detailed discussion of individual poems.

12 'I like (or do not like) the poetry of Derek Mahon'.

Respond to this statement, referring to the poetry by Derek Mahon on your course.

Reasons you could give for liking the poetry of Derek Mahon might include:

- his themes are wide-ranging and relevant to modern day life
- he refuses to be pigeon-holed as a poet from Northern Ireland
- he enters imaginatively into the minds of others in his poems
- he uses language in a precise and fresh manner, and often with the eye of a painter
- imagery and sound are used to great effect in his work
- he responds to the beauty of nature and the atmosphere of places.

Reasons you could give for not liking the poetry of Derek Mahon might include:

- the poet reveals very little about himself in his work
- he remains too detached from the historical issues and political questions of his time
- there is a certain lack of emotion in his work
- when he does engage with political issues, his approach is too indirect.

Sees himself as a
European rather than simply
an Irish poet.

Formal,
polished style.

Theme of history
in poems.

Poems appeal both to the
intellect and the emotions.

Sense of alienation and
distance in poems.

Derek Mahon

Wide range of
cultural reference.

Sees imaginative potential
of ordinary, concrete things.

Gives a voice to those who are
marginalised in society.

Keen sense of place.

Critics admire 'acute eye and
precise ear' in poems.

Painterly quality to the
imagery in poems.

JOHN MONTAGUE

B. 1929

BIOGRAPHY

John Montague was born in Brooklyn, New York, on 28 February, 1929. His parents were Irish emigrants. During the war of Independence, his father James was an Irish volunteer whose activities included participation in ambushes and house-burning. He emigrated to New York in 1925. In Ireland, he had been unsuccessful in business ventures financed from the sale of his farm. He became a ticket collector in the New York subway. His wife and two young sons joined him later.

John left New York at the age of four with his mother and two brothers when his father could no longer support the family. Although his mother also returned to Tyrone, she took little or no part in his upbringing. He was reared by two aunts who lived in his father's home in Garvaghey and he grew up without knowing his father.

He was educated at Garvaghey Primary School and later at St Patrick's College Armagh. In 1946, he won a scholarship to University College Dublin. He later studied at Yale and Berkeley, two famous American Universities. One of his teachers at St Patrick's College was Sean O'Boyle, a leading authority on Ulster folksong and Irish poetry. O'Boyle gave him a love of the Gaelic tradition, which was to have a profound influence on his life and on his poetry.

Montague published his first collection of poems, *Forms of Exile*, in 1958. In the 1960s, he taught Anglo-Irish literature at UCD and in 1967 he issued *A Chosen Light*. In the late 1960s he responded with enthusiasm to the Northern Ireland Civil Rights Movement and dedicated a collection of poems, *A New Siege*, to Bernadette Devlin, our of the leaders of the movement.

In 1972, he published *The Rough Field*, in which he explored Ulster and family history. Other important collections of his poetry include *A Slow Dance* (1975); *Poisoned Lands* (1977); *The Great Cloak* (1975); *Selected Poems* (1982) and *The Dead Kingdom* (1984). *A Slow Dance* is particularly interesting for its treatment of the Northern Ireland conflict. In one of the poems in that collection, 'Falls Funeral', there is a chillingly realistic account of the burial of a murdered Catholic child. In another, 'Northern Express', Montague shows how the horrors of the struggle can affect ordinary people. Some of the poems in *The Dead Kingdom* deal with his father's lonely life in Brooklyn.

Montague has held a wide variety of positions throughout his adult life. He has been a film-critic, a proof-reader, an editor, a university lecturer and a writer-in-residence at many American universities. In 1998 he was appointed to The Ireland Chair of Poetry, which is supported by the Ireland Fund. Since the 1970s, he has been based in Cork, lecturing at University College there and running poetry workshops. He was the first significant twentieth-century poet writing from a Northern Irish Catholic background. He established a tradition which has been followed by others from a similar background, including Seamus Heaney.

SOCIAL AND CULTURAL CONTEXT

Montague's poetry reflects his lifelong interest in the history, mythology and landscape of his ancestral home in Co. Tyrone. It was natural for a poet born in exile to display more than an ordinary interest in the world in which his father and mother grew up, as well as in their neighbours and relatives. In one of his most distinguished early poems, 'Like Dolmens Round My Childhood, The Old People', he combines reference to the ancient landscape of Tyrone and its prehistoric burial customs with an exploration of the mysterious old characters who fired his imagination during his childhood in Tyrone. In this poem, the people and their way of life are of much greater interest to the poet than are the relics of ancient times. Montague does, however, suggest an intimate link between past and present. His old and eccentric neighbours have inherited ancient customs from their primitive past. This makes it possible for him to feel that the past still lives through the lives of Jamie Mac Crystal, Maggie Owens, the Nialls and Wild Billy Eagleson:

Ancient Ireland, indeed! I was reared by her bedside,
The rune and the chant, evil eye and averted head,
Fomorian fierceness of family and local fend.

In 'The Wild Dog Rose', Montague might have turned the Cailleach, the terrible woman who terrified him when he was a child, into a creature of myth. Instead, he discovers in her a creature in the grip of loneliness and fear.

Many of Montague's poems are based on the poet's own family history and are strongly autobiographical. Memories of his father are often his major themes. In 'The Cage', for example, he recalls his father's unhappy life in New York, trying to preserve his identity as 'a traditional Irishman by drinking neat whiskey'. His father's ultimately successful struggle with his addiction to alcohol made Montague proud. After his father's death, he paid envious tribute to his freedom from addiction for fifteen years, remarking that 'if you're an alcoholic that's quite heroic'. A second quality he admired in his father was that he was 'an intensely believing Catholic'. Montague remembered thinking his 'poor old battered father quite noble' when he saw him laid out in a Franciscan habit. He believed that the power of his religious faith 'enabled him to surmount in himself a life which, he said himself, he had frittered away'. In 'The Locket', the poet's relationship with his mother is affectionately explored. Montague constructs his poem out of the miserable life endured by his mother, partly the result of his father's inability to support a wife and family, and partly the result of adverse circumstances: she had arrived at her husband's doorstep just in time for The Great Depression of 1929.

Montague does not focus exclusively on the limited set of themes suggested in the poems mentioned above: family life in New York, family relationships and Tyrone relationships. 'A Welcoming Party' suggests a broader vision of the world. Here, Montague ironically explores the detachment of Irish children from the realities of total war, his own 'parochial brand of innocence' in the face of a film showing a concentration camp. In this poem, an individual experience takes on a universal meaning.

KILLING THE PIG

He was pulled out, squealing,
an iron cleek sunk in the roof
of his mouth.

(Don't say they are not intelligent:
they know the hour has come   5
and they want none of it:
they dig in their little trotters,
will not go dumb or singing
to the slaughter.)

That high pitched final effort,   10
no single sound could match it –
a big plane roaring off,
a *diva* soaring towards her last note,
the brain-chilling persistence of an electric saw,
scrap being crushed.   15

Piercing & absolute,
only high heaven ignores it.

Then a full stop.
An expert plants
a solid thump of a mallet   20
flat between the ears.

Swiftly the knife seeks the throat;
swiftly the others cleavers work
till the carcass is hung up
shining and eviscerated as   25
a surgeon's coat.

A child is given the bladder to play with.
But the walls of the farmyard still
hold that scream, are built around it.

2 *cleek*: a large hook or crook for catching hold of something. An iron-headed club with a straight narrow face and a long shaft

7 *trotters*: pig's feet

13 *diva*: a famous female opera-singer

14 *the brain-chilling persistence… saw*: the poet is comparing the effect of the doomed pig's squealing with the effect on the human brain of the constant buzzing of an electric saw

16 *absolute*: complete, unlimited

17 *only high heaven ignores it*: the squeals of the pig disturb human listeners, but the heavenly powers seem uninterested. There is also a suggestion that heaven is too far away to hear the noise made by the pig

20 *mallet*: a hammer with a wooden head

23 *cleavers*: heavy choppers used to divide large sections of meat

24 *carcass*: the dead body of an animal

25 *eviscerated*: with the intestines or bowels removed

GUIDELINES

A number of prominent twentieth-century poets, most notably Ted Hughes and Seamus Heaney, have written pieces on living, dead and dying birds animals and fish. The impact of many of these lies in their close, realistic, almost clinical descriptions, which do not strive for emotional responses on the part of the reader. This is from 'View of a Pig' by Ted Hughes:

Pigs must have hot blood, they feel like ovens
Their bite is worse than a horse's –
they chop a half-moon clean out
They eat cinders, dead cats.

Many such poets, particularly those dealing with the slaughter of animals, are content to describe, but slow to evaluate or judge, what is happening. Montague's 'Killing the Pig' is different in this respect: the poem resonates beyond the immediate situation, and leaves the reader to ponder some profound questions.

The poem combines detailed, objective description of the process of slaughtering a pig ('An expert plants / a solid thump of a mallet / flat between the ears') with attempts to interpret the event from the pig's point of view; pigs led to the slaughter 'know the hour is come / and they want none of it'. As evidence of this, the poet describes the terrible scream, 'piercing & absolute', which signals the pig's consciousness of its coming ordeal: the blow to the head, the knife in the throat, the cleavers cutting the carcass.

The metaphors chosen by Montague to convey the painful, disturbing sound of the pig's scream are interesting. There are four of these: a plane taking off with a roar, an opera-singer rising to her final high note, 'the brain-chilling persistence of an electric saw', and scrap-metal being ground down in a crusher. Two of the metaphors, those of the electric saw and the scrap-crusher, can be seen as appropriate to the situation: their destructive power is a reflection of the act of slaughter. The jet metaphor can also be defended because it gives the impression of a massive sound soaring heavenwards, while the diva's final note may be imagined as a human cry, perhaps of protest, having the same tragic finality as the pig's scream. All these cries, whether from the singer, the machines or the pig, are in their own way futile: 'high heaven' pays no attention to disturbing signals from earth.

The final three lines of the poem extend its scope backwards and forwards in time, beyond the single incident that inspired it. When the poet writes that the walls of the farmyard 'still hold the scream' of the pig after it has died, he does not merely suggest that he will always associate this farmyard with the pig's scream, or hear it in his mind whenever he visits the place. He also invites us to go back, in imagination, to a time before the farmyard walls were built, and to enter the mind of the builder. We can imagine this builder, conscious that in some future time pigs like this one would go screaming to their deaths in this farmyard, planning the wall as a means of confining the scream, and the life-force it represents.

QUESTIONS

1 How does this poem encourage the reader to feel sympathy for the pig? Give details from the poem in support of your answer.

2 Mention three details from the poem which you find disturbing. Say how the poet achieves this effect.

3 Why does the poet dismiss the idea that pigs are not intelligent?

4 Before it dies, the pig utters a high-pitched sound. The poet tries to convey this sound in four different ways. List these and say how effective each one is.

5 Why do you think the poet says that 'only high heaven ignores' the pig's scream?

6 Is the poet suggesting that the killing of the pig is unnecessarily cruel?

7 Why do you think the poet describes the person who thumps the pig's head with a mallet as 'An expert'?

8 How does the poet suggest that the killing of the pig is an impersonal ritual? How does he distance those who kill the pig from their actions?

9 Does the poem give us any idea of how the poet feels about what he is describing?

10 Give your own response to the poem, recording its effect on you, the feelings it arouses in you and your views on the kind of event it describes.

THE TROUT

Flat on the bank I parted
Rushes to ease my hands
In the water without a ripple
And tilt them slowly downstream
To where he lay, tendril light,   5
In his fluid sensual dream.

Bodiless lord of creation
I hung briefly above him
Savouring my own absence
Senses expanding in the slow   10
Motion, the photographic calm
That grows before action.

As the curve of my hands
Swung under his body
He surged, with visible pleasure.   15
I was so preternaturally close
I could count every stipple
But still cast no shadow, until

The two palms crossed in a cage
Under the lightly pulsing gills.   20
Then (entering my own enlarged
Shape, which rode on the water)
I gripped. To this day I can
Taste his terror on my hands.

5 *tendril light*: a tendril is a leaf or stem used by climbing plants to attach themselves to a support. This phrase suggests that the trout seems almost weightless

6 *fluid*: there are two suggestions here. The fluid dream may be one in which each part merges easily into the next. 'Fluid' may also mean 'watery'

6 *sensual*: giving pleasure to the senses

7–8 *Bodiless … above him*: the poet hovered above the trout like a god

GUIDELINES

Like 'Killing the Pig', this poem deals with one aspect of the relationship between human beings and other creatures. In some respects, 'The Trout' also has affinities with 'The Cage'. The fish in the former, imprisoned by 'two palms crossed in a cage', and the poet's father in the latter, fated to spend his working-life in a little underground office behind a grille, are both captives. In 'Killing the Pig' Montague becomes a somewhat troubled commentator on the ritual of slaughter. In 'The Trout' he is more restrained. It is not until the last two lines that he conveys deep feeling for the fish whose terror he can still feel to this day.

The poet's presentation of himself in relation to the trout is interesting, particularly in Stanza Two. Here, the key lines are the following:

Bodiless lord of creation
I hung directly above him
Savouring my own absence.

These lines suggest that the poet sees himself as a divine being with the power to control the created world. This sense of the poet as a god is conveyed by the image of a bodiless being who is able to hover over the trout and to experience a sense of physical absence. The divine image is further deployed in Stanza Three in the poet's description of himself as being 'preternaturally close' to the trout as he is on the point of capturing it.

The poem is not entirely objective in its presentation of the trout. Twice the poet projects his own feelings and emotions onto the fish. In Stanza One, for example, he imagines it lost in a 'fluid sensual dream'. In the final stanza, he attributes human emotion to the captured trout: 'To this day I can / Taste his terror on my hands'. This sense of terror experienced by creatures at the hands of human beings is also reflected in 'Killing the Pig'. The poet's ability to sympathise with the feelings of the trout is part of a pattern which may be observed in many of his poems. Montague is in close harmony with the natural world. He is able to catch the trout because he is in tune with its habitat and understands its way of life.

The poem needs to be read slowly and deliberately. The movement of the poem is relaxed, in keeping with the leisurely pace of the event it describes. Thus, rhythm and meaning are in close harmony. The second stanza contains a good description of the way in which the movement of the poem reflects its meaning:

Senses expanding in the slow
Motion, the photographic calm
That grows before action.

The movement of the poem is constantly arrested by the poet's use of breaks in the meaning at the ends of lines:

Flat on the bank I parted
Rushes to ease my hands
In the water without a ripple.

QUESTIONS

1 In this poem, what happens is partly seen from the poet's point of view and partly in terms of what the trout might have felt. Comment on this idea with reference to the poem.

2 Describe the poet's feelings as he stalks the trout and catches it.

3 Explain the poet's progress from his 'own absence' (line 9) to his 'own enlarged / Shape' (lines 21–22).

4 What do you think the poet means by 'the photographic calm / That grows before action'?

5 The poet tells us that the trout 'surged, with visible pleasure' (line 15) just before being caught. What do you think is meant here?

6 Give your own response to the poem.

7 Write out two images from the poem that you find particularly impressive. Explain your choice.

8 Discuss the ways in which Montague makes a simple incident exciting.

9 Does Stanza Four provide an effective ending for the poem? Give your reasons for agreeing or disagreeing.

10 The poem is about more than the capture of a trout. Suggest some other issues it raises.

THE LOCKET

Sing a last song
for the lady who has gone,
fertile source of guilt and pain.
The worst birth in the annals of Brooklyn,
that was my cue to come on,   5
my first claim to fame.

Naturally, she longed for a girl,
and all my infant curls of brown
couldn't excuse my double blunder
coming out, both the wrong sex,   10
and the wrong way around.
Not readily forgiven,

So you never nursed me
and when all my father's songs
couldn't sweeten the lack of money,   15
when poverty comes through the door
love flies up the chimney,
your favourite saying.

Then you gave me away,
might never have known me,   20
if I had not cycled down
to court you like a young man,
teasingly untying your apron,
drinking by the fire, yarning

Of your wild, young days   25
which didn't last long, for you,
lovely Molly, the belle of your small town,
landed up mournful and chill
as the constant rain that lashes it,
wound into your cocoon of pain.   30

Standing in that same hallway,
don't come again, you say, roughly,
I start to get fond of you, John,
and then you are up and gone;
the harsh logic of a forlorn woman   35
resigned to being alone.

And still, mysterious blessing,
I never knew, until you were gone,
that, always around your neck,
you wore an oval locket
with an old picture in it,   40
of a child in Brooklyn.

GLOSSARY

2 *the lady*: this is the poet's mother

3 *fertile source of guilt and pain*: the poet's mother inspired strong feelings of guilt and pain in him

4 *Brooklyn*: Montague was born in Brooklyn, New York

5–6 *that was … fame*: his troublesome birth was the first remarkable thing about him

12 *Not readily forgiven*: his mother did not easily forgive him for being a boy and for having caused her such pain at his birth

13 *you never nursed me*: you treated me coldly.

14–15 *and when … money*: his father did not have a well-paid job and also drank too much. His songs could not compensate for the poverty his mother was forced to live in

19 *Then you gave me away*: when he returned to Ireland at the age of 4, he was raised, not by his mother, but by two aunts

24 *yarning*: telling stories

27 *lovely Molly*: a reference to the Rose of Mooncoin, a famous Irish ballad

27 *belle*: beautiful girl

28 *landed up*: ended up

29–30 *as the constant … cocoon of pain*: her efforts to protect herself from grief were not successful

30 *cocoon*: a protective covering. In this case it means a retreat from the sorrows of life

35 *forlorn*: pitifully sad and lonely

38 *gone*: dead

GUIDELINES

This is one of a number of poems in which Montague deals with members of his family. For example, in 'The Cage' he writes about his father. His mother is the main subject of 'The Locket'; another is the unusual relationship between mother and son. The background of the poem is a sad one. His mother, having given birth to two boys, resented John's birth because she wanted a girl: he thus felt, and was made to feel, that he should carry a burden of guilt for having been born, more particularly as his birth was a difficult one for his mother. Following the return of both of them to Ireland, his mother refused to let him live with her; he was obliged to live with his parental aunts seven miles away and endure the emotional consequences of his parents' broken marriage.

The poem is a lament for the poet's dead mother. It is not a conventional lament for a dead person: the poet is much more interested in the influence of his mother on his life than in her significance as a woman. Through most of the poem, the emphasis is on the damaging influence of his mother on his own life and development. She did not welcome his birth and found it hard to forgive him for it. She never nurtured him, and gave him away rather than rear him. She discouraged his visits in order to avoid growing fond of him. In this she follows 'the harsh logic of a forlorn woman / resigned to being alone'.

Rejection is not, however, the entire story of the poem, which ends with the poet's experience of what he calls a 'mysterious blessing'. After her death, it transpires that his mother always wore an oval locket containing an old picture of the poet as a child.

In 'The Locket', as in many of Montague's poems, among them 'Like Dolmens Round my Childhood, The Old People' and 'The Wild Dog Rose', outward appearances can be profoundly deceptive.

On a first reading the fourth stanza of the poem may seem odd. The poet claims that his mother might never have known him if he had not cycled the seven miles separating his home from hers. The purpose of his visit was:

> to court you like a young man
> teasingly untying your apron,
> drinking by the fire, yarning …

These ritual visits are best explained by the idea that the young Montague is not making them merely in an attempt to heal the wound of being an unwanted child. There is a sense in which he sees himself as his father's double as he does in 'The Cage', and even more obviously in a poem called 'The Same Fault', where he remarks that he and his father have:

the same scar
in the same place
as if the same fault ran through us both.

The child's mental anguish at being a displaced, unwanted child is mirrored in his father's anguish at losing his family, since, as a husband, he is unwanted. His wife, having instinctively rejected their child, engages in a double rejection when she refuses to live in New York as an immigrant wife and leaves her husband to return to Ireland. The boy's understanding of his father's predicament may well help to explain why he is willing to assume the role of his father's double, wooing his mother as if on his own father's behalf and vainly trying to heal the wounds of family division.

QUESTIONS

1 The title of the poem and the last stanza emphasise the importance of the locket. Why is the locket so important to the poet?

2 How would you describe the tone of the first stanza?

3 When the poet describes his coming into the world as '*The worst birth in the annals of Brooklyn*' (line 4), are we to take him seriously? Explain your answer.

4 Montague describes his mother as a 'fertile source of guilt and pain' (line 3). How is this description illustrated in the rest of the poem?

5 Show how the poet explores the theme of rejection throughout the poem.

6 The poem gives us an idea of the poet's attitude to his mother. How would you describe this attitude?

7 What does the poem tell us about the mother's life?

8 How does the young Montague try to win his mother's affection? Does he succeed?

9 Write an account of the young Montague's relationship with his mother, based on this poem.

10 What has happened to make the mother of the poet 'a forlorn woman'? You might look particularly at Stanza Three.

11 Is the poet sorry for himself? Give reasons for your answer.

12 What is the happiest moment of the poem, and what is the saddest?

THE CAGE

My father, the least happy
man I have known. His face
retained the pallor
of those who work underground:
the lost years in Brooklyn   5
listening to a subway
shudder the earth.

But a traditional Irishman
who (released from his grille
in the Clark St I.R.T.)   10
drank neat whiskey until
he reached the only element
he felt at home in
any longer: brute oblivion.

And yet picked himself   15
up, most mornings,
to march down the street
extending his smile
to all sides of the good
(non-negro) neighbourhood   20
belled by St. Teresa's church.

When he came back
we walked together
across fields of Garvaghey
to see hawthorn on the summer   25
hedges, as though
he had never left;
a bend on the road

which still sheltered
primroses. But we 30
did not smile in
the shared complicity
of a dream, for when
weary Odysseus returns
Telemachus must leave. 35

Often as I descend
into subway or underground
I see his bald head behind
the bars of the small booth;
the mark of an old car 40
accident beating on his
ghostly forehead.

GLOSSARY

3 *pallor*: an unnatural paleness

5 *Brooklyn*: a borough of New York. Many Irish emigrants lived there

6 *subway*: New York underground rail system

7 *shudder*: to shake violently

9 *grille*: a metal screen with bars. His duties as a subway ticket collector meant that the poet's father had to work behind a grille. Here it refers to the subway ticket office where the poet's father worked

10 *the Clark St I.R.T.*: a New York subway station

11 *neat whiskey*: undiluted whiskey

12 *the only element*: the only condition

14 *oblivion*: forgetfulness

18 *extending*: reaching out with

19–21 *to all sides … … church*: the speaker's father was happy to smile at the white inhabitants of the white neighbourhood, served by the local Catholic Church

22 *came back*: returned to Ireland

24 *Garvaghey*: the birthplace of the poet's father, who returned to Ireland in 1952, nineteen years after John had been sent back

29–32 *But we …of a dream*: we did not share the same dreams, hopes or ambitions

31 *complicity*: involvement

32–34 *for when … must leave*: Odysseus, also called Ulysses, is the hero of Homer's Epic poem, *The Odyssey*. His adventures on land and on sea last twenty years. Telemachus is the son of Odysseus. In Homer's poem, Telemachus and his mother Penelope wait at their home in Ithaca for the return of Odysseus. When Odysseus comes home, Telemachus leaves Ithaca. There are obvious parallels between this story and that of the Montague family. The most striking one is that the younger Montague left for New York as soon as his father came back from there

39 *booth*: a small enclosed structure

GUIDELINES

The poem is about Montague's father, James. It is also about the father-son relationship, and about the effects of exile and return on a man described in Stanza Two as 'a traditional Irishman'. Montague's father, 'the least happy / man I have known', according to the poet, had every reason to be unhappy. His militant patriotism induced him to flee to New York. His failure to earn an adequate living and his fondness for drink alienated his wife for whom, as we learn in 'The Locket', all his songs 'couldn't sweeten the lack of money'.

Abandoned by his wife and family in the early 1930s, he was obliged to live alone in New York until his retirement from a menial job in 1952, when he returned to Ireland to live out the last seven years of his life in Omagh, Co Tyrone.

The first three stanzas of the poem provide a concise account of James Montague's life as an Irish emigrant in New York. It is significant that Montague describes his father's time in New York as 'the lost years'. The suggestion here is that exile from the place of his ancestors deprives his life of its essential meaning and robs him of his identity. The title of the poem is a metaphor for James Montague's plight. He spends his working life underground in a subway ticket office, a kind of miniature prison in which he must dispense tickets through the bars of a grille. He is pale-faced from lack of fresh air, his ears assaulted by the noise of the subway trains as they 'shudder the earth'. His pale colour suggests death, which is also brought to mind by the image of the underground. This word invokes thoughts of Hades, the home of the dead in Greek mythology. Compare the parallel imagery in 'All Legendary Obstacles'.

What he has lost through exile is suggested in Stanzas Four and Five: the fields of his native Garvaghey, 'hawthorn on the summer / hedges' and primroses sheltered by a bend in the road. Life in the infernal underground cage can be relieved only in the 'brute oblivion' of drunkenness, another kind of imprisonment. The contrast between these forms of physical and mental captivity and the freedom of the open fields of Garvaghey is central to the meaning of the poem. James Montague's underground life behind the grille of the Clark Street subway station becomes a metaphor for his life as an exile who cannot feel at home in New York and who tries to find a substitute home in a state of forget-fulness induced by neat whiskey. The cage suggests another kind of double life. He is visible through its bars and at the same time cut off from a world to which he does not fully belong.

Stanzas Four and Five refer to James Montague's return from America in 1952, when father and son could spend time together in Garvaghey. The end of the father's exile does not, however, mark the beginning of a happy relationship between father and son. They 'did not smile in / the shared complicity / of a dream'. When James Montague, like the weary Odysseus of Homer's ancient epic, comes home, his son, like Telemachus, son of Odysseus, must himself go into exile. His place of exile is New York, the one originally chosen by his father.

The final stanza of the poem is based on the notion that the father is a double for his son, just as the son is a double for him. To reinforce this point, Montague uses an image of his dead father behind the bars of a subway booth:

the mark of an old car
accident beating on his
ghostly forehead.

Elsewhere in his work, Montague is at pains to stress the physical resemblance between his father and himself, in particular the detail of a facial scar common to both as a means of suggesting that he sees his father as an image of himself. (See the reference to 'The Same Fault' in the commentary on 'The Locket'.)

QUESTIONS

1 Why do you think the poet chose 'The Cage' as the title of this poem? Explore the ideas associated with the image of the cage throughout the poem.

2 How would you describe the poet's attitude to his father? Refer to words or phrases in the poem.

3 Explain the reference to 'the lost years in Brooklyn'.

4 Why did the poet's father seek comfort in 'brute oblivion'?

5 The poet tells us that his father extended his smile 'to all sides of the good / (non-negro) neighbourhood'. Explain this reference.

6 How is the idea of imprisonment suggested in Stanza Two of the poem?

7 In Stanza Five, we are told that father and son did not smile in 'the shared complicity / of a dream'. Why do you think this was so? What was the dream?

8 Comment on the reference to Odysseus and Telemachus in Stanza Five.

9 Say what you like or dislike about this poem.

10 On the evidence of the poem, does the father's life seem to have served any purpose?

11 The poem features some significant examples of contrast. Discuss some of these, for example, the contrast between Brooklyn and Garvaghey.

12 What do the images in the final stanza of the poem suggest to you ('I descend'; 'underground'; 'bars'; 'ghostly forehead')?

WINDHARP

for Patrick Collins

The sounds of Ireland,
that restless whispering
you never get away
from, seeping out of
low bushes and grass,   5
heatherbells and fern,
wrinkling bog pools,
scraping tree branches,
light hunting cloud,
sound hounding sight,   10
a hand ceaselessly
combing and stroking
the landscape, till
the valley gleams
like the pile upon
a mountain pony's coat.   15

GLOSSARY

2–4 *that restless ... from*: breezes are a constant feature of the Irish climate

4–5 *seeping out of ... ... grass*: the breezes come through the bushes and the grass in the same way as water leaks slowly from porous materials

7 *wrinkling bog pools*: the wind causing ripples on the surface of the water in bog holes

9 *light hunting cloud*: the breeze blows the clouds across the sky so that they are replaced by light

10 *sound hounding sight*: the image is based on a hound chasing after its prey

11–13 *hand ... landscape*: these lines help to explain the title of the poem. The entire landscape is like a great harp that the wind is constantly playing on

15 *pile*: the soft projecting surface of hair on the pony's back

GUIDELINES

The poem is dedicated to the Irish artist Patrick Collins, whose 'atmospheric' landscape paintings find a poetic equivalent in 'Windharp'. The title of the poem is an allusion to ancient Greek mythology. Montague has in mind Aeolus, whom Zeus appointed keeper of the winds, and the harp named after Aeolus, the Aeolian harp or windharp. This harp was much favoured by the English Romantic poets. Its strings, of varying thickness, were all tuned to the same note. When the wind blew across the strings, it played the music of nature, much as it does when it blows across the Irish landscape in the poem.

The title may have another significance for Montague. The seal of the United Irish Society, founded in Belfast in October 1971, featured a harp. Montague linked this harp not only to the harp of Aeolus, but 'more immediately to the events of my own country'.

The structure of the poem is interesting: it consists of a single extended sentence. The rushing, onward movement of the verse perfectly reflects the restless activity of the wind. The poem is a sensitive response to the natural world: Montague evokes its many voices and varied musical sounds in familiar, commonplace images within a short compass.

The music of the landscape is not particularly pleasing to the ear. It has an unsettling effect on the listener, suggested by its 'restless whispering'. The dominant sounds are disturbing ('seeping', 'wrinkling', 'scraping'). At one point, the images of the wind's activity become menacing, even predatory: 'light hunting cloud, / sound hunting sight'.

At line 11, as tactile and visual imagery replaces the imagery of sound, the poem takes on a gentler aspect. The hand 'ceaselessly / combing and stroking / the landscape' represents the care nature takes of that landscape. The image of the hand humanises the action of the wind. The hand which combs the landscape is seen, by means of a charming simile, to comb the pony's back as well. Nature's fostering activity prepares us for the revelation of the full glory of the landscape as 'the valley gleams'. As often in Montague, this poem has implications which go deeper than the surface meaning. Montague, with the imagery of music in mind, has suggested that this music might be able to suggest, in a Northern Ireland political context, an inclusive, unpartitioned attitude in which all Irish people 'should be able to accept, or listen to, many voices, agreeable or disturbing, which haunt our land', and in that way 'blend, as a symphony contains its dissonances, structures of healing'.

QUESTIONS

1 This poem is dedicated to a famous landscape painter. In what ways do you think it might appeal to such a painter?

2 Is this poem an entirely happy one? Does it suggest any criticisms of the Irish landscape?

3 Why do you think the poet chose 'Windharp' as his title?

4 How do the final five lines contrast with what has gone before?

5 Do you think the poet captures some essential features of the Irish landscape? Explain your answer by referring to significant details in the poem.

6 Why does the poet refer to a hand 'combing and stroking / the landscape'? Is there a connection between this image, the title of the poem, and the pony's coat?

7 How does the poet suggest the ceaseless movement of the wind?

ALL LEGENDARY OBSTACLES

All legendary obstacles lay between
Us, the long imaginary plain,
The monstrous ruck of mountains
And, swinging across the night,
Flooding the Sacramento, San Joaquin,   5
The hissing drift of winter rain.

All day I waited, shifting
Nervously from station to bar
As I saw another train sail
By, the San Francisco Chief or   10
Golden Gate, water dripping
From great flanged wheels.

At midnight you came, pale
Above the negro porter's lamp.
I was too blind with rain   15
And doubt to speak, but
Reached from the platform
Until our chilled hands met.

You had been travelling for days
With an old lady, who marked   20
A neat circle on the glass
With her glove, to watch us
Move into the wet darkness
Kissing, still unable to speak.

GLOSSARY

2 *plain*: an area of low, generally flat land

3 *ruck*: heap or pile

5 *the Sacramento, San Joaquin*: rivers in California

10–11 *San Francisco Chief or / Golden Gate*: trains operating in California

12 *flanged wheels*: wheels protected by metal rims or flanges which keep them in place

15 *I was too blind with rain*: I could not see properly due to the falling rain

16 *And doubt to speak*: the speaker was not sure what to say and therefore said nothing

20–21 *who marked … glass*: by marking a circle on the glass the old lady duplicates what the porter does with his lamp, when he sheds a circle of light on the lovers' meeting

23 *wet darkness*: dark night with rain falling

GUIDELINES

Many of Montague's poems can be adequately understood only with the help of information on the circumstances of the poet's life, his family background, the neighbourhoods in which he grew up and the cultural, social and political history of Ireland. In particular, plantation, dispossession and emigration are matters which influenced Montague's thinking. Such poems include 'Like Dolmens Round my Childhood', 'The Windharp', 'The Locket' and 'The Cage'. 'All Legendary Obstacles', on the other hand, is relatively self-explanatory, apart from the references in lines 5, 10 and 11 on which non-Americans might need help. The poem is an account of separated lovers coming together. The woman has travelled across the American continent to where the speaker of the poem waits for her in San Francisco.

'All Legendary Obstacles' is a love poem. This helps to explain why its language is richer, less matter-of-fact than that in many of Montague's other poems. The opening stanza, for example, is grandly rhetorical and urgent in its rhythms. Lines 4–6 impressively reflect the movement of the rain across a wide geographical expanse. The 'legendary obstacles' separating the lovers are the great natural barriers, the long plain and 'The monstrous ruck of mountains', and to a lesser extent, perhaps, 'The hissing drift of winter rain'. In this stanza, Montague clearly does not want his high rhetorical flight to get out of control, as we discover in the opening two lines: 'All legendary obstacles lay between / Us, the long imaginary plain'. By placing the 'Us' at the beginning of line 2 rather than at the end of line 1, he temporarily slows the movement of the verse, only to quicken its pace again in the remainder of the stanza. The second line, with its reference to 'the long imaginary plain' poses a problem. The plain referred to is clearly a real one. It is being imagined by the waiting lover rather than being an imaginary thing. To make sense, the poet should have written 'the long imagined plain' or even 'the long-imagined plain'. This is one case in which Montague allowed his desire to achieve impressive sound effects to overrule the demands of meaning: 'imaginary' is rhythmically superior and provides a pleasant verbal echo for 'legendary' in line 1.

The two opening lines of Stanza Three call for comment: 'At midnight you came, pale / Above the negro porter's lamp'. The key word here is 'pale'. It is a word that Montague uses very often in his poetry. Here it is used with impressive effect. It contrasts sharply with the darkness of the porter's skin and with the midnight darkness. The word has another significance. Montague, like many of the Romantic poets, thought of 'pale' as the colour symbolising death. John Keats, for example, describes the dying knight in 'La Belle Dame Sans Merci' as 'palely loitering'. With this in mind, we may think of the woman of the poem surrounded by an aura of death, perhaps recovering from an illness which brought her near to death. This kind of interpretation is reinforced by the general melancholy of the midnight scene, the 'hissing drift of winter rain', the 'chilled hands' of the lovers and the 'wet darkness'.

At one level, the poem deals with the ordinary experience of two separated lovers. At a deeper level, as some of its details suggest, the woman's journey has disturbing implications. Are we, for example, to see a sinister meaning in the black porter? Is he a figure from the underworld? Or is the transcontinental crossing in which the pale woman participates a journey to the underworld, and has the train arriving at midnight, the fateful hour, been part of a funeral procession? The 'legendary obstacles' of the title are the obstacles which, in legend and fable, fate places between lovers as a means of separating them. Of such obstacles, the ultimate one is death, images of which seem to hover around the platform, which is the stage on which the events of the poem are enacted. The ending of the poem, however, may suggest a contrary view. The lady with her circle on the glass is an image of age, from which the two lovers slip away into the darkness. The moving train is an image of transience, from which the lovers retreat into what they must hope will be a permanent state of love.

QUESTIONS

1 What does the poem tell us about the poet's relationship with the person he is waiting for? How does he feel about her?

2 Why is the poet uneasy and nervous as he waits?

3 The poem features some striking contrasts. Comment on these.

4 Choose two images from the poem that appeal to you. Explain why you like them.

5 Why does the poet find it impossible to speak?

6 Do you think the old lady in the final stanza adds to the meaning of the poem? Explain your answer.

7 Write your own account of the poem, explaining what it means to you.

8 What does the title of the poem suggest? How does it relate to the overall impact of the poem?

9 Is this a sad or happy poem?

10 Does this poem have a single theme? If you think it has, give a brief outline of it.

THE SAME GESTURE

There is a secret room
of golden light where
everything – love, violence,
hatred is possible:
and, again love.   5

Such intimacy of hand
and mind is achieved
under its healing light
that the shifting of
hands is a rite   10

like court music.
We barely know our
selves there though
it is what we always were
– most nakedly are –   15

and must remember
when we leave, re-
suming our habits
with our clothes:
work, 'phone, drive   20

through late traffic
changing gears with
the same gesture as
eased your snowbound
heart and flesh.   25

GLOSSARY

1 *a secret room*: a room shared by the two lovers

10 *a rite*: a sacred ritual

11 *court music*: elegant, graceful music played for royal persons

15 *most nakedly are*: most obviously are, essentially are. There is a pun on 'nakedly'. In this context, it also has its literal meaning. See lines 19–20

24 *snowbound*: the poet is saying that the ritual of love, expressed in the 'shifting' roving hands of the lover, releases the trapped emotions of the woman he loves

GUIDELINES

This is a love poem. In traditional love poetry, it is possible to identify two distinct interpretations of the meaning of love. In many poems, we find a tension between them. The tradition of Platonic poetry emphasises the spiritual dimension of love as an image of God's love for human beings, and underplays its physical expression. In this poem, Montague is an anti-Platonic love-poet, who finds the fullest meaning of love only in its physical expression.

The 'secret room' imagined in the poem is the room shared by the two lovers. In this room, love, in its purely physical sense, excludes everything else from the consciousness of the two lovers. A 'healing light' shines on the lovers as they embrace and caress each other. Their loving gestures are seen by the poet as equivalent to a sacred ceremony or 'rite' in which sense and intelligence are intimately linked.

Montague sees the rooms, often in his case hotel rooms, in which he imagines the most intimate physical contact between himself and his lover, as sacred spaces or places of worship, in which the two lovers become closest to their true selves. For a while, the room they share becomes the whole world: it is a place where 'everything … is possible' and which contains everything that matters. A similar idea is at the heart of Donne's poem 'The Sunne Rising'. In that poem, Donne tries to persuade his readers that for him and his mistress confined to their room, their world consists of nothing but themselves ('Nothing else is'), and that the whole world has contracted to the size of a single room.

In Montague's poem, there are realities other than the intimacies described in the first three stanzas. These intimacies are passing, temporary events in a temporary space. They can linger only in the memory. The lovers must leave their sanctuary and return to the routines of everyday life ('re- / suming our habits / with our clothes / work, 'phone, drive'). The same hands that expressed loving gestures must soon be put to more everyday use. The same kind of gesture that eased the woman's 'snowbound / heart and flesh' is soon used by the poet to change gears as he drives through late traffic.

QUESTIONS

1 Why does the poet describe the light in the room as 'golden'?
2 Why is the room called 'secret'?
3 What is the significance of the 'healing light'? See the final stanza.
4 Is the kind of love described in the poem permanent? Base your answer on evidence offered by the poem.
5 Discuss the meaning of the title.
6 There is a contrast between the first three stanzas of the poem and the final two. Comment on this.
7 What is the theme of the poem?
8 Do you find this poem optimistic?
9 What does the poem tell us about the meaning of love? Do you share the point of view it expresses?
10 It might be suggested that this is an escapist poem, dealing with people who try to find a refuge from reality. Would you agree?

THE WILD DOG ROSE

I

I go to say goodbye to the *Cailleach*
that terrible figure who haunted my childhood
but no longer harsh, a human being
merely, hurt by event.

    The cottage,   5
circled by trees, weathered to admonitory
shapes of desolation by the mountain winds,
straggles into view. The rank thistles
and leathery bracken of untilled fields
stretch behind with – a final outcrop –   10
the hooped figure by the roadside,
its retinue of dogs

    which give tongue
as I approach, with savage, whining cries
so that she slowly turns, a moving nest   15
of shawls and rags, to view, to stare
the stranger down.

    And I feel again
that ancient awe, the terror of a child
before the great hooked nose, the cheeks   20
dewlapped with dirt, the staring blue
of the sunken eyes, the mottled claws
clutching a stick

    but now hold
and return her gaze, to greet her,   25
as she greets me, in friendliness.
Memories have wrought reconciliation
between us, we talk in ease at last,
like old friends, lovers almost,
sharing secrets   30

    of neighbours
she quarrelled with, who now lie
in Garvaghey graveyard, beyond all hatred;
of my family and hers, how she never married,
though a man came asking in her youth   35
'You would be loath to leave your own'
she sighs, 'and go among strangers' –
his parish ten miles off.

    For sixty years
since she has lived alone, in one place.   40
Obscurely honoured by such confidences,
I idle by the summer roadside, listening,
while the monologue falters, continues,
rehearsing the small events of her life.
The only true madness is loneliness,   45
the monotonous voice in the skull
that never stops

    because never heard.

II
And there
where the dog rose shines in the hedge   50
she tells me a story so terrible
that I try to push it away,
my bones melting.

    Late at night
a drunk came beating at her door   55
to break it in, the bold snapping
from the soft wood, the thin mongrels
rushing to cut, but yelping as
he whirls with his farm boots
to crush their skulls.   60

        In the darkness
they wrestle, two creatures crazed
with loneliness, the smell of the
decaying cottage in his nostrils
like a drug, his body heavy on hers,   65
the tasteless trunk of a seventy year
old virgin, which he rummages while
she battles for life

        bony fingers
reaching desperately to push   70
against his bull neck. 'I prayed
to the Blessed Virgin herself
for help and after a time
I broke his grip.'

        He rolls   75
to the floor, snores asleep,
while she cowers until dawn
and the dogs' whimpering starts
him awake, to lurch back across
the wet bog.   80

III
        And still
the dog rose shines in the hedge.
Petals beaten wide by rain, it
sways slightly, at the tip of a
slender, tangled, arching branch   85
which, with her stick, she gathers
into us.

        'The wild rose
is the only rose without thorns,'
she says, holding a wet blossom   90
for a second, in a hand knotted
as the knob of her stick.
'Whenever I see it, I remember
the Holy Mother of God and
all she suffered.'   95

Briefly
the air is strong with the smell
of that weak flower, offering
its crumbled yellow cup
and pale bleeding lips   100
fading to white

   at the rim
of each bruised and heart-
shaped petal.

GLOSSARY

1 *Cailleach*: Irish and Scots Gaelic for an old woman, a hag

3 *harsh*: cruel or severe

6 *admonitory*: warning

7 *desolation*: having a bleak and dismal appearance

8 *straggles*: comes gradually into view

8 *rank*: rotting

10 *outcrop*: part of a rock formation that is visible from the surface

12 *retinue*: group of followers

13 *give tongue*: to express themselves

16–17 *to stare … down*: to look with a fixed expression at the stranger until he is forced to look away

19 *awe*: feeling of great respect mixed with fear

21 *dewlapped*: having folds of skin hanging from the neck or throat

22 *mottled*: spotted

27 *wrought reconciliation*: brought about friendly relations

36 *loath*: unwilling

41 *Obscurely honoured …confidences*: in some vague way he was flattered that the old woman shared her private thoughts with him

43 *monologue*: a long speech by one person during a conversation

43 *falters*: slows down

44 *rehearsing*: repeating

46 *monotonous*: boring or tedious

50 *dog rose*: delicately scented wild rose with pink or white flowers

52 *I try to push it away*: I don't want to hear it

58 *cut*: bite

77 *cowers*: crouches in fear

78 *lurch*: to stagger

99 *crumbled*: crushed

100–101 *pale … white*: the dog rose is pink at the edges and white at the centre

102 *rim*: the outer edge

GUIDELINES

'The Wild Dog Rose' is best read in conjunction with 'Like Dolmens Round my Childhood'. The old woman who is the subject of the poem has much in common with the old people who made Montague fearful in his childhood and who troubled his dreams. In 'The Wild Dog Rose', as in 'Like Dolmens Round my Childhood', people are not what they seem. The early description of the old woman as a *cailleach*, the Irish word for hag, suggests that she was widely regarded as a sinister creature, almost a witch, because of her hideous appearance, her 'great hooked nose', her cheeks 'dewlapped with dirt', and 'her mottled claws'. As the poet explores her character and circumstances, we learn that far form being a witch, she is a lonely, suffering human being, harshly treated by circumstances.

Contrast is at the heart of 'The Wild Dog Rose'. Firstly, there is the contrast between past and present, between the poet's childhood view of the old woman as an object of terror and his mature view of her as an unfortunate victim in need of sympathy. This sympathy is strongly evoked by the poet. Instead of cowering in terror before her, he can now greet her in friendliness. The two of them can talk easily and naturally, 'like old friends, lovers almost, / sharing secrets'. He is honoured by her willingness to share the small events of her life with him, particularly the cause of her present loneliness: her refusal as a young woman of a proposal of marriage from a man who lived ten miles away. The poet who was terrified of her in his childhood now learns that she had to confront her own terrors, above all her isolation:

> The only true madness is loneliness,
> the monotonous voice in the skull
> that never stops
>
>   because never heard.

The climax of the poem is the terrible story of an attempt by a drunken man to rape her one night in her cottage. The incident is presented in realistic detail and the effect is shocking. There is a touch of ambiguity in the account, as the poet tries to understand the motives of the drunken aggressor and his miserable way of life:

> they wrestle, two creatures crazed
> with loneliness, the smell of the
> decaying cottage in his nostrils
> like a drug …

It is important to note that the woman's terrible ordeal does not result in madness or in the destruction of her will to survive. At the heart of her account of the attempted rape and her battle for life, she recalls that she prayed to the Blessed Virgin for help. She believes that as a result of this prayer she was able to break the assailant's grip. The reference to the Blessed Virgin becomes part of the symbolic meaning of the poem and of its title. The old woman gives the clue to this when she suggests an association between the wild dog rose and the Blessed Virgin. Whenever she sees the flower, she remembers 'the Holy Mother of God and / all she suffered'. Her cruel history of fear, attempted rape and isolation based on superstition is transformed when the dog rose still shines in the hedge reminding her of her stubborn faith in the Mother of God which permits her to survive the monotony of her life as well as her suffering.

Montague's comment on the central episode of the poem is worth bearing in mind. He points to a crucial distinction between the woman's interpretation of her experience and the more ambiguous way in which he, as the poet, may have intended to present it. Montague writes:

> After she is almost raped, the woman prays to the Blessed Virgin. The Blessed Virgin is symbolised for her by the Wild Dog Rose, but the end of the poem describes that as a 'weak flower'. This is her comfort. The poem doesn't say that it accepts that comfort, just that she has been able to draw strength from it as people do from whatever they can mange to believe in.

Just as the wild dog rose is viewed by the woman in terms of religious symbolism, the attempted rape is intended by the poet as a piece of political symbolism. When the poem first appeared in Montague's collection *Tides* (1970), it could be read as a grim account of a real-life situation. However, Montague made it part of another collection, *The Rough Field* (1972), which deals with the violent dispossession of the native inhabitants of Ireland of their land, language, heritage and identity at the hands of British colonists. In the context of this collection, 'The

Wild Dog Rose' necessarily takes on a political dimension, as an implied comment on an imperial rape of a weak subject people. In 1980, when *The Rough Field* was performed in a theatre, Montague approved of the playing of the traditional Irish patriotic tune *Roisin Dubh* (The Little Black Rose) as background music to the description of the rape. Montague remarked:

> *And so, as she's describing her rape or her attempted rape, you get this lovely song of Ireland's betrayal and Ireland's loss and Ireland's wrong. And it's very, very moving. Terribly moving.*

QUESTIONS

1 What happened to make the poet see the old woman as no longer harsh but as 'a human being / merely, hurt by event'?

2 Do you think the woman's environment has influenced the young Montague's attitude to her?

3 Is there a suggestion in the poem that the woman's physical appearance caused the poet to judge her harshly? Explain your answer with reference to the poem.

4 The *Cailleach* is a lonely woman. Is this important? Give reasons for your answer.

5 Why is the poet honoured as the old woman tells him about the small events of her life?

6 Write out two images from the poem that you find impressive. Give reasons for your choices.

7 Contrast the child's view of the old woman with the adult's view.

8 Why do you think the old woman greets the poet 'in friendliness'?

9 Give your own impression of the old woman as she appears in the poem.

10 What does the woman's account of the attempted rape tell us about her?

11 In Part III of the poem, it is clear that the wild dog rose has a symbolic meaning. How is this suggested in the poem? Give your own interpretation of the symbolism of the rose.

12 The Blessed Virgin plays an important part in the woman's account. Comment on this. How is the Virgin associated with the rose?

LIKE DOLMENS ROUND MY CHILDHOOD, THE OLD PEOPLE

Like dolmens round my childhood, the old people.

Jamie MacCrystal sang to himself,
A broken song without tune, without words;
He tipped me a penny every pension day,
Fed kindly crusts to winter birds   5
When he died, his cottage was robbed,
Mattress and money box torn and searched.
Only the corpse they didn't disturb.

Maggie Owens was surrounded by animals,
A mongrel bitch and shivering pups,   10
Even in her bedroom a she-goat cried.
She was a well of gossip defiled,
Fanged chronicler of a whole countryside:
Reputed a witch, all I could find
Was her lonely need to deride.   15

The Nialls lived along a mountain lane
Where heather bells bloomed, clumps of foxglove.
All were blind, with Blind Pension and Wireless,
Dead eyes serpent-flicked as one entered
To shelter from a downpour of mountain rain.
Crickets chirped under the rocking hearthstone   20
Until the muddy sun shone out again.

Mary Moore lived in a crumbling gatehouse,
Famous as Pisa for its leaning gable.
Bag-apron and boots, she tramped the fields
Driving lean cattle from a miry stable.   25
A by-word for fierceness, she fell asleep
Over love stories, Red Star and Red Circle,
Dreamed of gypsy love rites, by firelight sealed.

Wile Billy Eagleson married a Catholic servant girl   30
When all his Loyal family passed on:
We danced round him shouting 'To Hell with King Billy,'
And dodged from the arc of his flailing blackthorn.
Forsaken by both creeds, he showed little concern
Until the Orange drums banged past in the summer   35
And bowler and sash aggressively shone.

Curate and doctor trudged to attend them,
Through knee-deep snow, through summer heat,
From main road to lane to broken path,
Gulping the mountain air with painful breath.   40
Sometimes they were found by neighbours,
Silent keepers of a smokeless hearth,
Suddenly cast in the mould of death.

Ancient Ireland, indeed! I was reared by her bedside,
The rune and the chant, evil eye and averted head,   45
Fomorian fierceness of family and local feud.
Gaunt figures of fear and of friendliness,
For years they trespassed on my dreams,
Until once, in a standing circle of stones,
I felt their shadows pass   50

Into that dark permanence of ancient forms.

GLOSSARY

1 *dolmens*: prehistoric monuments usually consisting of several great stone slabs set edgewise in the earth to support a flat stone, which served as a roof. Dolmens were designed as burial structures

12 *She was ...defiled*: she told foul stories about her neighbours

13 *Fanged chronicler*: teller of bitter, biting stories

14 *Reputed a witch*: having the reputation of being a witch

15 *Was her lonely need to deride*: her loneliness caused her to mock other people

18 *All were blind ... Wireless*: those who were blind were entitled to a pension and a radio from the social welfare services

23 *gatehouse*: a house occupied by the caretaker of a larger house

24 *Pisa*: a reference to the leaning tower in that city

25 *miry*: muddy

27 *Red Star and Red Circle*: magazines featuring love stories

31 *Loyal family*: a family which supported the connection between Northern Ireland and the United Kingdom

32 *King Billy*: King William of Orange, a Protestant hero

34 *Forsaken by both creeds*: abandoned by members of both religions

35 *Until the Orange drums ... summer*: until the arrival of the Orange Order marching season

36 *bowler and sash*: these are worn by members of the Orange Order during their marches

37 *Curate*: Catholic priest

45 *rune and chant*: a rune was a song or set of words believed to have magic properties. The chant has a similar meaning

45 *evil eye and averted head*: people who had the evil eye were believed to have the power to bring disaster on those they looked at. To avoid this, people turned away or averted their heads

46 *Fomorian:* the Fomorians were a savage tribe of ancient settlers in Ireland

46 *feud*: long-standing dispute often involving several generations of the same families

47 *Gaunt*: thin

48 *trespassed on my dreams*: invaded my dreams

49 *standing circle of stones*: in ancient Ireland, stone circles were associated with the worship of the sun

50–51 *I felt their shadows pass ... forms*: the ancient forms that haunted him have passed away forever

GUIDELINES

This poem deals with some of the more unusual people who inhabited the world of Montague's childhood. Like many of Montague's poems, this one features fully human individuals, scarred by misery and suffering but also possessing faith and enjoying life. The main characters in the poem are isolated, lonely people. For the young Montague, their main significance was that they haunted his childhood dreams, conjuring up sinister and grotesque images associated with ancient pagan customs. In early adult life, when childhood gave way to manhood, the dark dreams no longer troubled him. He traces his liberation from their fearful grip to a single experience. Standing as a young man in a circle of stones, he feels the terrible shadow cast by the old people pass away and the dreams, which have troubled him are transformed into myth, 'that dark permanence of ancient forms'.

The dolmens mentioned in the title and in the first line of the poem have a symbolic meaning. By imagining the old people as dolmens, the poet is suggesting why Jamie Mac Crystal, Maggie Owens and the others dominated his life and troubled even his dreams. He was imprisoned by their influence in much the same way as the body of an ancient inhabitant of Ireland was buried beneath a dolmen. There is a further dimension to the comparison between dolmens and old people. To the poet's eye, the human figures are scattered around the landscape like figures of stone.

The poem, however, is one of liberation as well as of imprisonment. This becomes clear in the last stanza. Just as the dolmens represent the child's captivity, the standing circle of stones is associated with his release from the fearful dreams inspired by the old people. The last stanza tells us that his escape from the shadow cast on his young life by his elderly neighbours coincides with his entry into manhood. The act of making the old people present in his poetry serves a purpose similar to exorcism. They become in the end external to his mind and find their permanence in stone.

To the child's imagination all the characters of the poem are forbidding, abnormal and sometimes grotesque. Jamie Mac Crystal's song without tune and without words is sung to himself. Maggie Owens is thought to be a witch and keeps a she-goat in her bedroom. The Nialls are all blind. Mary Moore is remarkable for her fierceness, while Billy Eagleson is wild and wields a flailing blackthorn. These primitive people carry on some of the pagan traditions of ancient Ireland. There is, however, more to them than this. They may be 'Gaunt figures of fear', but as the last stanza admits they also appeal to the poet's imagination as figures of friendliness. In spite of their forbidding appearance the poet is able to feel sympathy for them and to understand the motives behind their behaviour. Jamie Mac Crystal is a poor man but still gives a penny to the young Montague every pension day and feeds hungry winter birds. Maggie Owens is a notorious gossip but the poet feels able to explain this by suggesting that frustration and loneliness cause her to speak ill of her neighbours. We find a similar attitude in 'The Wild Dog Rose' where the woman described as a hag is really an ordinary human being who has suffered much in her isolation.

QUESTIONS

1 In the title and in the first line, the poet relates the old people to dolmens. What is the significance of this relationship?

2 The old people mentioned in the poem have a few things in common. Mention as many of these as you can.

3 What is the poet's attitude to the people he is describing. Explain your answer by referring to words or phrases from the poem.

4 Which of the people do you think had a) the happiest life, and b) the saddest life. Refer to the poem for examples.

5 Maggie Owens is not the woman she seems. Explain this idea.

6 The old people are described as 'Silent keepers of a smokeless hearth / Suddenly cast in the mould of death'. What does this mean? Has 'mould' more than one meaning in this context?

7 Is the poem sad or comic or both? Explain.

8 Choose your favourite character from the poem. Give reasons for your choice.

9 Why is Billy Eagleson 'forsaken by both creeds'? What effect do the 'Orange drums' have on his attitudes?

10 What does the poet mean when he claims that he was reared by the bedside of 'Ancient Ireland'? Develop your answer by referring to the poem.

11 Why do you think the poet describes his neighbours as 'Gaunt figures of fear and friendliness'?

12 How did the old people trespass on the poet's dreams? How did he free himself from the influence of these dreams?

A WELCOMING PARTY

Wie war das möglich?

That final newsreel of the war:
A welcoming party of almost shades
Met us at the cinema door
Clicking what remained of their heels.

From nests of bodies like hatching eggs   5
Flickered insectlike hands and legs
And rose in ululation, terrible, shy;
Children conjugating the verb 'to die'.

One clamoured mutely of love
From a mouth like a burnt glove;   10
Others upheld hands bleak as begging bowls
Claiming the small change of our souls.

Some smiled at us as protectors.
Can these bones live?
Our parochial brand of innocence   15
Was all we had to give.

To be always at the periphery of incident
Gave my childhood its Irish dimension;
Yet doves of mercy, as doves of air,
Can falter here as anywhere.   20

That long dead Sunday in Armagh
I learned one meaning of total war
And went home to my Christian school
To kick a football through the air.

GLOSSARY

1 *newsreel*: type of news programme shown in cinemas before television became popular

1 *the war*: World War II; the final newsreel shows the discovery of death camps by Allied forces in 1945

2 *shades*: ghostly figures. The skeletal figures shown on the screen are little more than ghosts

4 *Clicking what remained of their heels*: in the context of a German camp, clicking the heels may be interpreted as a token of respect on the part of the inmates for their liberators. The heels of the welcoming party, however, have been worn down by starvation so that they can only click what remains of their heels. Notice the cruel irony of the title

5 *nests of bodies*: the bodies of the dead and dying were piled in heaps

6 *Flickered …legs*: the poet imagines that the heaps of bodies are newly-hatched eggs and that the twitching arms and legs of the camp victims are like the chicks emerging form the breaking shells

7 *an ululation*: loud cries of sorrow

8 *conjugating*: listing the various forms of death

9 *One clamoured …glove*: the silent attempt of the child to express love spoke more loudly and was more appealing than if it had been able to shout

11–12 *Others … souls*: other victims held up their skinny hands as if they were begging for the small amount of pity that we could offer them

13–16 *Some … give*: the surviving victims in the newsreel could expect nothing from the audience in the cinema except an innocent response based on a lack of understanding

17–18 *To be always at … dimension*: Irish children did not experience the horrors of the Second World War. Their only experience of the war was based on newsreel films. The Irish dimension to the poet's wartime childhood was his ignorance of the realities of the conflict

17 *at the periphery of incident*: not directly involved in the war

19 *doves of mercy*: people with kind feelings and intentions

19 *doves of air*: doves that fly

21 *That long dead Sunday*: that Sunday long ago. Given the nature of the film, is there a pun on 'dead'?

22 *total war*: the Second World War was an example of total war in which innocent civilians suffered as much as soldiers

GUIDELINES

In this poem Montague recalls a visit he made to a cinema with fellow-students when he was a pupil at St Patrick's College, Armagh. He was about 16 years old when the newsreel described in the poem was shown. At the end of the war, cinemas throughout the western world showed similar newsreels depicting the horrors of German concentration camps. The question raised in German following the title of the poem is the kind of one which a young audience might raise: how could a great European people like the Germans have descended to the barbarities depicted in the newsreel.

This poem combines description with reflection on what the details shown in the newsreel might have meant to a boy of 16 who had been insulated from the brutality of the Second World War. Earlier newsreels had shown the progress of the war, the victorious and defeated armies, navies and air-forces, the bombed cities and the millions of fleeing refugees. The final newsreel of the war shows the ultimate result of the combat: innocent civilians are degraded to a subhuman condition, most of them facing death from starvation and neglect. Montague presents the realities of the death-camps as depicted in the newsreel with frank realism in Stanzas Two and Three.

In the final three stanzas of the poem, the poet reflects on the meaning of what his younger self experienced on 'That long dead Sunday in Armagh'. The troubling question raised in these three stanzas concerns the inability of the young audience to do anything for the dying children in the newsreel. The latter hold their hands out and plead for help. In response, all that the audience can offer is sympathy. The poem gives an insight into the position taken by most Irish people during the Second World War. The Southern Irish State remained neutral while participation in the war remained optional for citizens of Northern Ireland. The poem reflects the detachment of people like the young Montague: 'To be always at the periphery of incident / Gave my childhood its Irish dimension'. The final stanza of the poem offers an ironic reflection on the boy's experience. On the playing-field of his 'Christian school' he enjoys the luxury of playing football while his contemporaries in Europe are raising 'insectlike hands and legs', begging for survival.

QUESTIONS

1 Why do you think the poet has chosen 'A Welcoming Party' as his title?

2 In the first stanza, the poet conveys a sinister and disturbing atmosphere. Explain how he does this.

3 Why are the hands and legs described as 'insectlike'?

4 What do the animal images in Stanza Two suggest?

5 What was the response of the cinema audience to what was shown on the screen?

6 How does the poet suggest that the cinema audience might have been as helpless as the victims?

7 Why did the victims suffer the fate described in the poem?

8 In the fifth stanza, the poet talks about the 'Irish dimension' of his childhood. Explain this reference. What has the 'Irish dimension' to do with the subject-matter of the poem?

9 What does the poet mean when he talks about being 'at the periphery of incident'?

10 Why is the epigraph to the poem in German?

11 Does the last stanza convey the idea that what he had seen on the cinema screen did not affect the young Montague very deeply?

12 Why do you think the poet mentions going back to his 'Christian school'? How would you describe the tone of the stanza?

GENERAL QUESTIONS ON MONTAGUE

1 Select two poems by Montague that deal with similar themes and issues. Discuss the poet's treatment of his subject matter in each case. Comment on any contrasts in approach between the two poems.

2 Name your favourite Montague poem. Give an account of the poem, its themes, language and imagery, indicating the qualities you most admire.

3 Do you find that Montague has a sad outlook on life? Base your answer on reference to a selection of his poems.

4 Montague's poems are notable for their descriptive qualities. Discuss two poems that you find outstanding in this respect.

5 Discuss Montague's treatment of women in his poetry.

6 In many of his poems, Montague deals with the past. Discuss one of the poems in the light of this comment, and explain why you think the past means so much to him.

7 Personal themes play a large part in Montague's poetry. Consider the autobiographical element in two of his poems.

8 Montague's poems give us a good picture of the kind of man who wrote them. Based on your reading of the poems you have studied, give your own impressions of the poet.

9 Discuss the theme of exile in the poetry of Montague.

10 In Montague's poetry there are numerous victims: (a) of society; (b) of other people; (c) of circumstances. Using these headings, write an essay on Montague's victims.

11 You are asked to give a talk on Montague's poetry. What would you say?

12 Montague's poetry displays an understanding of the problems people have to face in their daily lives and in their relationships. Explore this idea.

13 Montague's poems move easily between ancient and modern settings. Discuss this aspect of his work using appropriate reference/quotation.

14 What kind of impact do you think Montague's American background has on his poetry?

15 Consider Montague as a nature poet.

16 Write on Montague's exploration of the theme of love.

17 In his poems, Montague reflects a good deal on his childhood. Discuss his treatment of this topic.

18 'Montague is an Irish poet, but much more than that.' Discuss this statement.

19 The cruelties of life loom large in Montague's poetry. Examine the poet's treatment of these.

20 What do you think Montague's poetry can offer the young, modern reader?

EXAMINATION-STYLE QUESTIONS

21 You have been asked to select what you regard as the two best poems by Montague on your course, for inclusion in an anthology. Explain and justify your choice by means of reference to and quotation from the poems you have chosen.

22 Discuss Montague's treatment of:
a) the father-son relationship
and
b) the mother-son relationship.
In your discussion you should make detailed reference to poems by Montague on your course, and quote where necessary.

23 'Although Montague's poetry deals mainly with the sadder aspects of life, it also sounds many notes of hope.'
Examine this verdict, supporting your answer with quotation from, and reference to, relevant poems by Montague on your course.

Ability to see beneath
the surface of things.

Preoccupation with
family roots.

Theme of exile.

Interest in Irish history
and folklore.

Eccentric people as
favourite subjects.

Interested in
life's victims.

Theme of cruelty.

John Montague

More than one
layer of meaning in many of
Montague's poems.

Montague as a
landscape poet.

Theme of separation.

Concern for
people's suffering.

Poet is a
compassionate observer.

Poet is recorder of intimate
personal experience.

Childhood experiences
are important in
Montague's poetry.

SYLVIA PLATH

1932–1963

BIOGRAPHY

Sylvia Plath was born in a seaside suburb of Boston in 1932. Both her parents, Otto Plath and Aurelia Schober, were academics and had German ancestry. They believed in the virtues of hard work and were committed to education. Sylvia was a bright, intelligent child and won many school prizes and awards.

When Sylvia was eight, her father fell ill. Convinced that he had cancer, he refused to attend a doctor. When, eventually, a diagnosis was confirmed, he had to undergo an operation to amputate his leg. He died shortly afterwards. When Sylvia learned of his death, she declared, 'I'll never speak to God again'. Anxious to spare Sylvia and her younger brother Warren any unnecessary upset, their mother did not bring them to the funeral. Her father's death haunted Sylvia for the remainder of her life.

Otto Plath's death left the family in difficult financial circumstances. Aurelia Plath took up a full-time teaching job to support her children and Sylvia's grandparents moved in with the family in a house in the prosperous suburb of Wellesley. Later Sylvia wrote that the move to Wellesley marked the end of her idyllic childhood by the sea.

All through High School, Plath published poems and stories in local and national newspapers and in her school magazine. In her final year at school,

Seventeen, a national teen magazine, published her short story 'And Summer Will Not Come Again'. It was an important landmark in the young writer's life.

In 1951, Plath entered Smith College, an exclusive women's college in Massachusetts, with the help of two scholarships. Plath's first two years at Smith went well. Her talent and intelligence were nurtured by the teaching staff, her grades were excellent and she continued to have her work published. During her second year at Smith, she was awarded a fiction prize by *Mademoiselle,* a fashionable, upmarket magazine for young women. During this period she dated Dick Norton, a childhood friend from Wellesley who came from a wealthy background.

Despite these successes, academic, personal and social, Plath was deeply insecure about herself. The beginning of her third year in college saw her beset by many doubts and uncertainties. A four-week guest editorship at *Mademoiselle* in New York did little to improve matters. Failure to secure a place on a summer course run by Frank O'Connor at Harvard in 1953 caused a crisis, and she was sent for psychiatric treatment. A poorly supervised and administered series of electric shock treatments worsened her condition and she made an attempt to take her own life. She was missing for three days, unconscious in a narrow space under the family home. She recovered her health over a period of six months with the help of a sympathetic psychiatrist.

Smith College offered her a scholarship to allow her to finish her degree, and she returned to the college in spring 1954, graduating with distinction. By now she had acquired a growing reputation as a writer.

More success came her way in the form of a prestigious Fulbright scholarship to study at Cambridge University. She entered Newnham College in October 1955. It was in Cambridge that Sylvia Plath met the poet Ted Hughes. After a whirlwind romance, the couple married on Bloomsday, June 16, 1956. Plath returned to Cambridge to complete her studies in Autumn 1956, continuing all the while to write. At the same time she helped Hughes organise and send out his work. ('Black Rook in Rainy Weather' was written in this period.) The couple moved to America in summer 1957, and Plath taught for a year at Smith. She found the job taxing and considered herself to be a poor teacher. While Hughes continued to enjoy publishing success, Plath found it impossible to find time to devote to her writing in the way that she longed. At the end of the academic year in summer 1958, Plath resigned her teaching position at Smith, against her mother's wishes, and the couple rented a small apartment in Boston. The year was not without its difficulties. Plath suffered from writer's block and depression. 'The Times Are Tidy' was one of the few poems she completed. She was worried by financial concerns and tried to supplement their income by taking part-time secretarial work. By summer 1959, things had improved. Hughes continued to write and publish and Plath, too, completed both poems and short stories. The couple then decided to return to England. Before they left America, they spent two months at a writer's colony in New York State. Relieved of domestic duties, Plath wrote freely and finished a number of the poems that are included in *The Colossus*, the only collection published during her lifetime.

Frieda Rebecca Hughes, the couple's first child, was born in April 1960 in London. By this time, Heinemann had agreed to publish *The Colossus* and Hughes had won the prestigious Somerset Maughan Award. Plath, however, was disappointed by the lack of reaction to *The Colossus*, and while she loved her husband and new daughter, she found that the roles of mother and wife took her away from her writing.

The year 1961 was a topsy-turvy one for Sylvia Plath. It began with the sadness of a miscarriage, followed by an operation to remove an appendix. Her recovery from this she likened to a resurrection. A contract with the *New Yorker* magazine boosted her morale and she began work on her novel, *The Bell Jar*. When Plath became pregnant the couple decided to look for a house in the country, eventually moving in the autumn to Court Green in Devon. This was a rambling, crumbling old house with three acres of lawn, garden and orchard. Despite her pregnancy, the care of a young daughter and the practicalities of setting up home in an old house, Plath wrote with great energy in the first months in Devon, though the poems she completed, including 'Finisterre' and 'Mirror', are marked by a sense of threat, fear and menace.

In January 1962, Plath gave birth to her second child, Nicholas. Her experience of birth and her remembrance of her miscarriage in the previous year inform the radio play, *Three Women*, that she wrote for the BBC in the spring of 1962. The poems written later in 1962, most notably 'Elm', are dark meditations on love and self-knowledge.

By summer 1962 Plath's marriage to Hughes was beginning to unravel. Hughes became involved with Assia Wevill, the wife of a Canadian poet, and left Court Green. A holiday in Ireland in September failed to save the relationship.

Back in Court Green in October and November, Sylvia Plath, working early in the morning, wrote forty of the poems that make up the collection *Ariel*, including 'Poppies in July' and 'The Arrival of the Bee Box', published after her death. By any standards, these are remarkable poems. Writing to a friend, she said, 'I am living like a Spartan, writing through huge fevers and producing free stuff I had locked in me for years'. The strain of writing these intense, personal poems began to affect her health. Her letters to her mother from this period are touched with desperation. In November Plath decided to move back to London and found a flat in the house where W. B. Yeats had once lived. By December she had closed up Court Green and moved into her new home with her two young children. In the New Year, some of the worst weather seen in London for decades, allied to the delay in obtaining a phone and the colds and flu she and the children suffered, cast her down and left her feeling isolated. She was further disheartened by the fact that her new work was, on the whole, rejected by the editors to whom she sent it. The publication of her novel, *The Bell Jar*, under a pseudonym, did little to lift the gloom. Her final poems (including 'Child'), written in late January and early February, reveal that her will to live was almost spent. At this point Sylvia Plath sought medical help and was put on a course of anti-depressants and arrangements were made for her to see a psychiatrist. However, in the early hours of Monday morning, February 11, 1963, overcome by a despairing depression, Sylvia Plath took her own life.

Ariel, a collection of her final poems was published in 1965. Since that time, it has sold over half a million copies. Sylvia Plath's life, death and poetry have been the subject of much controversy. Understandably, given the tragic circumstances of her death, much of the response to her poetry has sought to relate her work to her life – to find clues in her poetry to explain her suicide or to attribute blame. The difference between the personality that Sylvia Plath reveals in her letters home to her mother and the darker personality of her journals has also attracted the attention of critics. Rarely has a poet left such a disputed body of work.

SOCIAL AND CULTURAL CONTEXT

The world into which Sylvia Plath was born in Boston, in 1932, was a male-dominated one. Her father ruled the family. Her mother was the wife and homemaker. Plath attended a college for girls. Here she wanted to achieve and be a perfect American girl. Magazines like *The Ladies Home Journal* defined this ideal. A woman should be a wife, a homemaker and a mother, but she was not expected to be a professional or to have her own career. She was to be respectable, that is, she was not expected to have sexual relations before marriage. There was, in this middle-class culture, a tolerance of male promiscuity but girls were expected to be modest and virginal. Not to marry was to risk being labelled 'unfeminine'. Throughout her life, Plath struggled to escape this ideal of perfection. Her letters to her mother are full of references to her attempts to make a home for herself and Ted Hughes and to win her mother's approval. She was conscious of this tendency in herself, noting in her journal: 'Old need of giving mother accomplishments, getting reward of love'.

Her biographer, Anne Stevenson, says of the letters Plath wrote to her mother:

Letters Home *can be seen as one long projection of the 'desired image' (the required image) of herself as Eve – wife, mother, home-maker, protector of the wholesome, the good and the holy, an identity that both her upbringing and her own instinctive physical being had fiercely aspired to.*

Linda Wagner's analysis of the advertisements and contents of *The Ladies' Home Journal*, a publication to which Plath submitted her stories, makes fascinating reading:

Judging from illustrations throughout the magazine (1949–54), women wear either formal gowns or bathing suits; and are interested only in romance or recipes. Or, perhaps, in mother-daughter fashions. Patterns for mother-daughter 'look alike' dresses, robes and sportswear abound in many of these issues, and one must conjecture that the message is not only the natural sexual affinity but the similarity in role: whether adult or child, the female is a doll-like object, needing protection, capable of only limited activities.

Much of Plath's poetry can be seen as a struggle to create a new identity for herself that transcended the cultural limitations imposed upon women. Given society's view of women, Plath found it difficult to find acceptance as a writer outside women's books and magazines. In her lifetime, her work won serious admiration from only a small number of people. She was more famous for being the wife of the poet Ted Hughes than for being a poet, novelist and short-story writer in her own right. Yet her ambition, dedication and determination to succeed as a writer, not to mention her talent, were as least as great, if not greater, than his.

Plath's desire to fit in at school and be an all-American girl was deepened by her consciousness of her German ancestry. Plath's use of Holocaust imagery and her reference to her father as a Nazi in her poem 'Daddy' indicate a feeling of displacement, a fear that she might, somehow, be tainted by her origins. And she employed Holocaust imagery to speak of the suffering of women. More than is sometimes acknowledged by critics, Plath was attuned, in a personal way, to the major historical issues of her time. Plath lived during the period of the Cold War and the threat of nuclear warfare between America and Russia. She was conscious of the dangers of a nuclear conflict and concerned for the future safety of her children. In a letter to her mother in December 1961, Plath wrote of these fears:

> *The reason I haven't written for so long is probably quite silly, but I got so awfully depressed two weeks ago by reading two issues of* The Nation *all about the terrifying marriage of big business and the military in America … and the repulsive shelter craze for fallout, all very factual, documented and true, that I simply couldn't sleep for nights with all the warlike talk in the papers, such as Kennedy saying Khrushchev would 'have no place to hide,' and the armed forces manuals indoctrinating soldiers about the 'inevitable' war with our 'implacable foe'…. I began to wonder if there was any point in trying to bring up children in such a mad, self-destructive world. The sad thing is that the power for destruction is real and universal.*

The fears expressed here find their way in her poetry in the terrifying imagery of her last poems.

For Sylvia Plath, the opportunity to live and study in England was a partly liberating experience. From England she could view with clarity the consumerism and militarism of American culture. However, she did not always feel at home in England and disliked the shabby inefficiency which she saw in English life. By the end of her life, Plath was caught between the two cultures, feeling ambivalent towards both. And her feelings of displacement are important in shaping the poetry she wrote.

BLACK ROOK IN RAINY WEATHER

On the stiff twig up there
Hunches a wet black rook
Arranging and rearranging its feathers in the rain.
I do not expect miracle
Or an accident   5

To set the sight on fire
In my eye, nor seek
Any more in the desultory weather some design,
But let spotted leaves fall as they fall,
Without ceremony, or portent.   10

Although, I admit, I desire,
Occasionally, some backtalk
From the mute sky, I can't honestly complain:
A certain minor light may still
Leap incandescent   15

Out of kitchen table or chair
As if a celestial burning took
Possession of the most obtuse objects now and then—
Thus hallowing an interval
Otherwise inconsequent   20

By bestowing largesse, honour,
One might say love. At any rate, I now walk
Wary (for it could happen
Even in this dull, ruinous landscape); sceptical,
Yet politic; ignorant   25

Of whatever angel may choose to flare
Suddenly at my elbow. I only know that a rook
Ordering its black feathers can so shine
As to seize my senses, haul
My eyelids up, and grant 30

A brief respite from fear
Of total neutrality. With luck,
Trekking stubborn through this season
Of fatigue, I shall
Patch together a content 35

Of sorts. Miracles occur,
If you care to call those spasmodic
Tricks of radiance miracles. The wait's begun again,
The long wait for the angel,
For that rare, random descent. 40

GLOSSARY

8 *desultory*: changing in a random way

10 *portent*: a sign or indication of a future event. An omen

15 *incandescent*: red hot or white hot; shining, luminous

17 *celestial*: heavenly

18 *obtuse*: dull, insensitive

19 *hallowing*: to make holy or sacred

20 *inconsequent*: trivial or insignificant.

21 *largesse*: generosity

23 *Wary*: alert, vigilant

25 *politic*: discreet, prudent

31 *respite*: rest or temporary relief

33 *Trekking*: making a long, hard journey

37 *spasmodic*: a word for something that happens for a sudden, brief spell

GUIDELINES

The poem comes from Plath's first collection, *The Colossus*. It was originally published in the English journal *Granta*, while she studied at Cambridge. The poem alerts us to many features of her style:

- the confident handling of rhyme and stanza form
- the exploration of emotions and states of mind
- the use of weather, colours and natural objects as symbols
- the dream-like or surreal world of the poem.

Although Sylvia Plath uses 'I' in the poem, there is no simple relationship between the persona of the poem and the writer. The poem explores the nature of poetic inspiration, and the necessity of such inspiration to ward off the speaker's fear of 'total neutrality'.

The poem begins with a clear description of the rook, sitting 'Arranging and rearranging its feathers in the rain'. The sight is ordinary. The speaker of the poem tells us that she does not expect a miracle or an accident to set the sight on fire. The words 'miracle' and 'fire' set up a contrast between the damp weather, the reality, and the fire of vision, the poet's imagination. But the poet/speaker is not expecting anything to happen. Her muse, her inner vision, seems to have deserted her. Therefore, she simply describes what she sees, telling us that she no longer looks to read or interpret the weather, but lets the world be as it is.

Although not stated directly, the poem suggests that poetic inspiration is like a gift from heaven. It is not within the control of the poet. It is not a matter of will or determination. Inspiration, when it happens, has the quality of accident, favour and giftedness about it. Nor is it that the poet is inspired, but rather that the world is transformed in the poet's presence. The adjectives 'incandescent' and 'burning' suggest the force and power of the experience of inspiration.

Without vision and the inspiration to write, the poet fears 'total neutrality'. The words suggest a state of non-being, a blank. (This kind of fear is expressed in a number of other poems, including 'Poppies in July'.) However, this is not the final word, for the poet's belief or desire to believe, or her need to believe, is expressed in the beautiful ending: 'The wait's begun again, / The long wait for the angel, / For that rare, random descent'.

What is clear from this poem is that for the speaker/poet, the threat to her well-being is posed by a fear of 'neutrality'. She is afraid that without moments of vision and the reassurance of her creativity, life and identity will be intolerable.

QUESTIONS

1 What attitude to the rook and the weather does the speaker of the poem express in the first two stanzas? What do these stanzas suggest to you about the speaker?

2 How do you understand the idea of celestial burning, as presented in the poem? In your experience can ordinary objects be seized in the way described between lines 14–22 of the poem?

3 Consider the character of the speaker of the poem, as suggested by the adjectives ('Wary', 'sceptical', 'politic') in lines 23–25. Having read the poem, what additional adjectives would you use to describe the speaker?

4 What is the fear referred to at the outset of Stanza 7? Consider the possible meanings of the word 'neutrality'. How might the rook allay this fear? What is the relationship between the rook and the celestial burning referred to in Stanza 4?

5 What is it that the speaker hopes to achieve 'with luck' (lines 32–36)? What is your reaction to this hope?

6 Comment on the phrase 'this season / Of fatigue' and what it tells us about the speaker.

7 What belief is expressed in the final stanza? How is the belief qualified?

8 'The wait's begun again.' Comment on the word 'again'.

9 The beauty of the last two lines of the poem has been remarked on by critics. What, in your view, makes them beautiful?

10 Examine the stanza form employed by the poet and comment on it.

11 a) Comment on the images of heat and light in the poem, and their relevance to the theme of the poem.
b) Consider the title of the poem and its relevance to the theme of the poem.
c) What does the poem say to you about imagination and the vision of the poet?

12 'The speaker of the poem is poised between hope and despair.' Comment on this view of the poem, supporting your answer by reference to the poem.

13 'Behind the controlled language of the poem, there is a glimpse of a fearful and nightmarish personal world.' Do you think this is a fair assessment of the poem?

THE TIMES ARE TIDY

Unlucky the hero born
In this province of the stuck record
Where the most watchful cooks go jobless
And the mayor's rôtisserie turns
Round of its own accord.   5

There's no career in the venture
Of riding against the lizard,
Himself withered these latter-days
To leaf-size from lack of action:
History's beaten the hazard.   10

The last crone got burnt up
More than eight decades back
With the love-hot herb, the talking cat,
But the children are better for it,
The cow milk's cream an inch thick.   15

GLOSSARY

2 *province*: in this context, a historical period. The word also carries the derogatory suggestion of a place that is culturally backward

2 *stuck record*: when the needle on the turntable gets stuck on the vinyl surface of a record. The image suggests something that is going nowhere

3 *watchful cooks*: from the Middle Ages onwards, the poisoning of food was common in attempts on the lives of the powerful. Thus, cooks had to be vigilant, wary and politic

4 *rôtisserie*: traditionally, a pointed rod with a turning handle on which meat is skewered and roasted. Today, an electric cooking apparatus, with a rotating spit

7 *lizard*: used here as a synonym for dragon

10 *hazard*: danger or risk

11 *crone*: withered old woman, witch

GUIDELINES

'The Times Are Tidy' was published in the 1960 collection, *The Colossus*. The poem was written during the summer of 1958 after Plath had resigned her job as a teacher at Smith College. This is one of the few poems in which the 'I' persona does not appear. The poem is a straightforward social comment on the blandness of contemporary culture compared to the fairy-tale world of the past. As a way of keeping up her German, the language of her ancestors, Plath read Grimm's Fairy Tales.

Interestingly, around the time Plath wrote 'The Times Are Tidy', she and Ted Hughes were experimenting with an Ouija board. Plath found these sessions both intriguing and entertaining. She also shared Hughes' interest in tarot cards and horoscopes. The consumer culture, rapidly developing in urban America, was removed from the superstitious beliefs that attracted her. Perhaps the poem hints at the difference between Hughes's Yorkshire, where superstitions still survived, and the urban culture of America, where it had disappeared. As in 'Black Rook in Rainy Weather', there is a contrast between a world of mystery and adventure and the blandness and neutrality of the present.

The poem shows Plath's interest in the craft of poetry. The stanzas and rhymes are carefully worked.

QUESTIONS

1 How is the disappearance of the world of fairy-tale adventure suggested in the first stanza?

2 Comment on the phrase 'the stuck record' and the attitude it conveys.

3 Give examples of the people of whom it might be said that they rode 'against the lizard'.

4 What do you think is the meaning of the statement 'History's beaten the hazard.'

5 How do you interpret the references to the 'love-hot herb' and the 'talking cat' in the third stanza?

6 Do you think the speaker believes that the gains referred to, in the last two lines, compensate for the losses mentioned in the rest of the poem?

7 Describe the tone and mood of the poem and the attitude it expresses towards the contemporary world. Refer to the title of the poem, in your answer.

8 Do you think this is a well crafted poem? Explain your answer.

9 The poem is dismissed by some critics as a mere 'exercise'. What is your assessment of the poem?

MORNING SONG

Love set you going like a fat gold watch.
The midwife slapped your footsoles, and your bald cry
Took its place among the elements.

Our voices echo, magnifying your arrival. New statue.
In a drafty museum, your nakedness   5
Shadows our safety. We stand round blankly as walls.

I'm no more your mother
Than the cloud that distils a mirror to reflect its own slow
Effacement at the wind's hand.

All night your moth-breath   10
Flickers among the flat pink roses. I wake to listen:
A far sea moves in my ear.

One cry, and I stumble from bed, cow-heavy and floral
In my Victorian nightgown.
Your mouth opens clean as a cat's. The window square   15

Whitens and swallows its dull stars. And now you try
Your handful of notes;
The clear vowels rise like balloons.

GLOSSARY

4 *New statue*: the newborn baby resembles a small statue (a perfect work of art?) in a museum, which people gaze upon with wonder

5–6 *your nakedness / Shadows our safety*: the nakedness of the child causes the parents to doubt their ability to keep the child safe and secure? This is a line that will support many interpretations

8–9 *the cloud that distils a mirror to reflect its own slow / Effacement*: the rainwater from the cloud forms a pool in which is reflected the dispersal of the cloud by the wind. A complex image of the relationship between mother and daughter

11 *flat pink roses*: presumably the patterned wallpaper

13 *cow-heavy and floral*: the poet's amused reference to herself in her matronly nightdress, with her breasts heavy with milk

GUIDELINES

Plath wrote 'Morning Song', a poem on the birth of her daughter, in spring 1961, ten months after Frieda's birth and shortly after a miscarriage. It was first published in *The Observer* newspaper in May and included in her posthumous collection. *Ariel*, published in 1965. In November 1962, Plath arranged the poems for her collection, placing 'Morning Song' first so that the manuscript would begin with the word 'love' and end with the word 'spring' from the poem, 'Wintering'. (The published collection does not follow her wishes.) 'Morning Song' is clearly a celebration of birth, but there is also a suggestion of loss and separation in the imagery of the poem.

'Morning Song' explores the feelings of a mother after the birth of her child. It begins with the word 'Love' and ends with the music of the child's cry rising 'like balloons'. In between it charts the mother's journey from her initial disorientation to her joyful acceptance of her baby.

The poem also rehearses an often-expressed fear in Plath's work – the fear of effacement or of annihilation. She fears, perhaps, that the birth will rob her of her identity, just as the rain creates a mirror in which the cloud can see its own effacement.

The sound of the child's breath at night, symbolising her fragile, though insistent, hold on life, evokes the mother's protective response. After the estrangement of the opening stanzas, where the mother's response was frozen into an attitude of a blank wall in a museum setting, a more recognisable, domestic world appears. Now the new mother is involved with her child, filled with wonder as, 'Your mouth opens clean as a cat's'. The image resonates with amused delight.

The quality of happiness continues in the imagery of the growing light. The light swallows the stars as the child swallows her mother's milk. The poem ends on a note of elation as the child's 'clear vowels rise like balloons.'

QUESTIONS

1 Comment on the importance of the words 'Love' and 'elements' in the first stanza of the poem.

2 In what way is the child a 'New statue'?

3 Explain, as clearly as you can, the museum imagery in Stanza 2. What does it suggest about the relationship between the adults and the newborn child?

4 Tease out the meaning of the statement, 'your nakedness / Shadows our safety'.

5 What is the tone of the declaration, 'I'm no more your mother'?

6 What kind of relationship between mother and child is described in the cloud/mirror/wind imagery? Do you think it is a distinctive view or does it express a general truth?

7 What does the moth imagery suggest about the child in Stanza 4?

8 What picture of the new mother is created in Stanzas 4 and 5?

9 What is your favourite image in the poem?

10 'Although tender in tone, the poem is clear-sighted and unsentimental.' Discuss this view of the poem.

11 'Even though the poem celebrates motherhood, the mother appears as an isolated and estranged figure.' Do you agree with this assessment of the poem? Support your answer by reference to the poem.

12 How do you imagine Frieda Hughes reacting to this poem about her birth?

FINISTERRE

This was the land's end: the last fingers, knuckled and rheumatic,
Cramped on nothing. Black
Admonitory cliffs, and the sea exploding
With no bottom, or anything on the other side of it,
Whitened by the faces of the drowned.   5
Now it is only gloomy, a dump of rocks—
Leftover soldiers from old, messy wars.
The sea cannons into their ear, but they don't budge.
Other rocks hide their grudges under the water.

The cliffs are edged with trefoils, stars and bells   10
Such as fingers might embroider, close to death,
Almost too small for the mists to bother with.
The mists are part of the ancient paraphernalia—
Souls, rolled in the doom-noise of the sea.
They bruise the rocks out of existence, then resurrect them.   15
They go up without hope, like sighs.
I walk among them, and they stuff my mouth with cotton.
When they free me, I am beaded with tears.

Our Lady of the Shipwrecked is striding toward the horizon,
Her marble skirts blown back in two pink wings.   20
A marble sailor kneels at her foot distractedly, and at his foot
A peasant woman in black
Is praying to the monument of the sailor praying.
Our Lady of the Shipwrecked is three times life size,
Her lips sweet with divinity.   25
She does not hear what the sailor or the peasant is saying—
She is in love with the beautiful formlessness of the sea.

Gull-coloured laces flap in the sea drafts
Beside the postcard stalls.
The peasants anchor them with conches. One is told: 30
'These are the pretty trinkets the sea hides,
Little shells made up into necklaces and toy ladies.
They do not come from the Bay of the Dead down there,
But from another place, tropical and blue,
We have never been to.   35
These are our crêpes. Eat them before they blow cold.'

GLOSSARY

1 *the land's end*: the literal meaning of 'Finisterre' is the land's end. From earliest times it was believed that the horizon marked the end of the created world

1 *the last fingers*: the rocks jutting into the sea are compared to fingers striving to find a hold. The imagery suggests the desperate clinging of a drowning person

3 *Admonitory*: warning

7 *old, messy wars*: at nearby Berck-Plage, Plath saw the wounded, maimed, veterans of the Algerian war. This influenced her view of the landscape of Finisterre

10 *trefoils, stars and bells*: wildflowers, identified by shape rather than name

13 *the ancient paraphernalia*: the ancient bits and pieces (of belief). Plath is referring to the belief that the mists are the souls of the dead. She sees this belief as one of the many superstitions associated with Finisterre

19 *Our Lady of the Shipwrecked*: as a twelve-year-old, Plath saw Shakespeare's *The Tempest*, a play that begins with a shipwreck. Later on she associated Ariel's song, 'Full fathom five, thy father lies; / Of his bones are coral made' with her own dead father

GUIDELINES

'Finisterre' was among a group of poems that Plath wrote in autumn, 1961, shortly after moving to Devon with her husband and daughter, Frieda. Although this was one of the happiest periods of her personal life, the poems she wrote are dark.

In June 1960, Plath and Hughes motored through Brittany, swimming along the rocky coastline of Finisterre. They also stopped at Berck-Plage, a seaside resort with a sanatorium for soldiers wounded in the Algerian war. Plath saw maimed soldiers limp among the holiday makers. The experience made a profound impression and called to mind her father's death, following the amputation of his leg. The poems she wrote about Brittany, 'Finisterre' and 'Berck-Plage', share a sense of death and menace, contrasting images of permanence and stability with those of formlessness and annihilation. In this regard, it is worth bearing in mind that 'Finisterre' was written during a period when there was a serious risk of nuclear conflict between Russia and America. Plath wrote of her fears in this regard in a letter to her mother in December 1961.

The ocean played an important part in Plath's childhood and is a constant in the imagery of the poems. In a letter to her mother, written in 1958, she said, 'I am going back to the ocean as my poetic heritage'. She also wrote in her journal a note on the title of her poem, 'Full Fathom Five', which gives an insight into the importance of the sea for her:

> 'Full Fathom Five' … has the background of The Tempest, the association of the sea, which is a central metaphor for my childhood, my poems and the artist's subconscious, of the father image … and the pearls and coral highly wrought to art; pearls sea-changed from the ubiquitous grit of sorrow and routine.

At one level, 'Finisterre' is a description of a visit to a seaside resort. It describes the rocky shoreline and the cliffs that surround the bay known as the Bay of the Dead. It describes the mists that rise from the sea. It describes the statue of Our Lady of the Shipwrecked, a memorial to the sailors who died at sea. The poem concludes with a description of the stalls and the trinkets sold by local traders to tourists. At another level, 'Finisterre' is a symbolic poem, in which the meeting of ocean and land is presented in terms of the recurrent drama of death and rebirth, or of entrapment and freedom. As with other of Plath's poems, the symbolic language sends the reader off in many directions. Thus 'Finsterre' can support different interpretations.

The vocabulary of the opening stanza suggests a pattern of force and annihilation – 'knuckled', 'Cramped', 'exploding', 'cannons', 'end', 'last', 'nothing', 'black' and 'bottom'. It is as if the Bay of the Dead is a site of battle between the sea and the land.

Plath sees in the relationship between the sea mist and the rocks an archetype or symbol of death and resurrection. In describing the rocks and the sea mist, the poem juxtaposes the fixed and the fluid. The fixed forms of the rocks seem threatened by the formlessness of the sea and the mist, but they survive.

There is a shift of tone in the final stanza. We are back in the world of the living, on firm land, where the locals sell 'pretty trinkets' to the tourists. The locals are anxious to disassociate the souvenirs from the Bay of the Dead, telling the speaker of the poem that the trinkets come from 'another place, tropical and blue'.

This place is like the world of Plath's childhood or the world of her poetry. She takes elements from the sea of her unconscious and makes them into poems. The poem ends with the peasants offering her some sustenance. They urge her to eat before the food goes cold. Although eating is associated with human nurture, the final word of the poem, 'cold', brings us back to the idea of death which haunts the poem.

QUESTIONS

1 The first five lines give a vivid account of the beliefs/fears once held about the sea. Describe these. Is there a relationship between these fears/beliefs and private fears?

2 How is Finisterre regarded now, according to lines 6–9? Comment on the rock imagery in these lines.

3 Examine the description of the flowers and the mist in Stanza 2. How are both associated with death?

4 Comment on Plath's use of the verb 'bruise' in line 15. Is it effective?

5 'I walk among them, and they stuff my mouth with cotton. / When they free me, I am beaded with tears' (lines 17–18). What do you make of these lines and the drama they describe? (Are the mists/souls presented as hostile? Do they prevent her from speaking? Is the speaker in the poem more in sympathy with the ancient or the modern view of the place…?)

6 How is Our Lady of the Shipwrecked presented in the third stanza? Is it a surprising representation?

7 Comment on the phrase 'the beautiful formlessness of the sea' (line 27).

8 In lines 31–35, the peasants speak of the pretty trinkets that the sea hides, which come from a place far away. How do you interpret these lines? What, for example, is the other place 'tropical and blue'?

9 Does the poem end on a hopeful note?

10 In your view is the speaker of the poem attracted to the sea? Plath regarded the sea as an image of the artist's subconscious. What does the description of the sea in the poem suggest about Plath's subconscious and its concerns?

11 The poem arose from a holiday visit to a seaside resort. What does her treatment of this visit in the poem suggest to you about the personality and imagination of the poet? Support the points you make by quotation from the poem.

MIRROR

I am silver and exact. I have no preconceptions.
Whatever I see I swallow immediately
Just as it is, unmisted by love or dislike.
I am not cruel, only truthful—
The eye of a little god, four-cornered.   5
Most of the time I meditate on the opposite wall.
It is pink, with speckles. I have looked at it so long
I think it is a part of my heart. But it flickers.
Faces and darkness separate us over and over.

Now I am a lake. A woman bends over me,   10
Searching my reaches for what she really is.
Then she turns to those liars, the candles or the moon.
I see her back, and reflect it faithfully.
She rewards me with tears and an agitation of hands.
I am important to her. She comes and goes.   15
Each morning it is her face that replaces the darkness.
In me she has drowned a young girl, and in me an old woman
Rises toward her day after day, like a terrible fish.

GLOSSARY

title *Mirror*: Sylvia Plath was well read in folk and fairy tales and may have taken the
idea of the talking mirror from this tradition

GUIDELINES

'Mirror' was one of a group of poems written in autumn 1961, days before Sylvia
Plath's twenty-ninth birthday and shortly after she and Ted Hughes moved to
Court Green in Devon. Plath was pregnant with her second child at the time. This
was one of the last poems she wrote before the birth of her baby, Nicholas. As in
'Elm', Plath employs the technique of personification to achieve a sinister effect.

The poem begins with a statement, in language that is very precise: 'I am silver and exact'. 'Silver' suggests something valuable but it is also something inanimate and, therefore, heartless. The adjective 'exact' is ambiguous. It suggests accuracy and correctness. However, there is a more sinister meaning to the verbal form of the word. 'To exact' is to extort or demand payment. So the opening statement can be read in quite different ways. On one hand there is the surface meaning – 'I am valuable and accurate'. Or the other there is an implied meaning – 'I am heartless and demand payment'. The opening statement succeeds in expressing both meanings simultaneously, moving back and forth between ordinary and symbolic meaning.

If we identify the mirror with the perceiving self, then the opening statement suggests a harsh and unforgiving way of viewing oneself. It suggests a lack of self-love. Is the voice of the mirror to be interpreted as the voice of the woman whose image the mirror reflects? Is the voice of the poem an aspect of Sylvia Plath's own voice? Or should we keep a distance between the poet and the speaker of the poem? There are no correct answers to these questions. Different readers read the poem in different ways. Moreover, Plath's poetry succeeds in communicating on a number of levels in any individual poem, without losing its sense of focus.

In the final image of the poem (the old woman rising like a terrible fish), Plath suggests many fears and insecurities:

- the fear of time and old age
- the fear of annihilation
- the fear of entrapment and alienation
- the fear of losing control
- perhaps also a daughter's fear of her mother (this is the reading that the critic David Holbrook gives to these lines).

The world of the poem is a bleak and unloving one. The perceiving and recording intelligence is cold and inhuman. It gives nothing creative, warm or assuring to the woman. The woman is alone and has no one else to turn to, except the moon and the candles.

Mirrors occur in many of Plath's poems. Perhaps, they suggest the dangers of judging ourselves too harshly, or seeking for perfection. Or they may suggest the lonely drama of living and dying, as it was, in the end, for Plath herself.

QUESTIONS

1 What qualities does the mirror attribute to itself in the first four lines of the poem? What is your reaction to the claims the mirror makes for itself? What is your reaction to the tone of these lines?

2 In what sense might a mirror be said to 'swallow' what it sees (line 2)?

3 'I am not cruel, only truthful' (line 4). Consider this statement. Is the voice of the poem cruel? Is it a masculine or a feminine voice? Are mirrors always truthful? What governs what a person may or may not see in a mirror?

4 Why does the mirror refer to the moon and candles as 'liars' (line12)?

5 What is the woman's attitude to the mirror and the mirror's attitude to the woman? What is your attitude to the woman?

6 Comment on the images of the final lines of the poem and the impact they have on you. Where else is there a sense of dread or panic in the poem?

7 What does the poem say to you about fear and insecurity and the prospect of growing old?

8 'The exact and precise nature of the mirror is reflected in the language and structure of the poem.' In the light of this statement, comment on the language and form of the poem.

9 'The world reflected by the mirror is one in which the female persona suffers and is alone.' Do you agree with this reading of the poem? Support the points you make by quoting from the poem.

10 'The voice of the mirror is the harsh inner voice that every woman carries within herself.' Give your response to this statement, supporting the points you make by quotation from the poem.

PHEASANT

You said you would kill it this morning.
Do not kill it. It startles me still,
The jut of that odd, dark head, pacing

Through the uncut grass on the elm's hill.
It is something to own a pheasant,   5
Or just to be visited at all.

I am not mystical: it isn't
As if I thought it had a spirit.
It is simply in its element.

That gives it a kingliness, a right.   10
The print of its big foot last winter,
The tail-track, on the snow in our court—

The wonder of it, in that pallor,
Through crosshatch of sparrow and starling.
Is it its rareness, then? It is rare.   15

But a dozen would be worth having,
A hundred, on that hill—green and red,
Crossing and recrossing: a fine thing!

It is such a good shape, so vivid.
It's a little cornucopia.   20
It unclaps, brown as a leaf, and loud,

Settles in the elm, and is easy.
It was sunning in the narcissi.
I trespass stupidly. Let be, let be.

GLOSSARY

1 *You*: the 'You' of the poem is often identified with Ted Hughes, Sylvia Plath's husband. Hughes came from a Yorkshire family, well used to hunting and fishing

3 *The jut of that odd, dark head*: the jerky, forward movement of the head; the way the head of the pheasant leaned forward

12 *our court*: courtyard. Court Green is the name of the house in Devon, where the poem is set. 'Court' also suggests a royal court and picks up on the mention of the kingliness of the bird

13 *pallor*: paleness

14 *crosshatch*: to crosshatch is to shade by drawing a series of intersecting parallel lines. The prints left by the pheasant intersect those left by the sparrow and starling in a crosshatch pattern

20 *cornucopia*: the literal meaning is 'horn of plenty'. A goat's horn or similar vessel overflowing with fruit, flowers and corn. A Roman symbol of abundance and plenty

23 *narcissi*: narcissi are daffodil-like plants, with white or yellow flowers. There were thousands of bulbs planted around Court Green

GUIDELINES

Sylvia Plath wrote 'Pheasant' in April 1962, in a period of enormous creativity in which she wrote a number of fine poems within days of each other.

The poem opens in a dramatic fashion. The narrator reports the intention of the 'You' to kill the pheasant, which she has seen on the hill behind their house. The narrator pleads for the pheasant's life. Her plea is direct and simple, 'Do not kill it' (line 2). This is not an order as she feels obliged to supply reasons for her request.

To the narrator's mind, the pheasant is in its element (line 9) and belongs here. It left its footprint and the track of its tail in the snow last winter. These are its signature, drawn in their 'court'. The narrator feels the wonder of these markings in the snow, criss-crossing the marks of the smaller sparrow and starling.

As she watches, the pheasant 'unclaps' its wings and settles in the elm 'and is easy'. This ease is not shared by the narrator. The tone of the poem takes on an edge in the final stanza as the narrator describes herself as trespassing stupidly on the pheasant. The emotion, which has been controlled throughout 'Pheasant', breaks out in the urgent plea of the final words of the poem, 'Let be, let be'. The repeated phrase and the echoing rhyme of the last line capture the anguish and intensity with which the speaker makes her plea.

For some critics, the plea is not for the pheasant but for the poet herself. Plath wrote 'Pheasant' in April 1962 during a tense period in her relationship with Ted Hughes. Some critics read the poem as being about Plath's marriage. She is the narrator and Ted Hughes is the 'You' whom she addresses. The pheasant represents the marriage itself, under threat from the male. It is he who is intent on destroying it. The female pleads for it. She pleads for its beauty and wonder, and for the life and passion which animate it. The fact that it s the female who makes the plea suggests that the relationship of power is an unequal one, with the male possessing the authority to take or spare life as he wills. For Linda Wagner-Martin, 'Pheasant' rests on the fear that the male will not listen to the female's plea for the life that deserves to exist. The male is a silent, powerful presence in the poem. The female is the pleading supplicant.

'Pheasant' is a beautifully achieved poem. It has a conversational quality. Yet, apart from the final line, Plath uses a nine-syllable line, and there are subtle rhymes and half-rhymes throughout the poem.

QUESTIONS

1 What is the dramatic situation as outlined in the first two lines of the poem?

2 What reasons does the 'I' give to support her plea, in stanzas 1–2?

3 From the evidence of Stanzas 3 to 5, is the speaker sure of her reasons for wanting the pheasant spared? Quote from the poem in your answer.

4 In Stanzas 7 and 8, what is the speaker's attitude to the pheasant and where is it most evident?

5 'At the end of the poem, it is the speaker who feels like an outsider.' Do you agree with this reading of the poem? Give reasons for your answer.

6 'The difference between "Pheasant" and "Black Rook in Rainy Weather" is that in the former there is no movement from the outside to the inside. It is the bird, rather than the poetic persona who is the centre of the poem.'
OR
'In "Pheasant", the poetic persona pleads for herself in pleading for the bird.' Which of the above readings of the poem is closest to your own. Support the points you make by quotation from the poem.

7 In writing about 'Pheasant' Ted Hughes speaks of Sylvia Plath achieving a 'cool, light, very beautiful moment of mastery'. Write a note on the kind of mastery achieved by Plath in 'Pheasant'. You might like to consider some or all of the following in your answer:
 - the choice of verbs and their effect
 - the descriptions of the pheasant
 - the dramatic language
 - line length and syllable count
 - the stanza form.

8 In considering the above, be alert to the sounds of the poem and their effect.

9 If, as some critics suggest, the poem describes the relationship between the poet and her husband, what kind of relationship is portrayed? (In the above questions, it is assumed that the speaker of the poem is a woman. Do you think this is a fair assumption? Does the poem support it?)

10 If you were encouraging someone to read 'Pheasant' for the first time, how would you describe the poem and your reaction to it?

ELM

for Ruth Fainlight

I know the bottom, she says. I know it with my great tap root;
It is what you fear.
I do not fear it: I have been there.

Is it the sea you hear in me,
Its dissatisfactions? 5
Or the voice of nothing, that was your madness?

Love is a shadow.
How you lie and cry after it
Listen: these are its hooves: it has gone off, like a horse.

All night I shall gallop thus, impetuously, 10
Till your head is a stone, your pillow a little turf,
Echoing, echoing.

Or shall I bring you the sound of poisons?
This is rain now, this big hush.
And this is the fruit of it: tin-white, like arsenic. 15

I have suffered the atrocity of sunsets.
Scorched to the root
My red filaments burn and stand, a hand of wires.

Now I break up in pieces that fly about like clubs.
A wind of such violence 20
Will tolerate no bystanding: I must shriek.

The moon, also, is merciless: she would drag me
Cruelly, being barren.
Her radiance scathes me. Or perhaps I have caught her.

I let her go. I let her go   25
Diminished and flat, as after radical surgery.
How your bad dreams possess and endow me.

I am inhabited by a cry.
Nightly it flaps out
Looking, with its hooks, for something to love.   30

I am terrified by this dark thing
That sleeps in me;
All day I feel its soft, feathery turnings, its malignity.

Clouds pass and disperse.
Are those the faces of love, those pale irretrievables?   35
Is it for such I agitate my heart?

I am incapable of more knowledge.
What is this, this face
So murderous in its strangle of branches?—

Its snaky acids hiss.   40
It petrifies the will. These are the isolate, slow faults
That kill, that kill, that kill.

GLOSSARY

title *Elm*: the elm of the title was a wych elm which grew on a prehistoric mound at
the back of Court Green, the house in Devon which Sylvia Plath shared with
Ted Hughes, before the break-up of their marriage. In silhouette, the branches
of the wych elm make strange, tangled shapes. Plath described the branches of
the tree as an 'intricate nervous system'. Plath plays upon the visual
appearance of the elm and its great age in giving it human characteristics.
As Anne Stevenson, one of Plath's biographers, observes, the wych elm
becomes 'witch' elm in the poem, a frightening, sinister presence

1 *the bottom*: the bottom is the furthest point that can be reached. In this
context, it is the subterranean world. The 'bottom' can also refer to the worst
periods in a person's life. It also suggests the bottom of a lake or river where
the mud and sludge gathers, or the unconscious where the debris of a personal
life is stored. The imagery here is reminiscent of the imagery in 'Mirror'

1 *tap root*: the main root that goes deep into the soil

4 *the sea*: the sea is an important and complex symbol in Plath's poetry. It often represents formlessness and annihilation, as in 'Finisterre', or it represents Plath's childhood before the death of her father. After he died, Plath thought of him as drowned. For Plath, the creation of pearls came from the 'grit of sorrow and routine'. Thus the sea represents creativity and the subconscious of the artist

6 *Or the voice of nothing, that was your madness?*: silence, the absence of inspiration, was the cause of severe depression in Plath. She constantly feared that her poetic gift had deserted her

7 *Love is a shadow*: as with 'Pheasant', written during the same month, it is worth bearing in mind that Plath's marriage to Ted Hughes was in crisis at the time she wrote 'Elm'

8 *lie*: there is an interesting ambiguity in the choice of the verb

13–15 *Or shall I bring you the sound of poisons … like arsenic*: Plath worried about the threat of nuclear warfare and the poisoning of the environment. Her fear and concern are reflected in the imagery, with its suggestions of, acid rain; nuclear dust, the silence induced by chemicals in the atmosphere and in the soil (arsenic is a component in many weed and insect killers), or the hush following a nuclear explosion

18 *My red filaments burn and stand, a hand of wire*: the imagery, with its references to suffering, 'Scorched', 'wires', 'violence' and 'shriek,' suggests the suffering endured by Sylvia Plath's body in the electric shock treatment she received for depression, as much as it describes the violence endured by the body of the elm. From this point on, the narrator seems identifiable with the poet herself

19 *clubs*: stout-ended sticks used as weapons

22–23 *The moon also, is merciless: she would drag me / Cruelly, being barren*: the moon is associated with women but it cannot create life. 'Barren' is an adjective Plath uses often to suggest a strong dislike or horror of someone. A barren woman is, Plath suggests in another poem, like an empty museum. In another poem, Plath writes that the moon 'drags the sea after it like a dark crime'. In all, there are 61 references to the moon in Plath's poetry and none of them are benevolent

26 *Diminished and flat, as after radical surgery*: the startling and disturbing image suggests a woman after a mastectomy

38–41 *What is this, this face…petrifies the will*: the imagery recalls Medusa, the Gorgon, whose hair was a tangle of snakes. Anyone who looked upon her was turned to stone. It also recalls the serpent in the Garden of Eden and suggests a correspondence between the elm and the Tree of Knowledge

42 *That kill, that kill, that kill*: the repetition of the verb 'kill' suggests both a violent frenzy and a hysterical fear of that violence. It is interesting to note that the verb 'kill' also appears in the first line of 'Pheasant'

GUIDELINES

'Elm' is a poem that went through numerous drafts before Plath completed it in April 1962. It follows on from the last line of 'Pheasant', in which the bird settles in the elm, a tree at the back of their house, 'and is easy'. Plath took up the word 'easy' at the end of 'Pheasant' and began to explore the elm as something that is not easy.

In the poem, as in many others, Plath personifies a natural object – here the elm – and gives it a voice. The voice is at once the 'voice' of a tree and the voice of a woman. The voice of the elm is knowledgeable, distressed, and, arguably, cruel. The elm addresses a 'You', the poetic persona of the poet, on the subject of fear, love and suffering. Many critics read the second half of the poem as spoken by this 'You' and perceive the voice as anguished and fearful. The second part of the poem speaks of the need for love, its absence and a destructive inner force. However, to describe the poem in this way is possibly misleading. In each utterance of the tree, we can catch a trace of the woman's voice and, in effect, the voices blur and merge.

The technique of personification creates a surreal, even nightmarish effect. The world of 'Elm' is not unlike the world of a Grimm's fairy tale, or the world of the subconscious. It is also worth bearing in mind that, in the heightened atmosphere of the Cold War, there was much discussion about the prospect of nuclear warfare, so much so that Plath wrote to her mother about the 'mad, self-destructive world' in which they lived, a couple of months before she completed 'Elm'. This atmosphere may also have contributed to the imagery of the poem.

In another poem, 'The Moon and the Yew Tree', Plath says that the trees of the mind are black. The elm is black and expresses some of the dark, incomprehensible fears that occupy the narrator's mind. It is as if she is a stranger to herself, terrified by forces she cannot control and a destructive need for love.

As with many of Plath's poems, the poetic persona seems very harsh in her view of herself. The end of the poem suggests the recognition of some inner faults that may lead to her death. The absence of love intensifies the activity of the dark owl-like thing, whose malignity she fears. As in 'Child', 'Mirror' and 'Poppies in July', the poetic persona is wretched and speaks in a voice that is, by the end of the poem, anguished and fearful.

Compared to the careful structure of 'Pheasant', 'Elm' is written in a looser manner. Interestingly, the critic Hugh Kenner believes that Plath's abandonment of formal structures in the later poetry encouraged her to explore states of mind and emotions that were unsafe and which, ultimately, contributed to her suicide.

QUESTIONS

1 What impression of the elm is created by her statements in the first stanza?

2 Examine the questions posed by the elm in Stanza 2. What do they suggest about the elm and the person she addresses?

3 What image of love is created in Stanzas 3–4? Is the elm comforting or cruel in these stanzas?

4 Stanzas 5–9 describe the elements of rain, sun, wind and moon and their relationship to the elm. What aspect of each is emphasised? How does each affect the elm? What, in your view, is the most striking image in these stanzas?

5 What is the elm's attitude to the moon? Where is this attitude most apparent?

6 What do the Stanzas 5–9 suggest about the nature of the elm's existence? Select the words or phrases that strike you most forcefully.

7 'How your bad dreams possess and endow me' (line 27). What relationship is suggested between the elm and the 'You' of the poem in this statement? The line can be read as either the elm addressing the woman or the woman addressing the elm. What is the effect of each reading? How do you read it?

8 The last five stanzas are rich, complex and difficult. How does the speaker view herself? What images strike you as particularly disturbing or vivid? What is your reaction to the use of the word 'faults'? What is the tone of the extraordinary last line of the poem?

9 'In "Elm", the boundary between outside and inside is blurred. It is as if the "You", the poetic persona, takes the elm into herself.' In the light of this statement, describe the poetic personae of 'Elm' and the nature of the world, physical and psychological, that they inhabit. Refer to the imagery and vocabulary of the poem in your answer.

10 There is no single reading of 'Elm' that will do justice to its rich complexity. Here are three of the many readings proposed for the poem. Give your opinion of each:

■ *The poem's narrator confesses that she is searching desperately for someone to love. Because of this hysteria, she realises that some deadly force within her has been triggered into action by the loss of love. The disintegration of love, the poem says, is a sure death warrant for the speaker.* (Paul Alexander)

- *'Elm' describes the effects of nuclear and chemical damage upon a tree and a woman. 'I have suffered the atrocity of sunsets', the speaker explains, and further, 'My red filaments burn and stand, a hand of wires' … 'Elm' is one of the many poems in which Plath explores the consequences of isolation, and argues against the impulse to hold oneself as separate from the rest of the world.* (Tracy Brain)
- *In the poem, originally titled, 'The Elm Speaks', the wych elm becomes a witch elm, a frightening mother-double of the poet, who offers death as the only possible love substitute. Between the taproot of the tree and the murderous face of the moon, the poet, 'incapable of more knowledge' is forced into a terrible acknowledgement of 'faults' – suddenly a new word in Sylvia's poetic lexicon. The poem suggests them as somehow built into her nature, bent like a crooked tree by traumatic childhood events: 'These are the isolate, slow faults / That kill, that kill, that kill'.* (Anne Stevenson)

11 '"Elm" vividly conveys suffering, self-doubt and despair.' Give your response to this assessment of the poem, supporting the points you make by quotation from the poem.

12 'Elm' is a poem with many striking visual images. Perhaps you might like to offer your own creative response to, or interpretation of, the poem, in visual form.

POPPIES IN JULY

Little poppies, little hell flames,
Do you do no harm?

You flicker, I cannot touch you.
I put my hands among the flames. Nothing burns.

And it exhausts me to watch you   5
Flickering like that, wrinkly and clear red, like the skin of a mouth.

A mouth just bloodied.
Little bloody skirts!

There are fumes that I cannot touch.
Where are your opiates, your nauseous capsules?   10

If I could bleed, or sleep!—
If my mouth could marry a hurt like that!

Or your liquors seep to me, in this glass capsule,
Dulling and stilling.

But colourless. Colourless.   15

GLOSSARY

title *Poppies in July*: red poppies are a common sight in the English countryside in
summer. In England, the poppy is a flower of remembrance for the war dead.
In Keats' 'To Autumn', the poppy is associated with sleep and ease. As Plath
develops the symbolism of the poppy, it takes on a dark and destructive
resonance, indicative of a troubled state of mind

7 *A mouth just bloodied*: Plath often associated red with love as a form of violent
emotion that incorporated danger, excitement, and vitality

8 *Little bloody skirts*: a reference to the stain of menstrual blood? The phrase could also be an oblique and derogatory reference to Assia Weevil, the woman with whom Ted Hughes was having an affair. Ronald Hayman, one of Plath's biographers, suggests that 'Poppies in July' is directed at Assia Weevil

10 *your opiates*: opium comes from the unripe seed of the poppy

12 *If my mouth could marry a hurt like that*: a startling line which encompasses all the related imagery at work in the poem – life, death, violence, sexuality, addiction, sickness

13 *liquors*: a liquor is a solution of a drug or chemical in water

13 *glass capsule*: a bell jar, of the kind used in scientific experiments or to hold specimens. The image suggests that the subject is trapped. The references to bell jar and liquor suggest hospital and museum specimens, kept in chemical solutions, in bell jars. Plath witnessed such specimens when she posed as a medical student and observed an anatomical dissection. The experience proved traumatic

GUIDELINES

Sylvia Plath wrote 'Poppies in July' in July 1962 at Court Green in Devon, during the break-up of her marriage to Ted Hughes. In the poem, the poetic persona addresses the flowers in a voice that is overwrought and anguished. The poem concludes with a chilling wish for annihilation.

From the first line we realise that the persona of the poem is troubled. The opening greetings, 'Little poppies, little hell flames' seem to be spoken by two different people. The first, 'Little poppies', suggests a sentimental relationship to the flowers. However, no sooner is this relationship established than it is destroyed by the energy and surprise of 'little hell flames'. The association of the poppies with hell suggests an excited and disturbed psychological state. This disturbed state seems poised between two extremes – violent intensity and annihilation. The violent intensity is associated with the red of the poppies; the annihilation with the poppies' colourless opiates.

Anne Stevenson sets the poems written in the final months of Plath's life in a biographical context. She says:

As absorbed and intent as a cartographer, Sylvia reported in her poems on the weather of her inner universe and delineated its two poles: 'stasis' and rage. At the depressed pole there was a turning in on herself, a longing for non-being, 'dulling and stilling,' as in 'Poppies in July'.

QUESTIONS

1 From the first two lines of the poem, what is the state of mind of the speaker? Consider, in particular the phrase,' little hell flames'.

2 'Nothing burns.' What, in your view, is the tone of this statement? What does it reveal about the speaker of the poem? Explain your answer.

3 Look at lines 5–8 and trace how the thought develops through a series of associative leaps. What do these lines reveal about the speaker of the poem?

4 Lines 10–14 present a series of wishes. How similar or different are they? Consider, for example, line 11: 'If I could bleed, or sleep!'

5 'If my mouth could marry a hurt like that.' Consider the ideas suggested by the imagery and vocabulary of this line, and describe its impact upon you.

6 What is the effect of the glass capsule image of line 13?

7 What is the effect of the repetition of the word 'colourless' at the end of the poem?

8 As with all her work, 'Poppies in July' is a carefully crafted poem. Examine the use and effect of repetition in the poem, and comment on any other examples of the poet's craft that you think worthy of note.

9 Do you agree that the end of the poem expresses a desire for non-being, for annihilation? Explain your point of view.

10 The critic Judith Kroll suggests that the poppies offer two possible kinds of death:

One is the impulse toward a vital, gaudy, and bloody physical death, a natural affinity with the poppies as 'hell flames' and 'bloody skirts'… The other possible resolution, a kind of death … symbolised by paleness or colourlessness, is also embodied in the poppies. This second death is promised by the poppies' opium: a colourless, rather than a bloody death; the achievement of even greater stasis, not a violent catastrophe; a death of consciousness which does not necessarily entail physical injury.

Do you agree with this reading of the poem? Support the points you make by quotation from the poem.

11 What, in your opinion, is gained or lost by identifying the poetic persona of the poem with Sylvia Plath?

12 '"Poppies in July" has little to do with poppies and a great deal to do with the mind that perceives them.' Give your response to this statement, supporting the points you make by quotation from the poem.

THE ARRIVAL OF THE BEE BOX

I ordered this, this clean wood box
Square as a chair and almost too heavy to lift.
I would say it was the coffin of a midget
Or a square baby
Were there not such a din in it.   5

The box is locked, it is dangerous.
I have to live with it overnight
And I can't keep away from it.
There are no windows, so I can't see what is in there.
There is only a little grid, no exit.   10

I put my eye to the grid.
It is dark, dark,
With the swarmy feeling of African hands
Minute and shrunk for export,
Black on black, angrily clambering.   15

How can I let them out?
It is the noise that appals me most of all,
The unintelligible syllables.
It is like a Roman mob,
Small, taken one by one, but my god, together!   20

I lay my ear to furious Latin.
I am not a Caesar.
I have simply ordered a box of maniacs.
They can be sent back.
They can die, I need feed them nothing, I am the owner.   25

I wonder how hungry they are.
I wonder if they would forget me
If I just undid the locks and stood back and turned into a tree.
There is the laburnum, its blond colonnades,
And the petticoats of the cherry.   30

They might ignore me immediately
In my moon suit and funeral veil.
I am no source of honey
So why should they turn on me?
Tomorrow I will be sweet God, I will set them free.   35

The box is only temporary.

GLOSSARY

13–14 *the swarmy feeling …export*: Plath was influenced by the surrealist painter
Giorgio de Chirico, and his use of symbols taken from the subconscious to
create ominous, disturbing images. She was also interested in African sculpture
and folktales. Both interests, surrealism and Africa, come together in the
imagery of the stanza

19 *a Roman mob*: the Roman mob demanded public killings for their amusement.
The comparison suggests the potential for destruction that the speaker senses
in the bee box

29 *blond colonnades*: the flower-covered branches of the laburnum are compared to
blond ringlets

30 *my moon suit and funeral veil*: Plath compares the protective suit worn by
bee-keepers to the suit of an astronaut, while she associates the veil with
the traditional veil worn by women mourners at a funeral

GUIDELINES

In summer 1962, Sylvia Plath and Ted Hughes decided to take up bee-keeping.
(Plath's father had been an expert on bees.) In October, following her separation
from Ted Hughes, Plath wrote a sequence of bee poems which explore the nature
of the self and self-identity, personal fears, complex relations and attitudes
towards freedom and control. Of the five poems in the sequence, 'The Arrival of
the Bee Box' is the most self-contained and narrative. The poem may be taken at
face value – it describes the arrival of the bee box and the poet's response to it.
However, the bee box is sometimes interpreted as a metaphor for the inner life
of the poet.

The bee box, and all it represents, both frightens and attracts the speaker of
the poem, who is fascinated with its unknown and dangerous content. As the
poem progresses, the persona grows confident and determines to set the bees
free. She is still fearful of what they might do and fearful, perhaps, that in freeing

the bees she may lose something vital. However, if the persona risks losing something, she also has something to gain – the feeling of exercising her power in a generous way. There is a note of optimistic triumph in the final line of the poem.

If the bee box is a metaphor for what Carol Ferrier describes as 'the fertile, swarming and potentially destructive chaos that the poet sense within herself', how do we interpret the ending of the poem? Is the persona facing up to her own fears and finding a strength of purpose and resolve? Does the ending of the poem suggest that she will control her fears rather than allow her fears to control her? However, if the bees represent the inner life of the poetic persona, then the box may represent the body which contains it. 'The box is only temporary' may suggest that the inner life will be freed when it is released from the containing body – when the body dies. If the end of the poem suggests liberation, the precise nature of the liberation is unclear.

David Holbrook gives this interesting reading of the poem:

> In 'The Arrival of the Bee Box' Sylvia Plath achieves a significantly developed sense of distinction between herself and the bees – she discovers resources in herself by which to deal with reality, to care for the bees, as for children. The poem's images are of a rebirth, beginning with a dead baby, ending with free bees, and the escape from death. By her recognition of the bees not merely as aspects of her identity, but as creatures in themselves, she, as 'sweet God', can release them to be themselves (as in the end she released her children).

QUESTIONS

1 Do you find the imagery of the first stanza strange, disturbing, amusing? Explain your answer.

2 'In line 7, "I have to live with it overnight", we see that the bee box represents the speaker's unconscious and is linked to the imagery of 'the dark thing that sleeps in me', referred to by the speaker in "Elm".' Do you agree with this reading of the line? Support the points you make by reference to the poem.

3 What impression is created of the box and its contents in Stanzas 3–4? What phrase or image strikes you as particularly effective?

4 In Stanza 5, the speaker seems to gain a sense of control over the box. What brings this about? What change of heart is apparent in Stanza 6?

5 In Stanzas 6–7, the speaker contemplates her own self-effacement as a way of avoiding the threat of the bees. What does this suggest about the speaker?

6 'Tomorrow I will be sweet God, I will set them free' (line 35). What is the importance of this line in the poem, and what impact does it have on you?

7 'In the poem, there is both a desire to trust the bees and a fear of trusting them, but in the end, the fear is overcome.' Do you agree with this reading of the poem? Explain your answer.

8 'The poem is remarkable for its humour; the confident handling of language; and its stanza form and organisation.' In light of this statement, comment on the form and language of the poem.

9 The critic Carole Ferrier says that: 'In this poem the box of bees becomes a metaphor for the fertile, swarming, and potentially destructive chaos that the poet senses within herself'. Comment on this assessment of the poem and the assumption that the persona of the poem is the poet.

10 In your view does the poem end on a note of optimism? Explain your answer.

CHILD

Your clear eye is the one absolutely beautiful thing.
I want to fill it with colour and ducks.
The zoo of the new

Whose names you meditate—
April snowdrop, Indian pipe,   5
Little

Stalk without wrinkle,
Pool in which images
Should be grand and classical

Not this troublous   10
Wringing of hands, this dark
Ceiling without a star.

GLOSSARY

title *Child*: Sylvia Plath's second child, Nicholas, was born in January 1962. 'Child' was written shortly after his first birthday and less than two weeks before her death

4 *meditate*: the word means 'to reflect upon' and is used to pick up the imagery of reflection begun in line 1, 'clear eye' and continued in line 8 with 'Pool'

5 *snowdrop*: small, white-flowering plant that blooms in spring

5 *Indian pipe*: small woodland flower

10 *troublous*: taking up the idea of classical and grand in the preceding line, Plath uses an old-fashioned, literary word, which means agitated or unsettled

GUIDELINES

'Child' appeared in Plath's posthumous collection 'Winter Trees', published in 1971, although it was written at the end of January 1963, less than two weeks before she took her own life at the age of thirty. The poetic persona expresses her frustrated wishes for her child. The poem is beautifully phrased and composed.

The mother wants her child's eye to be filled with delightful things. She would like his eye to be filled with images that are 'grand and classical'. However, what he witnesses is the classical gesture of despair – the wringing of hands by his mother. This gesture is both troubled and troubling. In the poem, the power of the self is reduced to expressing its own anguish. The mother inhabits a world without hope. Her failure to fill the child's world with joy adds to her darkness and distress.

It is difficult not to read this poem in the biographical context in which it was written – two weeks before Sylvia Plath took her own life. The self that the poem presents is a self that has lost confidence in its own ability to create joy. It is a self that is shadowed by its own anguish. The mother is aware of her despair and anxious to spare her child the sight of it. The mother does not want the child's clear eye to witness the pain she endures, yet lacks the strength and self-belief – not the humour, imagination or inventiveness – to make things otherwise.

'Child' is a testimony to Sylvia Plath's skill as a poet. Every word is carefully chosen. The placing of 'Little' (line 6) and 'dark' (line 11) is perfectly judged. The despair that underlies it is managed and controlled. 'Poppies in July' and 'Mirror' also present a persona who is tormented and anguished.

QUESTIONS

1 How does the mother regard her child in line 1? What is the significance of describing the child's eye as 'clear'?

2 What does line 1 tell us about the world that the poetic persona inhabits?

3 What wish does the mother express in lines 2–3? What ideas and mood are generated by the use of the word 'zoo'?

4 What is the effect of the names recited by the mother? In what sense might the child 'meditate' the names? What is the relationship between the names and the child, in the mother's world?

5 What are the conditions in which the images in a pool might appear 'grand and classical'? Do these conditions exist in the child's life?

6 What does Stanza 4 tell us about the mother? What feeling does the mother have in relation to her child? What feeling do you have for the mother?

7 'As with all Plath's poetry, "Child" reveals her mastery of movement and phrasing.' Give your view of this assessment of the poem.

8 '"Child" can be placed with "Mirror" and "Poppies in July" in presenting an individual in tormented anguish.' Give your view of this interpretation of the poem, supporting the points you make by quotation from the poem.

GENERAL QUESTIONS ON SYLVIA PLATH

1 What in your view are the emotions and the emotional experiences explored in the poetry of Sylvia Plath? Support the points you make by quotation from the poems you have studied.

2 'The poetic techniques employed by Plath succeed in making the world of her poetry a strange and terrifying one.' In the light of this statement, discuss the world of Sylvia Plath's poetry. Support your answer by quotation from the poems you have studied.

3 'Sylvia Plath's poems make most sense when they are read as biographical.' Do you agree with this view of Sylvia Plath's poetry? Explain your answer, supporting the points you make by quotation from the poetry by Plath on your course.

4 'Death and annihilation are the themes that dominate Plath's poetry.' Do you think this is an accurate assessment of Sylvia Plath's poetry? Support your point of view by quotation from the poems you have studied.

5 'Sylvia Plath's poetry presents a vivid portrait of an individual whose life is tormented and anguished.' Do you agree with this reading of Plath's work? Support the points you make by quotation form the poems by Plath on your course.

6 'The movement of Sylvia Plath's poetry is from the outside world to the inner world, from landscape to mindscape.' Discuss this statement in relation to **two** of the poems by Sylvia Plath on your course.

7 'In Plath's poetry, of course, this slightly old-fashioned point of view of the sanctity of domesticity is wedded to a tormented modern consciousness.'
(Margaret Dickie)
'For all her harrowing and courageous record of suffering, Sylvia Plath died in the end because she could not sustain confidence in her true potentialities which could free her.'
(David Holbrook)
Write an essay on the poetry of Sylvia Plath in support of **one** of the views above. Support the points you make by quotation from the poems you have studied.

8 Select your favourite poems by Sylvia Plath and explain what it is you admire about them. Support the points you make by quotation from the chosen poems.

9 'Sylvia Plath – A Personal Response.' Give your personal response to the poetry of Sylvia Plath describing the impact of the poems upon you. Support your answer by relevant quotation from the poems you have studied.

Guidelines

Your answer might consider some or all of the following:

- her themes, for example, love and despair
- the anguished voice of some of her poems
- the startling imagery and symbolism employed in the poems
- her skill as a poet
- the emotional intensity of the poems
- the relationship between her life and her poetry.

10 Write an essay in which you outline your reasons for liking or not liking the poetry of Sylvia Plath. You must refer to the poems of Plath on your course.

Guidelines

Some possible reasons for liking the poetry:

- the uniqueness of the poetic voice
- the striking imagery and symbolism
- the vitality and energy of the writing
- the exploration of emotions and extreme states of mind
- the exploration of women's experience
- the impact of the poetry upon the reader
- the variety of themes
- Plath's skill as a poet.

Some possible reasons for not liking the poetry:

- the themes of isolation and estrangement
- the cruelty of the world of many of the poems
- the absence of happiness in many of the poems
- the obscurity of the imagery
- the troubled nature of the poetic persona
- the complexity of the relationship explored in the poetry
- the feeling of despair in many of the poems
- the effect of the poems upon the reader.

Poems have a dreamlike or surreal quality.

Imagery influenced by the threat of nuclear warfare.

Died when she was 30.

All her poems were written within seven years.

The importance of love.

Voice of the poem is sometimes anguished.

Sylvia Plath

Writes about her life, but there's no simple relationship between her life and her poetry.

Explores extreme emotions and states of mind. Poised between celebration and despair.

The importance of motherhood.

Poems are carefully composed and beautifully phrased.

Images of entrapment and release.

Writes about nature, the weather and children.

ADRIENNE RICH

B. 1929

BIOGRAPHY

Adrienne Rich's most recent books of poetry are *The School Among The Ruins: Poems 2000–2004*, and *Fox: Poems 1998–2000* (Norton). A selection of her essays, *Arts of the Possible: Essays and Conversations*, was published in 2001. A new edition of *What is Found There: Notebooks on Poetry and Politics*, appeared in 2003. She is a recipient of the Lannan Foundation Lifetime Achievement Award, the Lambda Book Award, the Lenore Marshall/Nation Prize, the Wallace Stevens Award and the Bollingen Prize in Poetry, among other honours. She lives in California.

SOCIAL AND CULTURAL CONTEXT

As one of the leading American poets of the twentieth century, Adrienne Rich has engaged with many of the controversial ideas of her time. Almost from the beginning she saw poetry not as a means of expression for its own sake solely, but also as a way in which to bring about change. She has blended poetry with politics throughout her career.

As a young woman she struggled with the conflict between the traditional roles of marriage and bringing up children, and artistic ambition. The poems in her first collection were famously praised by W. H. Auden as being 'neatly and modestly dressed; speak quietly but do not mumble; respect their elders but are not cowed by them'. This is an ironic comment in the light of her subsequent career when she became committed to what the critic Albert Gelpi calls 'the poetics of change'.

In 1950s America, as elsewhere in the western world, women poets were not encouraged to share in the same aspirations as their male counterparts. When poets such as Sylvia Plath and Adrienne Rich began to describe their experiences as women and mothers, there was as yet no wider cultural recognition that these experiences could be legitimate themes for poetry. Rich later recognised that her own work had been influenced primarily by male writers. Attitudes began to change when the women's liberation movement gathered force in the 1960s. Feminists began to enquire into the rights of women and their position in society. They analysed what they called 'the patriarchal society' in which males are the dominant power and found it wanting. Adrienne Rich was in the forefront of the movement, as her poems testify. In exploring sexual politics, Rich developed influential theories of the relationship between language, power and sexuality. These issues continue to be explored to this day.

Although it was to the women's movement that Rich gave her greatest attention, she and her husband Alfred Conrad were politically involved in the Civil Rights movement also sweeping the USA in the 1960s. Issues concerning education, especially that of Black Americans and other ethnic minorities, were highly controversial. Rich's involvement with disadvantaged students led her to further examination of the relation of language to power and the class struggle.

Throughout the 1960s, too, an anti-war movement constantly protested against American involvement in Vietnam. Rich, by this time a radical feminist fully committed to social justice, was immersed in this.

In her poems Rich records her journey with searing honesty from compliant daughter, to wife and mother, to feminist and political activist. She has not tried to diminish the emotional upheavals that accompanied her disintegrating marriage, her ex-husband's suicide, or her realisation of her lesbian sexuality. Stylistically, her poems seem to echo the tumultuous times in which she reached the peak of her career, from the formalism and control of her earlier work to the looser, more experimental style of her later poems.

Now in her seventies, Adrienne Rich continues to write, give lectures and interviews, and play an active role in political debates. Asked in 1994 if she thought writing political poetry (what the interviewer referred to as 'poetry of witness') was a good use of her time, she answered:

> I wouldn't say it isn't a good use of my time because it's really at the very core of who I am. I have to do this. This is really how I know and how I probe the world ... I happen to think [poetry] makes a huge difference.

STORM WARNINGS

The glass has been falling all the afternoon,
And knowing better than the instrument
What winds are walking overhead, what zone
Of gray unrest is moving across the land,
I leave the book upon a pillowed chair   5
And walk from window to closed window, watching
Boughs strain against the sky

And think again, as often when the air
Moves inward toward a silent core of waiting,
How with a single purpose time has traveled   10
By secret currents of the undiscerned
Into this polar realm. Weather abroad
And weather in the heart alike come on
Regardless of prediction.

Between foreseeing and averting change   15
Lies all the mastery of elements
Which clocks and weatherglasses cannot alter.
Time in the hand is not control of time,
Nor shattered fragments of an instrument
A proof against the wind; the wind will rise,   20
We can only close the shutters.

I draw the curtains as the sky goes black
And set a match to candles sheathed in glass
Against the keyhole draught, the insistent whine
Of weather through the unsealed aperture.   25
This is our sole defense against the season;
These are the things that we have learned to do
Who live in troubled regions.

GLOSSARY

1 *the glass*: the barometer
11 *undiscerned*: not seen or noticed
23 *sheathed*: enclosed in
25 *aperture*: opening

AUNT JENNIFER'S TIGERS

Aunt Jennifer's tigers prance across a screen,
Bright topaz denizens of a world of green.
They do not fear the men beneath the tree;
They pace in sleek chivalric certainty.

Aunt Jennifer's fingers fluttering through her wool   5
Find even the ivory needle hard to pull.
The massive weight of Uncle's wedding band
Sits heavily upon Aunt Jennifer's hand.

When Aunt is dead, her terrified hands will lie
Still ringed with ordeals she was mastered by.   10
The tigers in the panel that she made
Will go on prancing, proud and unafraid.

GLOSSARY

1 *prance*: to bound from the hind legs, to move proudly

2 *topaz*: a precious stone of yellow/tangerine colour

2 *denizens*: inhabitants

4 *chivalric*: knightly, courtly

10 *ordeals*: severe trials

THE UNCLE SPEAKS IN THE DRAWING ROOM

I have seen the mob of late
Standing sullen in the square,
Gazing with a sullen stare
At window, balcony, and gate.
Some have talked in bitter tones   5
Some have held and fingered stones.

There are follies that subside.
Let us consider, none the less,
Certain frailties of glass
Which, it cannot be denied,   10
Lead in times like these to fear
For crystal vase and chandelier.

Not that missiles will be cast;
None as yet dare lift an arm.
But the scene recalls a storm   15
When our grandsire stood aghast
To see his antique ruby bowl
Shivered in a thunder-roll.

Let us only bear in mind
How these treasures handed down   20
From a calmer age passed on
Are in the keeping of our kind.
We stand between the dead glass-blowers
And murmurings of missile-throwers.

GLOSSARY

title *drawing-room*: sitting –room

7 *follies*: foolish things

16 *grandsire*: grandfather

16 *aghast*: horrified

LIVING IN SIN

She had thought the studio would keep itself;
no dust upon the furniture of love.
Half heresy, to wish the taps less vocal,
the panes relieved of grime. A plate of pears,
a piano with a Persian shawl, a cat   5
stalking the picturesque amusing mouse
had risen at his urging.
Not that at five each separate stair would writhe
under the milkman's tramp; that morning light
so coldly would delineate the scraps   10
of last night's cheese and three sepulchral bottles;
that on the kitchen shelf among the saucers
a pair of beetle-eyes would fix her own –
envoy from some village in the moldings …
Meanwhile, he, with a yawn,   15
sounded a dozen notes upon the keyboard,
declared it out of tune, shrugged at the mirror,
rubbed at his beard, went for cigarettes;
while she, jeered by the minor demons,
pulled back the sheets and made the bed and found   20
a towel to dust the table-top,
and let the coffee-pot boil over on the stove.
By evening she was back in love again,
though not so wholly but throughout the night
she woke sometimes to feel the daylight coming   25
like a relentless milkman up the stairs.

GLOSSARY

title *Living in Sin*: living together without being married

1 *studio*: one-room apartment used also as artist's work room

3 *heresy*: opinion opposed to the usual belief

6 *picturesque*: beautiful as in a picture

8 *writhe*: to twist violently; here, to creak

10 *delineate*: draw

11 *sepulchral*: gloomy, like a tomb

14 *envoy*: messenger

14 *moldings*: mouldings, strips of wood used for decorative purposes

26 *relentless*: non-stop

THE ROOFWALKER

Over the half-finished houses
night comes. The builders
stand on the roof. It is
quiet after the hammers,
the pulleys hang slack.   5
Giants, the roofwalkers,
on a listing deck, the wave
of darkness about to break
on their heads. The sky
is a torn sail where figures   10
pass magnified, shadows
on a burning deck.

I feel like them up there:
exposed, larger than life,
and due to break my neck.   15

Was it worth while to lay-
with infinite exertion-
a roof I can't live under?
-All those blueprints,
closings of gaps,   20
measurements, calculations?
A life I didn't choose
chose me: even
my tools are the wrong ones
for what I have to do.   25
I'm naked, ignorant,
a naked man fleeing
across the roofs
who could with a shade of difference
be sitting in the lamplight   30
against the cream wallpaper
reading-not with indifference-
about a naked man
fleeing across the roofs.

GLOSSARY

dedication *for Denise Levertov:* Levertov was a poet (1923–97) born in England but who moved to America . Rich may be responding, in part, to Levertov's poem 'From the Roof', in which a woman bringing in the washing on her Manhattan rooftop becomes the transformer and the transformed, watching and taking part in the sensuous, teeming life beneath her.

5 *pulleys:* machine for lifting heavy weights

7 *listing:* leaning to one side

19 *blueprints:* a guide or model of how things should be done

OUR WHOLE LIFE

Our whole life a translation
the permissible fibs

and now a knot of lies
eating at itself to get undone

Words bitten thru words   5
meanings burnt-off like paint
under the blowtorch

All those dead letters
rendered into the oppressor's language

Trying to tell the doctor where it hurts   10
like the Algerian
who walked from his village, burning

his whole body a cloud of pain
and there are no words for this

except himself   15

GLOSSARY

2 *permissible*: allowable

5 *thru*: American version of 'through'

8 *dead letters*: undelivered letters

9 *oppressor*: one who governs tyrannically

TRYING TO TALK WITH A MAN

Out in this desert we are testing bombs,

that's why we came here.

Sometimes I feel an underground river
forcing its way between deformed cliffs
an acute angle of understanding   5
moving itself like a locus of the sun
into this condemned scenery.

What we've had to give up to get here—
whole LP collections, films we starred in
playing in the neighbourhoods, bakery windows   10
full of dry, chocolate-filled Jewish cookies,
the language of love-letters, of suicide notes,
afternoons on the riverbank
pretending to be children

Coming out to this desert   15
we meant to change the face of
driving among dull green succulents
walking at noon in the ghost town
surrounded by a silence

that sounds like the silence of the place   20
except that it came with us
and is familiar
and everything we were saying until now
was an effort to blot it out—
coming out here we are up against it   25

Out here I feel more helpless
with you than without you

You mention the danger
and list the equipment
we talk of people caring for each other   30
in emergencies—laceration, thirst—
but you look at me like an emergency

Your dry heat feels like power
your eyes are stars of a different magnitude
they reflect lights that spell out: EXIT   35
when you get up and pace the floor

talking of the danger
as if it were not ourselves
as if we were testing anything else.

GLOSSARY

4 *deformed*: misshapen

5 *acute angle*: sharp, pointed

6 *locus*: place. Also a term in geometry, meaning a location defined by a group
of elements

17 *succulents*: juicy, fleshy plants

31 *laceration*: torn flesh

34 *magnitude*: measure of star's brightness

DIVING INTO THE WRECK

First having read the book of myths,
and loaded the camera,
and checked the edge of the knife-blade,
I put on
the body-armor of black rubber   5
the absurd flippers
the grave and awkward mask.
I am having to do this
not like Cousteau with his
assiduous team   10
aboard the sun-flooded schooner
but here alone.

There is a ladder.
The ladder is always there
hanging innocently   15
close to the side of the schooner.
We know what it is for,
we who have used it.
Otherwise
it's a piece of maritime floss   20
some sundry equipment.

I go down.
Rung after rung and still
the oxygen immerses me
the blue light   25
the clear atoms
of our human air.
I go down.
My flippers cripple me,
I crawl like an insect down the ladder   30
and there is no one
to tell me when the ocean
will begin.

First the air is blue and then
it is bluer and then green and then   35
black I am blacking out and yet
my mask is powerful
it pumps my blood with power
the sea is another story
the sea is not a question of power
I have to learn alone   40
to turn my body without force
in the deep element.

And now: it is easy to forget
what I came for
among so many who have always   45
lived here
swaying their crenellated fans
between the reefs
and besides
you breathe differently down here.   50

I came to explore the wreck.
The words are purposes.
The words are maps.
I came to see the damage that was done
and the treasures that prevail.   55
I stroke the beam of my lamp
slowly along the flank
of something more permanent
than fish or weed.

the thing I came for: 60
the wreck and not the story of the wreck
the thing itself and not the myth
the drowned face always staring
toward the sun
the evidence of damage   65
worn by salt and sway into this threadbare beauty
the ribs of the disaster
curving their assertion
among the tentative haunters.

This is the place.   70
And I am here, the mermaid whose dark hair
streams black, the merman in his armored body
We circle silently
about the wreck
we dive into the hold.   75
I am she: I am he

whose drowned face sleeps with open eyes
whose breasts still bear the stress
whose silver, copper, vermeil cargo lies
obscurely inside barrels   80
half-wedged and left to rot
we are the half-destroyed instruments
that once held to a course
the water-eaten log
the fouled compass.   85

We are, I am, you are
by cowardice or courage
the one who find our way
back to this scene
carrying a knife, a camera   90
a book of myths
in which
our names do not appear.

GLOSSARY

1 *myths*: folklore, legends

8 *Cousteau*: Jacques Cousteau (1910–2001) French underwater explorer and film-maker

9 *assiduous*: diligent, hard-working

10 *schooner*: a swift-sailing vessel

19 *maritime floss*: thread used at sea

21 *sundry*: various

43 *element*: the water (one of the four elements – earth, air and fire are the others)

48 *crenellated*: notched with round or scalloped projections

49 *reefs*: a chain of rocks at or near the surface of water

56 *prevail*: triumph

70 *tentative*: done provisionally

80 *vermeil*: gilded metal

85 *log*: daily record of ship's progress

FROM A SURVIVOR

The pact that we made was the ordinary pact
of men & women in those days

I don't know who we thought we were
that our personalities
could resist the failures of the race   5

Lucky or unlucky, we didn't know
the race had failures of that order
and that we were going to share them

Like everybody else, we thought of ourselves as special

Your body is as vivid to me   10
as it ever was: even more

since my feeling for it is clearer:
I know what it could and could not do

it is no longer
the body of a god   15
or anything with power over my life

Next year it would have been 20 years
and you are wastefully dead
who might have made the leap
we talked, too late, of making   20

which I live now
not as a leap
but a succession of brief, amazing movements

each one making possible the next

GLOSSARY

   1 *the pact*: agreement i.e. of marriage

POWER

Living in the earth-deposits   of our history

Today a backhoe divulged   out of a crumbling flank of earth
one bottle   amber   perfect   a hundred-year-old
cure for fever   or melancholy   a tonic
for living on this earth   in the winters of this climate   5

Today I was reading about Marie Curie:
she must have known she suffered   from radiation sickness
her body bombarded for years   by the element
she had purified
It seems she denied to the end   10
the source of the cataracts on her eyes
the cracked and suppurating skin   of her finger-ends
till she could she no longer hold   a test-tube or a pencil

She died   a famous woman   denying
her wounds   15
denying
her wounds   came   from the same source as her power

GLOSSARY

2 *backhoe*: mechanical digger

3 *flank*: side

4 *Melancholy*: sadness, depression

6 *Marie Curie*: Polish-born chemist and physicist (1864–1934). Having come to
France and married Pierre Curie, she did pioneering research on radioactivity.
The Curies discovered radium. Marie Curie was the first person to be awarded
the Nobel Prize twice. She died of leukaemia caused by exposure to high
levels of radiation

8 *bombarded*: attacked

11 *cataracts*: a condition in which the lens of the eye becomes opaque, causing
partial blindness

12 *suppurating*: oozing pus

GENERAL QUESTIONS ON ADRIENNE RICH

1 Write an essay on the poetry of Adrienne Rich with the title: 'Adrienne Rich: woman of our time'.

2 'Adrienne Rich: a poet of conflict.' Write an essay on this aspect of Adrienne Rich's poetry.

3 Adrienne Rich has been called 'witness, visionary, prophet'. Would you agree that these words apply to her as a poet?

4 'Adrienne Rich's poems are more interesting for what she says rather than how she says it.' Would you agree with this view of Adrienne Rich's work?

5 'Adrienne Rich has documented her development as a woman and as a poet with great honesty.' Would you agree with this view?

6 'Adrienne Rich's early poems are more appealing than her later ones'. To what extent would you agree with this view?

7 'Rich's poems tell us a great deal about the society in which she lives.' Discuss this view of her poetry.

8 'Adrienne Rich's poems portray men in an unfair light'. Do you agree with this view?

EXAMINATION-STYLE QUESTIONS

9 'The appeal of Adrienne Rich's poetry.' Using the above title, write an essay outlining what you consider to be the appeal of Rich's poetry. Support your points by reference to the poetry of Adrienne Rich on your course.

In your answer, you could consider some of the following points:
- her choice of themes is interesting and contemporary e.g. relations between men and women, the nature of power, political issues
- she confronts the issues she deals with honestly and fearlessly
- her use of language is always fresh and exciting
- she reveals her own personality and concerns in many of her poems etc.

10 Write about the feelings that Adrienne Rich's poetry creates in you and the aspects of her poetry (content and/or style) that help to create those feelings. Support your points by reference to the poetry by Adrienne Rich on your course.

You might include some of these points in your answer:
- you respond well to the issues she deals with – they are relevant to people's lives, including your own

- you share in the anger she expresses, whether directly or indirectly, at oppression of women and the politically powerless
- you sympathise with the personal problems she has faced, as expressed in her work e.g. her husband's death
- you appreciate the way in which the form of her poetry changed in response to changes in her own life e.g. from her early to her later work etc.

NB Of course, it may be that the feelings her work creates in you are negative! In this case, you could make some of the following points:

- you consider the issues she deals with irrelevant to the present day
- you find her attitudes to certain issues (e.g. the relations of men and women) inflexible and exaggerated
- you feel she depicts men unfairly
- you find her use of language too detached
- you react negatively to her desire to change the world.

Early poems formal
and polished.

Explores nature of
power in poems.

Later poems closer to
speech rhythms.

Language is direct
and clear.

Challenges role of
women in society.

Adrienne Rich

Wrote about women
in history.

Interested in relations
between the sexes.

Interested in role of myth and
legend in reflecting reality.

Blends private experience and
public life in poems.

Came to see
language as inadequate in
expressing meaning.

Sees poetry as having a
political purpose.

MAYA ANGELOU

B. 1928

BIOGRAPHY

Maya Angelou was born on April 4, 1928 in St. Louis, Missouri, USA. She grew up in segregated rural Arkansas. She is a writer, actress, playwright, civil-rights activist, producer and director. She lectures throughout the USA and abroad and has been Reynolds Professor of American Studies at Wake Forest University in North Carolina since 1981.

Maya Angelou began her career in drama and dance. She married a South African freedom fighter and lived in Cairo where she was editor of *The Arab Observer*, the only English-language news weekly in the Middle East. In Ghana, she was features editor of the African review and taught at the University of Ghana. In the 1960s, at the request of Dr Martin Luther King, Jr, Angelou became the northern coordinator for the Southern Christian Leadership Conference. In 1993 she read one of her poems at the inauguration of President Bill Clinton.

Her account of her traumatic childhood and youth, *I Know Why the Caged Bird Sings*, became a bestselling book, as well as achieving critical acclaim in the 1970s. She has written and produced several prize-winning documentaries and screenplays. In theatre, she has produced, directed and acted in many plays. Her performance of her own poetry is highly entertaining and popular.

PHENOMENAL WOMAN

Pretty women wonder where my secret lies.
I'm not cute or built to suit a fashion model's size
But when I start to tell them,
They think I'm telling lies.
I say,   5
It's in the reach of my arms
The span of my hips,
The stride of my step,
The curl of my lips.
I'm a woman   10
Phenomenally.
Phenomenal woman,
That's me.
I walk into a room
Just as cool as you please,   15
And to a man,
The fellows stand or
Fall down on their knees.
Then they swarm around me,
A hive of honey bees.   20
I say,
It's the fire in my eyes,
And the flash of my teeth,
The swing in my waist,
And the joy in my feet.   25
I'm a woman
Phenomenally.
Phenomenal woman,
That's me.
Men themselves have wondered   30
What they see in me.
They try so much
But they can't touch
My inner mystery.

When I try to show them,   35
They say they still can't see.
I say,
It's in the arch of my back,
The sun of my smile,
The ride of my breasts,   40
The grace of my style.
I'm a woman
Phenomenally.
Phenomenal woman,
That's me.   45
Now you understand
Just why my head's not bowed.
I don't shout or jump about
Or have to talk real loud.
When you see me passing   50
It ought to make you proud.
I say,
It's in the click of my heels,
The bend of my hair,
The palm of my hand,   55
The need for my care,
'Cause I'm a woman
Phenomenally.
Phenomenal woman,
That's me.   60

GLOSSARY

title *Phenomenal*: extraordinary

GUIDELINES

The title says almost everything about the theme and feeling in the poem. The speaker is full of pride and confidence in herself, although, as she suggests, she may not be 'pretty' in a conventional sense. Her confidence arises from her ease with her own body. People react positively to her, she tells us, particularly men, like bees to honey. By repeating the words 'phenomenally' and 'phenomenal' she makes sure the reader gets the point!

But she also suggests that her attraction goes beyond the physical. Its source is in her 'inner mystery', which is connected with being a woman but also with her personality – how she smiles, her sense of style.

In the final section of the poem, she says that she feels people should be proud to see her passing by, just because she is who she is, a 'phenomenal' woman, not just someone looking for attention. There is an indirect reference here to the difficulties she has had to overcome in her life, as an emotionally damaged and abused child whose head you might expect to be 'bowed', or defeated by her experiences. This woman is not prepared to let her past determine how she feels in the present, as the final lines make clear.

QUESTIONS

1 How does the speaker suggest that she is not like other 'pretty women'?
2 How do the physical images help to convey the theme of the poem?
3 What sort of woman is the speaker of the poem, in your view?
4 Would you agree that there is a tremendous sense of energy in the poem? How is it created?
5 Do you think you would like this woman, if you met her?
6 Maya Angelou has performed this poem on the stage. Even if you have not seen it, or a televised version, try to describe how you think she may have done so.
7 Do you think this poem has anything to teach people, both men and women? If so, can you say what it might be?
8 Write a short note to Maya Angelou describing your response to her poem.

SIMON ARMITAGE

B. 1963

BIOGRAPHY

Simon Armitage was born in 1963 in Huddersfield and grew up in West Yorkshire. He studied geography at Portsmouth Polytechnic and later social work and psychology at Manchester University. He has worked as a shelf stacker, disc jockey and lathe operator. For some time he worked as a probation officer. He is now a freelance writer.

He has presented poetry programmes for the BBC, worked as an editor and taught at the University of Leeds and the University of Iowa, USA. In 2000 he was writer-in-residence at the Millennium Dome in London.

Armitage is the author of nine volumes of poetry, including *Zoom!* (1989), *Kid* (1992) and *Cloudcuckooland* (1996). He has also written four stage plays and two novels. He has received many awards for his writing, including the Forward Poetry Prize in 1992. In 1994 he was named *Sunday Times* Writer of the Year.

IT AIN'T WHAT YOU DO
IT'S WHAT IT DOES TO YOU

I have not bummed across America
with only a dollar to spare, one pair
of busted Levi's and a bowie knife.
I have lived with thieves in Manchester.

I have not padded through the Taj Mahal,   5
barefoot, listening to the space between
each footfall picking up and putting down
its print against the marble floor. But I

skimmed flat stones across Black Moss on a day
so still I could hear each set of ripples   10
as they crossed. I felt each stone's inertia
spend itself against the water; then sink.

I have not toyed with a parachute chord
while perched on the lip of a light aircraft;
but I held the wobbly head of a boy   15
at the day centre, and stroked his fat hands.

And I guess that the tightness in the throat
and the tiny cascading sensation
somewhere inside us are both part of that
sense of something else. That feeling, I mean.   20

3 *Levi's*: a brand of jeans

3 *bowie knife*: a strong, one-edged dagger knife

5 *Taj Mahal*: the most famous building in India, the magnificent mausoleum at Agra

9 *Black Moss*: a river on the border between Yorkshire and Lancashire.

11 *inertia*: stillness

18 *cascading*: falling (like a waterfall)

GUIDELINES

'It Ain't What You Do It's What It Does To You' is from the collection *Zoom!* (1989). The title of the poem echoes the song 'It ain't what you do it's the way that you do it'. Simon Armitage's work as a probation officer helps to explain some of his references in the poem.

The poem tells us about some of the adventurous things other people have done that the poet has not. For example, he hasn't travelled across America with little or no money, visited the Taj Mahal in India (one of the seven wonders of the world) or made a parachute jump from an aeroplane. Even though he has not been to India, he describes it in some detail, as if someone had told him about it. You can sense a certain regret, perhaps, that he has missed out on this particular experience, from the language he uses to convey its quietness and spirituality.

But he has his own experiences to relate. The things he has done may seem ordinary, such as living among thieves (we remember that he was a probation officer for a time), or skimming stones across a river. As in the description of the Taj Mahal, he makes use of the sounds of words to help us share in the experience of skimming stones. Notice the amount of 's' sounds he uses that create a musical effect, echoing the sound of water. It is as if this simple action was as significant to him as a visit to India would have been.

In the fourth stanza he mentions perhaps the most thrilling or dangerous thing he has not done – the parachute jump. But what he *has* done is communicate with, and comfort, another human being. The words suggest that this boy is special, perhaps unable to communicate by speech. It is a moving image that contrasts with the danger and excitement of the first two lines of the stanza.

In the last stanza the poet tries to express the effect that his own, more ordinary experiences have had on him. He uses his senses to get across the idea that these experiences have caused him to feel as emotional as more exciting adventures might have done. He suggests, too, that these feelings may also have a deeper, more spiritual significance, what he calls 'that / sense of something else'. The words are vague, as if he is attempting to describe the indescribable, and realises how difficult it is.

THE THEME OF THE POEM

The title of the poem gives us a good idea as to what its theme may be. What we actually do may not matter very much. What matters is how we respond to it and what effect it has on us as human beings. That is how we achieve fulfilment.

QUESTIONS

1 Why do you think the poet chooses the particular experiences that he has missed? What do they have in common with each other?

2 Do you think he regrets not having these experiences? Explain your answer.

3 Why did skimming the stones across the river and holding the boy's head at the day centre mean so much to him? What might these experiences have in common with each other, if anything?

4 What kind of feeling do you think Armitage is describing in the last stanza? Does he describe it well, in your opinion?

5 Which of the experiences described in the poem would you yourself like to share? Explain your answer.

6 From your reading of the poem, what sort of person do you imagine the speaker to be?

7 Does this poem make you think about life in a new way?

8 Do you think this poem appeals to young people in particular? Give reasons for your view.

CAROL ANN DUFFY

B. 1955

BIOGRAPHY

Carol Ann Duffy was born in Glasgow in December 1955. She grew up in Staffordshire where she was educated at Stafford Girls' High School. She studied philosophy at university in Liverpool before moving to London to work as a freelance writer. She has written plays as well as poems, edited books of poetry and been a writer-in-residence at the Southern Arts, Thamesdown. She has lived in Manchester where she lectured in poetry at Manchester Metropolitan University.

Duffy has published several volumes of poems, among them *Standing Female Nude* (1985), *Selling Manhattan* (1987), *The Other Country* (1990) and *Mean Time* (1993). In 2000 she published *The World's Wife*, a collection of dramatic monologues in the voices of the wives of famous men (Mrs Midas and Mrs Aesop, for example). She has edited two anthologies for teenagers, *I Wouldn't Thank You for a Valentine* and *Stopping for Death*.

Carol Ann Duffy has been awarded many prizes for her work, among them the Forward Poetry Prize and the Whitbread Poetry Award. In 1995 she was awarded an OBE in the Queen's Birthday Honours List. She is one of the most popular women poets writing today.

VALENTINE

Not a red rose or a satin heart.

I give you an onion.
It is a moon wrapped in brown paper.
It promises light
like the careful undressing of love.   5

Here.
It will blind you with tears
like a lover.
It will make your reflection
a wobbling photo of grief.   10

I am trying to be truthful.

Not a cute card or a kissogram.

I give you an onion.
Its fierce kiss will stay on your lips,
possessive and faithful   15
as we are,
for as long as we are.

Take it.
Its platinum loops shrink to a wedding-ring,
if you like.   20

Lethal.
Its scent will cling to your fingers,
cling to your knife.

GUIDELINES

'Valentine' is from the collection *Mean Time* (1993). Like a traditional valentine, the poem contains a proposal of marriage. But unlike a traditional valentine, the proposal is expressed in unromantic terms.

The title prepares us for a romantic love poem, but what we find is rather different. Instead of the usual sorts of gifts like red roses and satin hearts, the lover gives her beloved an onion.

The speaker makes a case for the onion as an appropriate gift. The metaphors are unusual, in that ordinary things (brown paper) are mixed with romantic images (the moon). This mixture of ordinary and romantic continues through the poem and gives it its ironic, bittersweet tone, so that we are never quite sure what exactly the feelings of the speaker are. For instance, the speaker never allows us to forget that the gift is an onion, so that we find references to its layers of skin, its colour, the fact that peeling onions makes us cry, and yet each of these aspects is made to fit the speaker's view of love: that it is sexual, that it offers light and happiness, but that it can also make you cry.

The speaker thinks that an onion is a more 'truthful' symbol of love than any other more conventional Valentine's Day gift. She reveals even more clearly what she thinks love is. The smell and taste of the onion, its 'fierce kiss', will last on the lips of the beloved, just as the speaker's love will last – as long as the love they share will last. Here she seems to recognise that love may not last forever, another more honest view of love than is usually found in a valentine.

There is a sense that the speaker is appealing to her beloved – 'Take it' – as she reveals another aspect of the onion that makes it appropriate. Its white rings, as it is cut up, may become 'platinum hoops' like a wedding ring, as the speaker says rather uncertainly 'if you like'. It is as if she is not totally confident about the relationship, so that the proposal comes across as rather off-hand and casual.

You can read the final three lines in a number of ways. 'Lethal' might suggest the fierceness of love, but it has underlying suggestions of destruction. And is there a threatening tone in the image of the onion's scent that 'clings'? 'Knife' is a strange word to finish with in a poem about love. Does it have suggestions of bitterness and betrayal?

How we respond to the poem may depend on our own personal experience, but we cannot fail to see how original and honest it is.

QUESTIONS

1 Why, according to the poem's speaker, is the onion suitable as a gift for the beloved on Valentine's Day?
2 Which of the metaphors and similes that the poet uses do you find the most unusual and effective?
3 Do you think the relationship between the lovers in this poem is a happy one?
4 What attitude to love and relationships in general is suggested in this poem?
5 Do you find the speaker's vision of love honest, bitter, refreshing, off-putting? Perhaps you would prefer to use another word?
6 Imagine you are the person who has received the onion (and the poem) as a valentine. Write out the response you would make.

PAUL DURCAN

B. 1944

BIOGRAPHY

Paul Durcan was born in Dublin in October 1944. He studied first at UCD, but left without taking a degree. Later, he graduated with a BA in Archaeology and Medieval History from University College, Cork.

Durcan has published many collections of poetry, among them *The Berlin Wall Café* (1985), *Daddy, Daddy* (1990), *Crazy about Women* (1991), *Greetings to our Friends in Brazil* (1999) and *Cries of an Irish Caveman* (2001). *Daddy Daddy* won the prestigious Whitbread Prize for Poetry.

Paul Durcan has given readings of his poetry throughout Ireland and Britain and in many other parts of the world, including Russia and Brazil. His poetry readings are dramatic, entertaining occasions. He regularly broadcasts on RTÉ, reading his own work and speaking about literature.

Paul Durcan has lived in London and Barcelona as well as Dublin, where he now resides. He is one of Ireland's most well-known poets.

GOING HOME TO MAYO, WINTER, 1949

Leaving behind us the alien, foreign city of Dublin
My father drove through the night in an old Ford Anglia,
His five-year-old son in the seat beside him,
The rexine seat of red leatherette,
And a yellow moon peered in through the windscreen.   5
'Daddy, Daddy,' I cried, 'Pass out the moon,'
But no matter how hard he drove he could not pass out the moon.
Each town we passed through was another milestone
And their names were magic passwords into eternity:
Kilcock, Kinnegad, Strokestown, Elphin,   10
Tarmonbarry, Tulsk, Ballaghaderreen, Ballavarry;
Now we were in Mayo and the next stop was Turlough,
The village of Turlough in the heartland of Mayo,
And my father's mother's house, all oil-lamps and women,
And my bedroom over the public bar below,   15
And in the morning cattle-cries and cock-crows:
Life's seemingly seamless garment gorgeously rent
By their screeches and bellowings. And in the evenings
I walked with my father in the high grass down by the river
Talking with him – an unheard-of thing in the city.   20

But home was not home and the moon could be no more outflanked
Than the daylight nightmare of Dublin city:
Back down along the canal we chugged into the city
And each lock-gate tolled our mutual doom;
And railings and palings and asphalt and traffic-lights,   25
And blocks after blocks of so-called 'new' tenements –
Thousands of crosses of loneliness planted
In the narrowing grave of the life of the father;
In the wide, wide cemetery of the boy's childhood.

   2 *Ford Anglia*: a brand of car

   4 *rexine*: artificial leather used in upholstery

  10 *Kilcock …Elphin*: Kilcock is in Co. Kildare; Kinnegad is in Co. Westmeath; Strokestown and Elphin are in Co. Roscommon

  11 *Tarmonbarry, Tulsk, Ballaghaderreen, Ballavarry*: Co. Roscommon

  12 *Turlough*: village in Co. Mayo, the birthplace of Paul Durcan's father

  17 *rent*: torn

  21 *outflanked*: passed out

  24 *lock-gate*: gate for opening or closing a lock in a canal

  25 *palings*: fences

  25 *asphalt*: paving

  26 *tenements*: houses divided into flats

GUIDELINES

Paul Durcan's parents came from Co. Mayo, where he spent many happy summer holidays as a child. In this poem he looks back to his childhood experience of travelling to Mayo with his father and his feelings about being there and returning to Dublin. Durcan's father was a circuit court judge, with whom the poet later had a rather troubled relationship.

From the beginning the speaker seems to see Dublin as an 'alien, foreign' place, possibly echoing his father's view of it (as a Mayoman). He describes the excitement of travelling in the car as a child, the childish desire to 'Pass out the moon', the sense of 'magic' as he names the towns through which they passed.

Vivid images of what he saw and heard bring to life his experience of actually being in Mayo on his holidays. Repetition of 'and' echoes his childish excitement. But there is a certain sadness in the image that ends the first stanza: he and his father, talking together, relax in a way that would not have happened in Dublin.

The atmosphere of the second stanza contrasts utterly with the first. Whereas life in Mayo was magical, life in Dublin was a 'daylight nightmare'. As the poet and his father return home through the city we can almost feel the weight of depression descending on him. Now the images suggest a sense of being trapped ('railings', 'palings'), the blocks of new tenements or Corporation flats becoming a metaphor for a kind of death and burial, for both himself and his father. The word 'loneliness' suggests that their return marked the end of the closeness that they had in Mayo.

QUESTIONS

1 What impression do you get of the relationship between the poet and his father as they travel to Mayo?

2 Do you think the use of placenames adds to the effect of the poem? Give reasons.

3 Contrast the poet's attitude to Mayo with his attitude to Dublin. Look carefully at the poet's use of language.

4 Do you think Durcan describes his childhood experience well? Give reasons for your view.

5 How would you describe the tone of the poem? Angry? Disappointed? Nostalgic? Sad? Perhaps you would suggest another word?

6 Do you like this poem? Give reasons for your answer.

7 You want to make a short film of this poem. Describe the sort of atmosphere you would like to create, and say what music, sound effects and images you would use.

KERRY HARDIE

B. 1951

BIOGRAPHY

Kerry Hardie was born in 1951 in Singapore, Malaysia, but grew up in County Down. She studied English at York University, England and then came back to work as a researcher and radio interviewer for the BBC in Belfast and Derry. She writes:

> This period coincided with the most violent years of the Troubles, and through my job I had access to situations and people I might not otherwise have known. I became fascinated with people who found themselves in a hard place and with how they reacted to this place. Some people adapted astonishingly fast to their new realities, but others spent their energies resisting and could only change to meet them when they had in some way been broken by them.

Because of her background and because she now lives in Kilkenny, she says her writing is 'one way of joining up the island, of subverting the separateness that eighty years of government under different systems has reinforced'.

She has published three collections of poetry: *A Furious Place* (1996), *Cry for the Hot Belly* (2000) and *The Sky Didn't Fall* (2003). Her first novel, *A Winter Marriage*, was published by in 2002, and her second novel, *The Bird Woman*, in 2005.

Kerry Hardie has won major literary awards, including the Friends Provident National Poetry Prize, the 1995 Hennessey Award for Poetry, the 1996 UK National Poetry Prize and a 2004 James Joyce Foundation Award (which took her to China and Australia). She has also collected awards from American universities.

Kerry Hardie's first collection, *A Furious Place*, from which 'May' is taken, includes poems that record people in their own landscapes and explore the way in which landscape permeates their lives. In her novel, *A Winter Marriage*, the landscape and climate of an Irish winter is unbearable to the foreign woman who marries a local farmer. Other poems in A *Furious Place* dwell on the hardships and lessons of a chronic illness. Kerry Hardie suffers from ME (chronic fatigue syndrome):

> *Being chronically sick makes you an observer rather than a participant. Before I was sick, I lived very hard and my life was very outgoing; now my life is quiet and disciplined and reflective .. .It took me a long time to come to terms with the change, but now I find my life immensely rich and rewarding.*

Kerry Hardie lives in Kilkenny with her husband, Sean, who is also a writer.

MAY

For Marian

The blessèd stretch and ease of it –
heart's ease. The hills blue. All the flowering weeds
bursting open. Balm in the air. The birdsong
bouncing back out of the sky. The cattle
lain down in the meadows, forgetting to feed.   5
The horses swishing their tails.
The yellow flare of furze on the near hill.
And the first cream splatters of blossom
High on the thorns where the day rests longest.

All hardship, hunger, treachery of winter forgotten.   10
The unfounded conviction: forgiveness, hope.

GLOSSARY

3 *Balm*: a healing and soothing fragrance

7 *furze*: gorse, a prickly shrub with an abundance of yellow flowers which grows
  wild on hills and mountains

10 *treachery*: deceit or betrayal

11 *unfounded conviction*: a strong belief that has no foundation

GUIDELINES

'May' is an intriguing poem. Who speaks the words – the poet, or a persona, like
a character in a novel? Is it a man or a woman? A stranger or a native? Someone
who is content or someone who is unhappy? Does the speaker speak for all of
us? Experiment with different readings of the poem until you find the voice
which you think works best.

   At first glance this is a simple poem about the effect of the weather and the
seasons on our moods and emotions. It is a hymn of celebration to the long days
of May and the sense of well-being they bring after winter. However, there are

elements in the poem which may hint at a darker, more complicated meaning, although this is not necessarily a better reading of the poem than a more straight-forward one.

The speaker of the poem treats the long, easeful days of May as something blessed, as days which provide ease for the heart. The phrase, 'hearts' ease', may suggest that the speaker's heart is not easy and May brings respite from a life that is troubled. The word 'Balm' may also suggest that the speaker is in need of soothing or healing. The images of May evoke colour ('blue', 'yellow' and 'cream') and also the countryside ('weeds', 'furze' and 'thorns') bursting into flower. The energy of May is caught in the colourful verbs and the alliteration and onomatopoeia of the descriptive language. There is birdsong and the cattle and the horses take their ease in the fine weather. The cattle are so content that they forget 'to feed', something that would not happen in the hungry months of winter. The word 'rests' in line 9, taken alongside 'ease' (line 1), 'heart's ease' (line 2) and 'Balm' (line 3), seem to suggest a life that is in need of restoration or recuperation.

The two lines that conclude the poem put the previous nine lines in context. May is blessed because it finally puts paid to the hardship, hunger and treachery of winter, and although these are forgotten, they cast a long shadow over the poem. 'Hardship' and 'hunger' describe the physical harshness of winter but they may also refer to the life of the heart and the spirit. In similar fashion the word 'treachery' describes the treacherous weather of winter but it may also refer to a human treachery. What is clear is that the speaker states that May brings the 'unfounded conviction' of 'forgiveness and hope'. The last line will repay careful thought. Are the hope and forgiveness of the final line real or merely longed-for? Are they understandable? Do we all feel them in May? What does the final line tell us about someone (all of us?) who cling to unfounded convictions? What does it tell us about the human heart?

QUESTIONS

1 Then first nine lines are a feast of sensuous responses to the month of May. Comment on each image and the sense it celebrates.

2 The images include references to 'weeds' (line 2), 'furze' (line 7) and 'thorns' (line 9). Why, do you think, were these plants chosen?

3 How is the energy of May reflected in the language of the first nine lines?

4 Select one phrase and comment on the way it sounds and the poetic techniques Kerry Hardie uses to achieve this sound.

5 Why does the poet associate May with 'heart's ease'?

6 In what way is line 10 surprising?

7 What word strikes you with most force in line 10?

8 Imagine the poem being spoken by a character in a novel. What kind of life does he or she live?

9 The hope and forgiveness of the last line are 'unfounded conviction'. Consider the meaning of the phrase. Do you think the speaker of the poem is an optimistic or a pessimistic person? Do you agree with the views expressed by the speaker of the poem?

SEAMUS HEANEY

B. 1939

BIOGRAPHY

Seamus Heaney was born on 13 April, 1939, on a farm in County Derry. He was the eldest of nine children. He went to the local primary school and then to St Columb's College, a boarding school in Derry, about forty miles from his home. After St Columb's, Seamus won a scholarship to Queen's University, Belfast, where he studied English Literature and Language, graduating with a First Class Honours degree in 1961. He then trained as a teacher and got a job in a secondary school in Ballymurphy, Belfast. The principal teacher was Michael McLaverty, the short-story writer, who introduced Heaney to the work of Patrick Kavanagh. At about this time – 1962 – Heaney began to write poems in a serious way, and the poetry of Kavanagh influenced the direction and style of his work. Heaney wrote, 'Kavanagh gave you permission to dwell without cultural anxiety among the usual landmarks of your life'.

In August 1965, Seamus Heaney married Marie Devlin and in the following year, the London publishers Faber & Faber brought out his first collection of poems, *Death of a Naturalist*. Since then Heaney has published ten collections of poetry, five books of critical essays and a number of translations, including the Anglo-Saxon poem *Beowulf* which became an unlikely bestseller. With his friend, the late Ted Hughes, he has co-edited two poetry anthologies, *The Rattle Bag* and

The School Bag. His version of the Greek play *Antigone* was produced at the Abbey Theatre in 2004. Since *Death of a Naturalist* won the Eric Gregory prize in 1966, Seamus Heaney has won countless awards for his poetry. Winning the Nobel Prize for Literature in 1995 was an experience which he compared to being 'hit by a mostly benign avalanche'.

In 1976, Seamus Heaney and his family moved to Sandymount in Dublin. He now divides his time between living in Dublin and living in America and England, where he teaches and lectures at Harvard and Oxford.

At this point in his career, Seamus Heaney is, without question, one of the most admired poets writing in English. He is also a man of wit and high spirits who is modest about his achievements and who is still open to what he describes as 'the pleasure and surprise of poetry, its rightness and thereness, the way it is at one moment unforeseeable and at the next indispensable'.

POSTSCRIPT

And some time make the time to drive out west
Into County Clare, along the Flaggy Shore,
In September or October, when the wind
And the light are working off each other
So that the ocean on one side is wild   5
With foam and glitter, and inland among stones
The surface of a slate-grey lake is lit
By the earthed lightning of a flock of swans,
Their feathers roughed and ruffling, white on white,
Their fully-grown headstrong-looking heads   10
Tucked or cresting or busy underwater.
Useless to think you'll park and capture it
More thoroughly. You are neither here nor there,
A hurry through which known and strange things pass
As big soft buffetings come at the car sideways   15
And catch the heart off guard and blow it open.

GLOSSARY

title *Postscript*: something added as an afterthought

2 *the Flaggy Shore*: portion of the Atlantic shoreline near Finvarra County Clare, where the flat slabs of Burren limestone run right to the sea

11 *Tucked or cresting*: some of the swans have tucked in their heads so that they rest on their bodies; some have their necks extended while others have their heads underwater

15 *buffetings*: gusts of wind which push or knock against the car

GUIDELINES

Reading 'Postscript' is like overhearing the end of a conversation in which someone offers advice to a friend (or a tourist) to take a car journey along the west coast of Clare and describes the beauty of the journey and the feelings it inspires, especially in September or October.

The journey is a dramatic one, with the wild sea on one side and a lake on the other, upon which a flock of swans appear like 'earthed lightning'. Like a painter, the speaker appreciates the interplay between the light and the wind; the way the wind ruffles the feathers of the swans. Like everything else in this landscape the swans are powerful with 'fully-grown headstrong-looking heads'.

The poem has a sonnet-like structure in the division between description and reflection. The first eleven lines consist of the advice to 'make the time to drive out west' and a description of what lies in store. The last five lines are more reflective. In these lines the speaker suggests there is little point in stopping the car in hope of capturing the experience more fully. The sense of hurrying through the landscape, of being in motion and subject to the gusts of wind which catch the car sideways, is an essential part of the experience. The gusts of wind are not dangerous or threatening. On the contrary, they are 'big soft buffetings' which 'catch the heart off guard and blow it open'. In the last line the speaker seems to be referring to an experience of greater significance than the momentary heart-in-the-mouth experience of a wind catching a moving car and blowing it slightly off course.

Like all journey poems, 'Postscript' can be read in a metaphorical way. The journey symbolises to some degree the journey of life, especially at those moments when we seems to be 'neither here nor there' but exist on the edge of things, just as the car travels in the space between the land and the sea and is blown off balance. So the observation that it is 'Useless to think you'll park and capture it' might well be read as the speaker's philosophy that life cannot be controlled or commanded and our hearts will be blown open by the surprising and unexpected in our lives.

Interestingly, in introducing the poem at a reading Seamus Heaney spoke of the significance of 'going west' and his remarks might lead you to read the poem in a new light:

The phrase, 'going west', from the First World War, has connotations of mortality, fatality, to 'go west'. And there's a very beautiful cadence in the last story of Joyce's Dubliners, 'The Dead', when Joyce says it was time for him to set out on his journey westward. So this is a memory of a vivid journey westward that we had.

QUESTIONS

1 The poem is rich in description. Select two images which you think are particularly effective and explain your choice.

2 Why, do you think, did Seamus Heaney decide to write the first eleven lines of description as one sentence?

3 Although conversational in tone, the poem has a feeling of strength about it. Examine the sounds of the poem and identify what you consider to be 'strong' sounds.

4 'A hurry through which known and strange things pass …'. In the overall context of the poem, what, do you think, is the meaning of this line?

5 'The speaker of the poem seems to enjoy the feeling of being off balance.' Do you agree with this statement? Explain your answer.

6 The poem reads like the advice of a wise man on how to lead your life. What is the wisdom that the speaker offers?

7 Why, in your opinion, is the poem entitled 'Postscript'? Does it suggest, for example, that the speaker is not claiming any great status for his advice and offers it modestly?

8 'The poem is written in ordinary language which seems to take flight and lifts off, just as the car seems to lift off as the wind catches it sideways.' Do you agree with this statement? Support your answer by reference to the poem.

9 Just as the phrase 'going west' strikes a chord in Heaney's imagination, the reference to swans on a lake is rich in connotations. What ideas does the image generate in your imagination?

10 Is the idea of a journey west a good metaphor for life? Explain your answer.

ELIZABETH JENNINGS

1926–2001

BIOGRAPHY

Elizabeth Jennings was born in Boston, Lincolnshire, the daughter of a physician. Roman Catholicism, the religion of her birth, was an important influence on her life and work. She read English at Oxford University, and afterwards worked in the Oxford Public Library. From the publication of her first collection of poems in 1953 onwards, her work won widespread critical acclaim. In the early 1960s, she suffered a severe nervous illness. The poems in her 1966 collection, the *Mind Has Mountains*, deal with her experiences in a psychiatric hospital. Before her illness, she worked in a publishing house in London. After her recovery, she continued to write poetry, as well as being a freelance critic, anthologist and lecturer on literary subjects.

Elizabeth Jennings found poetry an essential part of her life. Throughout her career, she remained a solitary person, relying on poetry as a vital link between her insecure private world and the seeming certainties of the world around her. Each poem could be seen as a temporary escape from isolation. There is an obsessive emphasis in her poetry on the theme of individual isolation. Some of her poems reveal a morbid fascination with the ultimate isolation – extinction in death. This poem from *Growing Points*, her 1975 collection, is a good example of this:

But better to be turned to earth
Where other things at least can grow,
I would be then a part of birth,
Passive, not knowing how to know.

Elizabeth Jennings was not an innovator. Her poetry has many of the characteristics associated with the group of poets who belonged to what is commonly
known as 'the Movement'. Its members included Philip Larkin, Kingsley Amis,
Donald Davie, D. J. Enright, Thom Gunn and John Wain. Like the work of these
poets, hers displays a simplicity of metre and rhyme and a search for honest
feeling. Like them too, she was influenced by Thomas Hardy rather than by T. S.
Eliot, avoiding radical experiments in poetic forms.

THE LADYBIRD'S STORY

It was a roadway to me.
So many meeting-places and directions.
It was smooth, polished, sometimes it shook a little
But I did not tumble off.
I heard you say, and it was like a siren,   5
'A ladybird. Good luck. Perhaps some money.'
I did not understand.
Suddenly I was frightened, fearful of falling
Because you lifted your hand.

And then I saw your eyes,   10
Glassy moons always changing shape,
Sometimes suns in eclipse.
I watched the beak, the peak of your huge nose
And the island of your lips.
I was afraid but you were not. I have   15
No sting. I do not wound.
I carry a brittle coat. It does not protect.
I thought you would blow me away but superstition

Saved me. You held your hand now in one position,
Gentled me over the veins and arteries.   20
But it was not I you cared about but money.
You see I have watched you with flies.

GLOSSARY

17 *brittle*: frail and easily broken
20 *Gentled*: moved me gently

GUIDELINES

The entire poem is spoken by the ladybird to the poet. In form, the poem is a dramatic monologue. This is a work in which a single speaker dramatises an incident or situation, and derives significance or meaning from it.

The situation is simply presented. A ladybird finds itself on the poet's hand, and fears for its safety. To its relief, the poet treats it kindly, making sure that it comes to no harm.

The interest of the poem lies in the significance the ladybird derives from the situation and its outcome. From the ladybird's point of view, the poet is a representative human being, enormous in magnitude when compared to an insect. The human hand is a roadway to the ladybird, the eyes are moons and suns, the 'huge nose' is a beak, and the lips are an island. The ladybird knows that its fragile shell will provide no defence against hostile human intentions. It cannot fight against these, as some creatures can, by stinging or wounding the human enemy.

The ladybird is clever enough to realise, however, that human beings, as well as ladybirds, have their own weaknesses. In the present case, the weakness is superstition. The ladybird has heard the poet say, 'A ladybird. Good luck. Perhaps some money'. It also senses that this human being acts tenderly towards it, not out of a sympathy for small creatures, but out of a belief that saving it will bring monetary reward. It has observed this and other human beings killing flies without mercy, and knows that people in general have little regard for the welfare of insect life.

Jennings has written a thought-provoking poem as much about human nature as about a ladybird. Notice the bare simplicity of the language, and the conversational tone of the ladybird's song.

QUESTIONS

1 The poem indicates that the ladybird has mixed feelings about its experience. Develop this idea.

2 'The poet raises questions which extend far beyond a single incident.' Discuss this statement.

3 The poet uses imagery to express the ladybird's point of view on a human being. Discuss this imagery and say how effective it is.

4 Is the ladybird fair to the person it is dealing with?

5 Was it a good idea for the poet to present the situation from the ladybird's point of view? What advantages does this kind of presentation have?

ROGER
McGOUGH

B. 1937

BIOGRAPHY

Roger McGough was born in Liverpool. He has married twice and has three sons and one daughter. He received his higher education at Hull University. He is a poet, dramatist, songwriter and performer. He was one of the group, along with Brian Patten and Adrian Henri, which became popularly known as 'The Liverpool Poets'. He became famous in the late 1960s as a member of the pop group Scaffold, and wrote many of their songs, including 'Lily the Pink' (1968). His poems were strongly influenced by the pop culture of the 1960s (the Mersey beat), and by the poets of the American Beat Generation. With his fellow-poets Brian Patten and Adrian Henri, McGough published the highly successful *Mersey Sound* poetry collection in 1967. His collections include *Gig* (1973) and *Waving at Trains* (1982). One of his fellow band members in Scaffold was Mike McCartney, whose brother Paul played in the world's most famous band, The Beatles.

McGough has written for theatre, film and television, and continues to write poetry: his latest collection, *Everyday Eclipses*, was published in 2002. His work has been widely translated. He is an international ambassador for poetry, and was awarded an OBE for his work in 1997. In 2001, he was made a freeman of the City of Liverpool. Much of his poetry has been written for live performances, which helps to explain why it is easily understood. The fact that it deals with the experiences and hopes of ordinary people has made it widely popular. It has a considerable appeal to children, since McGough speaks their language and understands their concerns and interests. This explains its widespread use in schools.

BEARHUGS

Whenever my sons call round we hug each other.
Bearhugs. Both bigger than me and stronger
They lift me off my feet, crushing the life out of me.

They smell of oil paint and aftershave, of beer
Sometimes and tobacco, and of women   5
Whose memory they seem reluctant to wash away.

They haven't lived with me for years,
Since they were tiny, and so each visit
Is an assessment, a reassurance of love unspoken.

I look for some resemblance to my family.   10
Seize on an expression, a lifted eyebrow,
A tilt of the head, but cannot see myself.

Though like each other, they are not like me.
But I can see in them, something of my father.
Uncles, home on leave during the war.   15

At three or four, I loved those straightbacked men
Towering above me, smiling and confident.
The whole world before them. Or so it seemed.

I look at my boys, slouched in armchairs
They have outgrown. See Tom in army uniform   20
And Finn in air force blue. Time is up.

Bearhugs. They lift me off my feet
And fifty years fall away. One son
After another, crushing the life into me.

5–6 *They haven't lived… tiny*: McGough married his first wife in 1970. When they were divorced in 1980, his wife got custody of their children

18 *Or so it seemed*: this suggests that whatever hopes the uncles might have had of a better future were shattered by the war, in which they may have suffered death or injury

GUIDELINES

Like the rest of McGough's poetry, 'Bearhugs' is a simple, straightforward account of a commonplace incident: a visit from two of his sons who no longer live with him, but with his first wife. 'Time is up' (line 21) suggests that the visit has to be of limited duration.

The visit is seen from the father's point of view. This, and all the other visits they make to him, are considered by him in two ways. Visits provide a means of assessing the boys, trying to discover what resemblances he can find between the two boys and other family members belonging to an earlier generation. They remind him, not of himself, but of his father and his uncles. This thought leads to a related one: the fine, upright stance of his uncles on leave from the front, and their disappointed hopes.

The visit has another significance for the father. It is, as he puts it, 'a reassurance of love unspoken' (line 9). The first three lines of the poem, along with the last three, show how this reassurance, so important to the father, is expressed. The repetition of 'Bearhugs' in these lines and in the title of the poem, suggests the urgent need felt by the father for confirmation of the love his sons have for him. Their vigorous expression of this love revives his spirit, and makes him feel young once more, as he relives the time when, as small children, they hugged him affectionately.

QUESTIONS

1 Does this poem help to explain why McGough has a wide appeal?
2 Comment on the language of the poem. What is its effect on you?
3 How does the poem make you feel about the father?
4 Why do you think the father needs reassurance? Does he get this from his sons?
5 Comment on the parallel between Stanzas Six and Seven.
6 Discuss the significance of the contrast between 'crushing the life out of me' (line 3) and 'crushing the life into me' (line 24).

PAUL MULDOON

B. 1951

BIOGRAPHY

Paul Muldoon was born in Portadown, Co. Armagh on 20 June, 1951. His mother was a teacher, his father a labourer and market gardener. He was educated at St Patrick's College, Armagh, and at the Queen's University, Belfast, where the poet Seamus Heaney was his tutor. Muldoon's first collection of poems, *New Weather*, was published in 1973 while he was 22 and still at university.

Muldoon has worked as a radio and television producer for BBC Northern Ireland and he has held writing fellowships at various universities including Cambridge University, Columbia University (New York) and the University of California at Berkeley. Since 1990 he has been a Professor of the Humanities and Creative Writing at Princeton University.

Muldoon has received many awards for his poetry, including the Sir Geoffrey Faber Memorial Award in 1991, the T. S. Eliot Memorial Prize in 1994 for his collection *The Annals of Chile* and the American Academy of Arts and Letters Award for Literature in 1996. In May 1999 he was appointed Professor of Poetry at Oxford University. His *New Selected Poems 1968–1994,* published in 1996, won the prestigious *Irish Times* Irish Literature Prize for Poetry in 1997. He has edited a number of poetry anthologies, among them *The Faber Book of Contemporary Irish Poetry* (1986), and he has also written a play for television, *Monkeys* (1989). His collection *Moy Sand and Gravel* (2002) was awarded the Pulitzer Prize in 2003.

He lives in the USA with his novelist wife Jean Hanff Korelitz and their daughter.

ANSEO

When the Master was calling the roll
At the primary school in Collegelands,
You were meant to call back *Anseo*
And raise your hand
As your name occurred.   5
Anseo, meaning here, here and now,
All present and correct,
Was the first word of Irish I spoke.
The last name on the ledger
Belonged to Joseph Mary Plunkett Ward   10
And was followed, as often as not,
By silence, knowing looks,
A nod and a wink, the Master's droll
'And where's our little Ward-of-court?'

I remember the first time he came back   15
The Master had sent him out
Along the hedges
To weigh up for himself and cut
A stick with which he would be beaten.
After a while, nothing was spoken;   20
He would arrive as a matter of course
With an ash-plant, a salley-rod.
Or finally, the hazel-wand
He had whittled down to a whip-lash,
Its twist of red and yellow lacquers   25
Sanded and polished,
And altogether so delicately wrought
That he had engraved his initials on it.

I last met Joseph Mary Plunkett Ward
In a pub just over the Irish border.   30
He was living in the open,
In a secret camp
On the other side of the mountain.
He was fighting for Ireland,
Making things happen.   35
And he told me, Joe Ward,
Of how he had risen through the ranks
To Quartermaster, Commandant:
How every morning at parade
His volunteers would call back *Anseo*   40
And raise their hands
As their names occurred.

GLOSSARY

title *Anseo*: the Irish word for 'present', in answer to a roll call

2 *Collegelands*: an area in Co. Armagh near where the poet was brought up

9 *ledger*: register, roll

10 *Joseph Mary Plunkett Ward*: the boy was clearly called after Joseph Mary Plunkett,
executed after the Rising of 1916

13 *droll*: amusing

14 *Ward-of-court*: a play on the phrase 'ward of court', to be in the care of the courts

22 *salley-rod*: a type of stick cut from the salley tree

24 *whittled down to a whip-lash*: pared down until it became like a whip

25 *lacquers*: varnishes

27 *wrought*: made

38 *Quartermaster*: a staff officer in the army (here, the IRA)

GUIDELINES

'Anseo' is from the volume *Why Brownlee Left* (1980). It was written when the
Northern Ireland conflict, known as 'The Troubles', seemed to have no solution.

Stanza One: Irish children have often used the Irish word 'Anseo', meaning
'present', during roll call at school, as the speaker and his classmates did at primary

school in Collegelands, Co. Armagh. One of the boys in the class, Joseph Mary Plunkett Ward, was often absent, a fact remarked on sarcastically by the teacher.

The boy's name is significant in the context of Irish history (see annotations above). As the poem is set in Northern Ireland it suggests that his parents' political views were those of the Irish Catholic Nationalists. The reasons why he was absent from school are not explained. Nor are we given any explanation why the 'Master' (schoolteacher) reacted as he did, with his rather feeble pun on the boy's last name.

Stanza Two: The speaker remembers how the teacher would send Joseph Mary Plunkett Ward out to cut a stick with which he would beat him. He describes in an unemotional way how the boy became so used to being beaten that he would arrive at school with the stick already cut. The sticks are described almost as if they were beautiful objects, 'Sanded and polished'. Even the boy himself seems immune to being punished. He has gone so far as to carve his own initials on the stick.

When you read these lines it is easy to gloss over the fact that corporal punishment was an accepted part of school life. Not only that, but to our modern minds it seems incredible that a child would be asked to prepare his own instrument of punishment, as he was. The speaker does not make any comment, underlining perhaps the fact that generations of children did not question the treatment they sometimes got at school.

Stanza Three: These lines suggest that his treatment at school had a profound effect on Joe Ward's later career. We see him as an adult, now a member of the Irish Republican Army, involved in the Northern Ireland conflict known as 'The Troubles'. It is clear that he is now in a position of power over others, as the teacher had once been over him. Ironically, he calls the roll in exactly the same way as the master had in school, so that the volunteers must answer '*Anseo*'.

THE THEME OF THE POEM

The poet/speaker makes no direct comment on Joe Ward (as he is now known) or his situation. The connection is clear, though, between the boy's treatment at school and his later life of violence. His experience of being brutalised by the schoolteacher has made him insensitive to the pain of others or the damage his actions may cause. Perhaps this is one of the themes of the poem: what happens to us in childhood affects the way we live later on and what we do. Ironically, though, Joe Ward seems unaware of this. Is this the worst irony of all?

QUESTIONS

1 What impression of primary school life does this poem give us?

2 What aspect of the story do you find most disturbing? Give reasons for your view.

3 Why do you think the poet describes the hazel-wand in such detail in the second stanza?

4 Do you think there is a connection between Joe Ward's early experiences at school and his activities in the IRA? Or is there a more complex reason for his activities? Might it have any connection with his personal circumstances, including the name given to him by his parents? Look again at the first stanza.

5 Which of these words would come closest to describing the tone of the poem, in your opinion: angry, disappointed, bitter, disgusted, detached? Refer to the poem in support of your views.

6 What, in your opinion, is the main point the poem makes? Do you agree with it?

7 Imagine you are one of Joe Ward's 'Volunteers'. Write a short account of the life you lead and say what you think of your leader.

RICHARD MURPHY

B. 1927

BIOGRAPHY

Richard Murphy was born in Galway. His father, Sir William Lindsay Murphy, was in the British Colonial Service, and Murphy spent his childhood in Ceylon and the Bahamas. He attended Oxford and the Sorbonne in Paris. He lived and worked in Crete before returning to Ireland in the early 1960s. He set up home on Inisbofin, making his living from an old sailing boat, which he restored. His 1963 collection, *Sailing to an Island*, won wide acclaim.

In 1985, Murphy's book, *The Price of Stone*, charted his colourful life through the houses and buildings he'd known. The book ranged over his colonial childhood, his English education and his life on a small island. His 1968 book on the Battle of Aughrim is of interest for many reasons, not least because his ancestors fought on both sides.

Murphy's work has always been highly regarded both at home and abroad. Among his most famous literary friends were the poets Ted Hughes and Sylvia Plath. Their visit to him in September 1962, a short time before Plath's death, has received much attention from her biographers.

Richard Murphy now divides his time between Dublin and Durban in South Africa. His *Collected Poems* was published in 2000.

THE READING LESSON

Fourteen years old, learning the alphabet,
He finds letters harder to catch than hares
Without a greyhound. Can't I give him a dog
To track them down, or put them in a cage?
He's caught in a trap, until I let him go,   5
Pinioned by 'Don't you want to learn to read?'
'I'll be the same man whatever I do.'

He looks at a page as a mule balks at a gap
From which a goat may hobble out and bleat.
His eyes jink from a sentence like flushed snipe   10
Escaping shot. A sharp word, and he'll mooch
Back to his piebald mare and bantam cock.
Our purpose is as tricky to retrieve
As mercury from a smashed thermometer.

'I'll not read any more.' Should I give up?   15
His hands, long-fingered as a Celtic scribe's,
Will grow callous, gathering sticks or scrap;
Exploring pockets of the horny drunk
Loiterers at the fairs, giving them lice.
A neighbour chuckles. 'You can never tame   20
The wild duck: when his wings grow, he'll fly off.'

If books resembled roads, he'd quickly read:
But they're small farms to him, fenced by the page,
Ploughed into lines, with letters drilled like oats:
A field of tasks he'll always be outside.   25
If words were bank notes, he would filch a wad;
If they were pheasants, they'd be in his pot
For breakfast, or if wrens he'd make them king.

8 *balks*: hesitates, refuses to go on

10 *jink*: dodge or move away

11 *mooch*: move in a half-hearted way

16 *scribe*: a person, usually a monk, who made copies of books. The Book of Kells was made by scribes

16–17 *a Celtic scribe's…sticks or scraps*: a remarkable feature of the poem is the way in which sounds are repeated and echoed across lines and stanzas, as in the tradition of poetry written in Irish

17 *callous*: hardened and thick-skinned

26 *filch*: steal, pilfer

GUIDELINES

The speaker of the poem describes giving a reading lesson to a 14 year-old boy. The poem uses a series of colourful images to suggest the boy's difficulty in mastering letters and words. The images are drawn from the boy's world.

The first line establishes the dramatic situation. The lesson is for a boy, who is almost a man in the Traveller culture to which he belongs, but who has not yet learned to read. The first line also establishes the style of the poem. It is written in lines of ten syllables, the traditional line length for poets writing in English, going back to the time of Shakespeare. However, the poem imitates some of the sound patterns of poetry written in Irish, thereby combining both an Irish and an English tradition of poetry.

In lines 2 and 3, the narrator introduces the first of many comparisons that describe what the boy cannot do by drawing attention to the things he can do. The boy feels trapped in the reading lesson. However, for the teacher, reading is a form of freedom. The final line of the first stanza, 'I'll be the same man whatever I do', illustrates the boy's pride, defiance and, perhaps, his vulnerability.

In the second stanza the comparison of the boy to a mule suggests the boy's awkward, stubborn, possibly belligerent attitude to the task of learning to read. The narrator continues to describe the boy's reaction to reading with images taken from the boy's world in which animals play a large part.

The reference to the scribe in Stanza Three is a reminder that the Travellers are inheritors of the Celtic tradition. Perhaps it suggests that the loss of reading and writing is a loss of the boy's birthright? The comment of the neighbour, 'You can never tame / The wild duck: when his wings grow, he'll fly off,' raises the question of whether the teacher is trying to turn the boy into something that he is not. However, the motivation of the teacher can be interpreted as a desire to save the boy from the rough, dirty life that lies ahead of him.

There is a change of tone in the final stanza. The teacher seems to have abandoned his or her efforts to teach the boy. The stanza is composed of a series of 'If only' statements which express regret at the failure to help the boy to read while speaking affectionately of him. The final image concludes the poem on a note of celebration and flight.

QUESTIONS

1 In the first stanza the speaker compares the boy's difficulty in reading to catching hares without a greyhound. In the context of the poem, is this a good image?

2 What, do you think, is the tone of the boy's remark, 'I'll be the same man whatever I do.' What does this line reveal to us about the boy?

3 What comparisons (similes) are used in Stanza Two to describe the way the boy looks at the page? What do they tell us about the boy?

4 a) What makes the job of teaching the boy so 'tricky'?
   b) What is the neighbour's attitude to the reading lesson (lines 20–21)?

5 What future does the speaker foresee for the boy (lines 16–19)?

6 'A field of tasks he'll always be outside' (line 25). The last stanza tells us much about the boy's world and way of life. Write a short piece describing this life, incorporating all the information given in the stanza.

7 Select three words, phrases or images that you like most in the poem. Explain your choice.

8 Take a stanza and count the number of syllables in each line. Examine the rhymes/half rhymes used by the poet. Look at any two lines and comment on the sounds in the lines and their effect.

9 'Should I give up?' (line 15). By the end of the poem, do you think the teacher has given up? Explain your answer.

10 It has been said that in his poetry Richard Murphy often celebrates people who are outsiders. Is the boy in this poem an outsider? Explain your answer.

SHARON OLDS

B. 1942

BIOGRAPHY

Sharon Olds was born in 1942 in San Francisco. She was educated at Stanford University and Columbia University. Her first book of poems, *Satan Says* (1980), received the San Francisco Poetry Center Award, while her second book, *The Dead and the Living* (1983) was the winner of the National Book Critics' Circle Award. Her other poetry collections include *The Gold Cell*, *The Father*, *The Wellspring* and *Blood, Tin, Straw*.

Sharon Olds has been writer-in-residence at a number of academic institutions in the USA. In recent years she has taught poetry workshops in the Graduate Program in Creative Writing at New York University and in the NYU workshop at Goldwater Hospital for the severely disabled in New York. She was appointed New York State Poet for 1998–2000.

LOOKING AT THEM ASLEEP

When I come home late at night and go in to kiss the children,
I see my girl with her arm curled around her head,
her face deep in unconsciousness—so
deeply centered she is in her dark self,
her mouth slightly puffed like one sated but   5
slightly pouted like one who hasn't had enough,
her eyes so closed you would think they have rolled the
iris around to face the back of her head,
the eyeball marble-naked under that
thick satisfied desiring lid,   10
she lies on her back in abandon and sealed completion,
and the son in his room, oh the son he is sideways in his bed,
one knee up as if he is climbing
sharp stairs up into the night,
and under his thin quivering eyelids you   15
know his eyes are wide open and
staring and glazed, the blue in them so
anxious and crystally in all this darkness, and his
mouth is open, he is breathing hard from the climb
and panting a bit, his brow is crumpled   20
and pale, his long fingers curved,
his hand open, and in the center of each hand
the dry dirty boyish palm
resting like a cookie. I look at him in his
quest, the thin muscles of his arms   25
passionate and tense, I look at her with her
face like the face of a snake who has swallowed a deer,
content, content—and I know if I wake her she'll
smile and turn her face toward me though
half asleep and open her eyes and I   30
know if I wake him he'll jerk and say Don't and sit
up and stare about him in blue
unrecognition, oh my Lord how I
know these two. When love comes to me and says
What do you know, I say This girl, this boy.   35

5 *sated*: fully satisfied

6 *pouted*: pushed forward in an attitude of sulkiness. Can also indicate seductiveness. Some of the language used to describe the girl has erotic connotations

8 *iris*: the round, coloured part of the eye

15 *quivering eyelids*: trembling. The movement of the eyelids is said to indicate the state of dreaming

20 *crumpled*: wrinkled

25 *quest*: an adventure, a journey, a search, especially that of a knight

GUIDELINES

In the poem the speaker describes her sleeping children and the feelings which she experiences as she looks at them asleep. Her daughter's sleep is more peaceful than her son's. She sleeps in a way that suggests a deep contentment. In her daughter's mouth and lips the speaker sees something of the girl's personality – someone who is satisfied even as she desires a little more.

In comparison to his sister, the boy's sleep is agitated. The speaker imagines him involved in some dream activity, a quest that involves physical effort and exertion. In his furrowed brow she reads tension and anxiety.

The speaker tells us that she knows how each of her children would react if she woke them. Her girl would smile at her but her boy would look at her without recognition, still involved in the world of his sleeping. And looking at her sleeping children, the speaker is overcome with a sense of her love for them and her knowledge of them.

The poem is rich in sounds and sound echoes and composed in carefully-crafted phrases. The language used to describe the girl's sleeping suggests sleep as the completion or end of activity ('sated', 'satisfied', 'sealed'), while the language used to describe the boy's sleep suggests endless activity ('climbing', 'quivering', 'panting').

There is an interesting tension in the poem between the idea of a parent's knowledge of his/her children and the dream world of these children to which the parent has no access. Examine, for example, the language used to describe the girl's sleep. She is 'deep in unconsciousness'; she is 'deeply centered in her dark self'. Her eyes are 'so closed' that the speaker imagines the iris rolled around to the back of the head. As the speaker looks at the girl she lies in 'sealed completion'. What these phrases suggest is the extent to which the child is in another place, far from the consciousness of the parent who observes her, so the claim to knowledge, made at the end of the poem, may be less strong than a claim to love.

QUESTIONS

1 The poem has no rhyme scheme and is written in lines of irregular length. What, in your opinion, are the poetic qualities it possesses?

2 '… so / deeply centered she is in her dark self …'. What do you think is the meaning of this line? Is the dark self something which can be known by others?

3 The speaker refers to 'my girl' and 'the son'. Is this a significant difference? Is it indicative a difference in the speaker's attitude to her daughter and to her son elsewhere in the poem?

4 Where, do you think, is the language of the poem most affectionate in relation to the children?

5 Describe difference between the girl's sleep and the boy's sleep. In the case of each, select two phrases that you think are particularly effective in describing their manner of sleep.

6 'On the evidence of this poem, the girl will lead a happier life than the boy.' Give your view of this statement.

7 What age do you think the children are in the poem? If you were one of the children who inspired the poem, how would you react to being described in this way? Explain your answer.

8 'The poem is a statement of a parent's love and loyalty.'
'The poem is an exercise in betrayal and exploitation.'
Give your view of these contrasting assessments of the poem.

9 'The speaker of the poem may love her children but the poem demonstrates that however much we love someone they remain a mystery to us.' Give your response to this statement.

10 Sharon Olds has said she wants to be accurate about thoughts and feelings in her poetry. In your opinion does she succeed in 'Looking at Them Asleep'?

11 Family life, parenthood, death and erotic love are the subjects of Sharon Olds' poetry. Do you think 'Looking at Them Asleep' contains elements of all four?

CHRISTINA ROSSETTI

1830–1894

BIOGRAPHY

Christina Rossetti was a member of one of the most famous families in Victorian England. Her father was the poet Gabriele Rossetti (1783–1854), professor of Italian at King's College from 1831. All the four children in the family became writers. Her brother, Dante Gabriel, also gained fame as a painter. Christina was educated at home by her mother, Frances Polidori, an intelligent woman, who was a devout Anglican. Christina shared her parents' interest in literature and was portrayed in the paintings and drawings of her brother and his friends. Based on the sketches made by her brother the young Christina was an attractive, even beautiful, woman.

When Gabriele Rossetti's failing health and eyesight forced him into retirement in 1853, Christina and her mother attempted to support the family by starting a day school, but had to give it up after a year or so. Like her mother, Christina was a devout Anglican and rejected two offers of marriage because of religious differences. Except for two brief visits abroad, she lived with her mother all her life.

After a serious illness in 1874, and recurrent bouts of Graves' disease, a disorder of the thyroid which altered her appearance, she rarely went outside her home. However, her circle of friends included some of the most important writers and artists of the day, including Whistler, Swinburne and Charles Dodgson (Lewis Carroll). Christina's religious feelings influenced how she led her life. For example, she gave up playing chess because she found she enjoyed winning too much!

She felt keenly the death of her beloved brother, Dante, in 1882 and, although she survived him by twelve years, she lived quietly, beset by bouts of ill health. In the weeks preceding her death, she disturbed her neighbours each night with her terrible screams of agony. Christina Rossetti died on December 29, 1894.

Christina Rossetti was composing stories and poems from before she could write, dictating her compositions to her mother. Her first collection of poetry was published in 1862, and was widely praised. It established her as a significant and distinctive voice in Victorian poetry. Several books followed: love poems and religious verse for adults, poetry and short stories for children. She wrote the words for the Christmas carol 'In the bleak midwinter' and she wrote pamphlets for the Society for Promoting Christian Knowledge. At its best, Christina Rossetti's poetry is remarkably clear and direct and her handling of form is masterful. Her recurrent themes are unhappy love, death and renunciation.

'REMEMBER ME WHEN I AM GONE AWAY'

Remember me when I am gone away,
Gone far away into the silent land;
When you can no more hold me by the hand,
Nor I half turn to go yet turning stay.
Remember me when no more day by day   5
You tell me of our future that you planned:
Only remember me; you understand
It will be late to counsel then or pray.
Yet if you should forget me for a while
And afterwards remember, do not grieve: 10
For if the darkness and corruption leave
A vestige of the thoughts that once I had,
Better by far you should forget and smile
Than that you should remember and be sad.

GLOSSARY

2 *the silent land*: usually taken as a metaphor for death. In the context of the poem as a whole, you might consider other possible meanings of the phrase

8 *counsel*: to give advice; to advise on matters of morality especially in relation to poverty, chastity and obedience

11 *the darkness and corruption*: usually interpreted as death. The speaker is referring to the darkness of her own death and the corruption of her body. However, if the terms 'darkness' and 'corruption' refer to the person she is addressing, then an entirely different reading emerges

12 *A vestige*: a trace; a hint; a slight amount of something that was once plentiful

GUIDELINES

'Remember me' was written in 1849 when Rossetti was just 19 years old. In the poem, a woman addresses her beloved before her death and urges him to remember her, or to forget her, if remembering makes him sad.

It is unwise to identify the speaker in the poem with the poet. This, in common with other poems that Rossetti wrote at this time, is a dramatic monologue. The most notable feature of the poem is the ambivalence which the speaker reveals towards the person she addresses. For some readers, the poem is marked by an unexpected irony and a note of anger. The speaker may well welcome death as a release from the lover's grasp and insensitivity, from the future that *he* planned for them both. This reading is dependent upon the tone in which certain key lines and phrases are read. Lines 3–4, 6, 8 and 11 are all open to different interpretations.

The dramatic situation (the speaker addressing her beloved before her death) is reminiscent of the poetry of Emily Dickinson. In 'After Death', another poem which Rossetti wrote in 1849, the speaker lies on a bed with a shroud on her face, observing the surroundings before her burial. It has a similar ambivalent quality to 'Remember me': 'He did not love me living; but once dead / He pitied me; and very sweet it is / To know he still is warm tho' I am cold.'

'Remember me' has little of the passionate declarations of love associated with Victorian love poetry. Instead it has a clarity and directness, an unsentimental, clear-eyed detachment that suggests that, for the speaker, her feelings of love have cooled, if not disappeared. Some traditional views of Rossetti have described her poetry as sincere and superficial. Recent criticism by feminist scholars suggest that Rossetti's poetry is far more subtle in its effects and intentions than has been understood or appreciated. 'Remember me', for example, is based on a paradox. The poem begins with an invitation to remember and concludes with an exhortation to forget!

'Remember me' is remarkable for the ease with which Rossetti rhymes and makes the thought fit the sonnet shape, while maintaining a dramatic voice, which gives the poem a contemporary feel.

Virigina Woolf's estimation of Christina Rossetti as a poet may help in reading 'Remember me':

You were not a pure saint by any means. You pulled legs; you tweaked noses. You were at war with all humbug and pretense. Modest as you were, still you were drastic, sure of your gift, convinced of your vision ... in a word, you were an artist.

The speaker of the poem may well share Rossetti's impatience with pretence and though she speaks simply and directly, there is a strength and confidence in her voice.

QUESTIONS

1 What is the speaker of the poem asking the 'you' to do after her death?

2 How does the speaker feel about the 'you' of the poem? What lines best reveal her feelings?

3 'It will be late to counsel then or pray.' What impression of the 'you' do you form from this line? Explain your answer. Where else do you think the character of the 'you' is suggested?

4 Describe a dramatic situation which you think fits the poem. Give a description of the speaker and the 'you' to whom she addresses her words.

5 Prepare two readings of the poem which offer contrasting views of the relationship between the speaker of the poem and the 'you'.

6 The poem has a number of opposites or contrasts. Identify these and comment on them.

7 What is your impression of the speaker of the poem? Support the points you make by quotation form the poem.

8 Is 'Remember me' a well-made poem? Support the points you make by quotation from the poem.

9 Do you like the poem? Explain your answer.

SIEGFRIED SASSOON

1886–1967

BIOGRAPHY

Sassoon was a member of a distinguished Jewish family which made its mark in English politics and finance. He was brought up as an English country gentleman, educated at a leading English grammar school and at Cambridge, from where he was sent down without taking a degree. Before the First World War he enjoyed tennis, foxhunting and writing poetry. When war broke out he enlisted and was posted to France as a junior officer. He displayed uncommon gallantry, was twice wounded and won the Military Cross. He was invalided home in 1917, and in protest against the inhumanity of war, announced publicly that he would not serve again. For this courageous stand he expected to be court-martialled, but was sent to a sanatorium instead. He went back to France, was again wounded, and ended the war as a Captain. In 1928, he published anonymously his prose classic, *Memoirs of a Fox-Hunting Man*, which provides a stimulating account of his war experiences. His war poems are often savagely satirical, exposing the sickening reality of war in the trenches. His main targets are complacent politicians and senior officers, whose incompetence and cynicism consigned millions of common soldiers to a living death. Although Sassoon wrote poetry after the war, his characteristic achievement belongs to the wartime period.

ON PASSING THE NEW MENIN GATE

Who will remember, passing through this Gate,
The unheroic Dead who fed the guns?
Who shall absolve the foulness of their fate—
Those doomed, conscripted, unvictorious ones?
Crudely renewed, the Salient holds its own.   5
Paid are its dim defenders by this pomp;
Paid, with a pile of peace-complacent stone,
The armies that endured that sullen swamp.

Here was the world's worst wound. And here with pride
"Their name liveth forever," the Gateway claims.   10
Was ever an immolation so belied
As these intolerably nameless names?
Well might the Dead that struggled in the slime
Rise and deride this sepulchre of crime.

GLOSSARY

title and line 1 *Gate*: the Menin Gate, in Flanders, Belgium, is an impressive memorial to massive numbers of British soldiers killed during the third battle of Ypres. This battle began on 31 July 1917, and lasted three months. The new Menin Gate was unveiled in 1927

2 *unheroic Dead*: British political and military leaders hailed the soldiers who died in battle as heroes. Sassoon's point is that war is far from being heroic. The battles in which the soldiers perished were sordid, bloody affairs, fought in muddy fields and filthy trenches

3 *absolve*: grant forgiveness for

5 *crudely renewed*: part of the memorial consisted of a crude reconstruction of part of the battlefield

5 *the Salient holds its own*: a Salient is a piece of land that juts out to form an angle. Here it is an outward bulge in a military line, which British troops had to defend with their lives. After death they are buried within the Salient, and so it can be said to hold its own

6 *dim defenders*: the defenders are 'dim' because they are obscure, because they are covered by the earth, and perhaps because they were stupid enough to fight for ruthless leaders

7 *peace-complacent stone*: the only reward the soldiers get is a stone-built monument erected by complacent (self-satisfied) survivors

8 *swamp*: the soldiers fought in mud and slime

9 *the world's worst wound*: the most violent assault on civilisation

11 *was ever an immolation so belied*: the poet wonders whether such human sacrifice was ever so casually treated

11 *immolation*: sacrificial slaughter

12 *intolerably nameless names*: the monument does not name any of the individuals who were sacrificed in the battle. The poet finds it intolerable that so many who died needlessly are now forgotten

13-14 *Well might ... crime*: no one could blame the dead soldiers if they rose from their graves to condemn this monument to their slaughter, which was a crime committed against them by those who led them into battle. Sassoon may have in mind Christ's reference to hypocrites as 'whited sepulchres'

GUIDELINES

The poem deals with what Sassoon thinks of as a futile, hypocritical attempt to commemorate the sacrifice of hundreds of thousands of British and Irish soldiers in and around Ypres in 1917. The three battles of Ypres, which formed part of the British offensive in Flanders, resulted in 324,000 British casualties. German casualties amounted to 202,000. Sassoon's poem focuses particularly on the third of these battles, popularly known as the Battle of Passchendaele, and described at the time by the British Prime Minister, Lloyd George, as the battle of the mud. The torrential rains of August 1917 turned the battlefield into a sea of mud. Soldiers struggled to advance up to their waists in slime. The British advanced four miles, and they evacuated the Salient when the Germans took the offensive in March 1918. The British tanks and artillery were useless in the mud of Flanders.

To understand this poem, one must take account of Sassoon's background and his experience of war. He served as an infantry officer in the First World War. Like many young fighting men of his generation, he had been taught by those who organised and backed the war to regard it as noble and heroic enterprise waged for a good cause. The horrible reality of war for those who fought shocked and repelled him, and inspired a series of bitter, often savage, anti-war poems. He was twice wounded seriously while serving in France. While still in the army, he published two collections of anti-war poetry, *The Old Huntsman* (1917) and *Counterattack* (1918). At the same time, he publicly asserted his pacifism. The authorities were fearful that the anti-war publicity generated by Sassoon, a war-hero who had been awarded the Military Cross for gallantry, might undermine the war-effort. His reluctance to fight was attributed to shell-shock, and he was confined to a sanitorium.

On Passing the New Menin Gate is an effective poem of protest. It is based on an ironic contrast between the glorification of war by those who do not have to take part in it, and the reality of war as this is experienced by the unfortunate volunteers and conscripts, many of whom are doomed to die anonymously. The main emphasis of the poem is on the real meaning of war for those who are forced to take part in it. The fate of hundreds of young conscripts is to be slaughtered in the mud. Their reward is a stone monument dominating a landscape of mass graves ('these intolerably nameless names').

Those responsible for erecting the monument want to suggest that the dead soldiers it honours (or dishonours as Sassoon believes) sacrificed their lives for a great ideal. Hence the inscription on the gateway, 'their name liveth forever'. But, as Sassoon argues in the poem, this inscription tells a lie. Their names do not live forever, because they are a massive dead collection of 'nameless names'. In its most fundamental aspect, war is a matter of leaders, many of them incompetent, converting young men into cannon-fodder, into 'the unheroic Dead who fed the guns'. The New Menin Gate is a monument not to the memory of heroes, but to the criminal folly of political and military leaders who sent young men to their deaths. This is why Sassoon refers to the memorial as 'this sepulchre of crime', and why he is able to suggest that if the soldiers could rise from the dead and speak, they would express their contempt for the 'pile of peace-complacent stone' erected in their memory.

QUESTIONS

1 Irony involves a contrast between what is said and what is meant, between the gesture and the reality. Examine some instances of irony in the poem.
2 Discuss the tone of the poem.
3 How does Sassoon compare the reward given to the soldiers with what they earned through their suffering?
4 The poem has three major questions. What answers does the poet expect us to give to these questions?
5 Is this poem an absolute condemnation of war?
6 Write your own response to the poem. Has it a meaning for our time?

WILLIAM SHAKESPEARE

1564–1616

BIOGRAPHY

One of Shakespeare's eighteenth-century editors, George Steevens, claimed that:

> all that we know of Shakespeare is that he was born at Stratford-on-Avon;
> married and had children there; went to London, where he commenced [as an]
> actor, and wrote plays and poems; returned to Stratford, made his will, and died.

Even in the eighteenth century, more of Shakespeare's life story was known than Steevens acknowledged, but there are still very large gaps indeed in his biography, in spite of centuries of patient and diligent scholarly effort.

Much of what passes for Shakespeare's biography is, in fact, largely a tissue of documentary records, mainly of trivial facts; traditions, legends and anecdotes, often of doubtful value; references to Shakespeare in the works of his contemporaries and, most unsatisfactory of all, assumptions based on passages in the plays and sonnets. In the absence of a substantial volume of undisputed facts, biographers are often forced to fall back on 'perhaps', 'it is probable', 'it is likely', 'it is almost certain', and so on.

There are, however, lives of Shakespeare that run to several hundred pages. It is known that Shakespeare's father, John, came into Stratford from a neighbouring farm in the 1550s, practised a variety of trades, achieved prosperity, owned property and became a leading citizen of the town, which at that time had a population of about one thousand. Shakespeare was christened at the parish church at Stratford on 26 April, 1564. It can be taken for granted that he attended the local grammar school, only half a mile from his home, until he was sixteen. In Shakespeare's day, grammar school education was focused almost exclusively on the study of the Latin language and its literature; students also learned rhetoric, which is the art of public speaking. In 1582, Shakespeare married Anne Hathaway. She was twenty-six; he was eighteen. They had three children. Their only son, Hamnet, died in 1596, aged eleven. No record of Anne Hathaway exists between the baptism of her children and the drafting of her husband's will in 1616, the year of his death, when he left her his second-best bed.

By the 1590s, Shakespeare had become a rising dramatist. By 1595, he was a sharer in an acting company. Two years later, he was able to buy New Place, the second largest property in Stratford. Between 1590 and 1603 he spent most of his time in London, writing plays, arranging for their performance and occasionally acting in them. Of the twenty-six plays he wrote during this period, *Hamlet* (1601) is the most celebrated. Between 1603 and his death thirteen years later in 1616, Shakespeare wrote his four other tragic masterpieces: *Othello* (1604), *King Lear* (1606), *Macbeth* (1606) and *Anthony and Cleopatra* (1607). The sonnets were published in 1609, but were almost certainly written over a decade before. His great plays were all first performed at the Globe theatre in London, in which he was a shareholder.

Shakespeare combined supreme creative ability with practical instincts and an impressive business sense. Records from the last decade of his life show him acquiring considerable property in and around his place of birth, and shrewdly protecting his legal interests there. In addition to houses, he purchased over one hundred acres of farmland and an interest in tithes which guaranteed a substantial income. When debts owing to him remained unpaid, he was quick to sue the defaulters, even in petty cases. Three years before he died, he bought a house in London as an investment.

Shakespeare appears to have taken far less interest in the fate of his writings than in his property and investment income. He did not oversee the publication of the editions of his plays published during his lifetime. These are carelessly printed and contain many errors. The sonnets were published without his supervision or consent. At his death, much of his most celebrated work was still in manuscript form, and remained so until his friends and colleagues John Heminges and Henry Condell published his complete plays in 1623 in an edition now known as the *First Folio*. This substantial volume contains all the plays now attributed to Shakespeare, except *Pericles*.

FEAR NO MORE THE HEAT O' TH' SUN

Guiderius	Fear no more the heat o' th' sun,	
	Nor the furious winter's rages,	
	Thou thy worldly task has done,	
	Home art gone and ta'en thy wages.	
	Golden lads and girls all must,	5
	As chimney-sweepers, come to dust.	
Arviragus	Fear no more the frown o' th' great,	
	Thou art past the tyrant's stroke,	
	Care no more to clothe and eat,	
	To thee the reed is as the oak:	10
	The sceptre, learning, physic, must	
	All follow this and come to dust.	
Gui.	Fear no more the lightening-flash.	
Arv.	Nor th' all-dreaded thunder-stone.	
Gui.	Fear not slander, censure rash.	15
Arv.	Thou hast finish'd joy and moan.	
Both.	All lovers young, all lovers must	
	Consign to thee and come to dust.	
Gui.	No exorciser harm thee!	
Arv.	Nor no witchcraft charm thee!	20
Gui.	Ghost unlaid forbear thee!	
Arv.	Nothing ill come near thee!	
Both.	Quiet consummation have,	
	And renowned be thy grave!	

2 *rages*: storms

8 *tyrant's stroke*: the power of a wicked, unjust dictatorial ruler to inflict the severest punishment, even death

11 *sceptre*: the king's staff of office, here standing for the king himself

learning: the scholar

physic: medicine, here referring to the doctor

14 *thunder-stone*: a meteorite, a mass of solid matter whose fall from the sky is accompanied by a sound like thunder

15 *slander*: a false, malicious statement intended to injure someone's reputation

censure rash: blame or condemnation without sufficient evidence

16 *moan*: complaint, lament

18 *Consign to thee*: agree to enlist or sign up in the ranks of death

19 *exorciser*: a person capable of conjuring up spirits

21 *Ghost … thee*: may you be left alone by spirits not yet banished or laid to rest

22 *ill*: evil

23 *consummation*: death

24 *renowned*: made famous, honoured

GUIDELINES

This song is taken from *Cymbeline*, a late play by Shakespeare. Cymbeline is the King of Britain. His two sons, Guiderius and Arviragus, are stolen from him and brought up in Wales by one of his nobles whom he has wronged. His daughter Imogen remains at his court, falls in love with Posthumus, the son of one of his warriors, and marries him. When Imogen's mother dies, Cymbeline marries a wicked widow with a brutal, foolish son named Cloten. The new queen decides that Cloten should marry Imogen. When it is discovered that Imogen has married Posthumus, the latter is banished. A wicked character named Iachimo convinces Posthumus that Imogen has been unfaithful to him in his absence. Mad with rage, Posthumus instructs his servant Pisanio to take Imogen to Wales and kill her. Moved by Imogen's goodness and innocence, Pisanio spares her, giving her a medicinal drug to comfort her. This drug turns out to be a powerful sleeping draught. Imogen puts on boy's clothes, and finds the cave where her unknown brothers, Guiderius and Arviragus, live. Imogen introduces herself to them as Fidele, a young man bound for Milford Haven. They show great kindness to their new acquaintance. When Imogen takes the drug given to her by Pisanio, she falls into a death-like sleep. Guiderius and Arviragus, thinking her dead, cover her with flowers and sing this lament.

The comments of Guiderius and Arviragus on the supposedly dead Fidele, whom they do not recognise as their sister, provide a moving context for the lament. Guiderius hopes that Fidele/Imogen may not, after all, be dead. He says (in Act 4, Scene 2, lines 216–19):

> *Why, he but sleeps:*
> *If he be gone he'll make his grave a bed.*
> *With female fairies will his tomb be haunted*
> *And worms will not come to thee.*

The events of the play unfold to make the beautiful lament of Imogen's brothers premature. *Cymbeline* is a romance, not a tragedy. The good characters are finally rewarded and the evil Cloten is decapitated. Imogen forgives her deceived and repentant husband, Posthumus. Cymbeline has his sons restored to him and all ends in happiness and peace.

The impulse behind this lament (or dirge) is to draw whatever consolation is possible from death, so that those who are left behind may not succumb to absolute despair. The varieties of consolation to be drawn from the event are expressed in the first four lines of each of the first three stanzas. In each of these groups of lines, the main idea is that the dead person is beyond the reach of misery, danger or misfortune, and is thus to be envied. The multiple dangers from which the dead are free include bad weather, the displeasure of great people, the danger to life posed by tyrants, the struggle to provide for bodily needs, the threat of sudden disaster, slander and criticism. This catalogue of mortal ills will no longer have meaning to the dead, thus inspiring the thought that death is to be welcomed rather than feared.

The dirge balances against this idea of welcome death another commonplace: that death is inevitable. This is expressed in the final two lines of the first three stanzas. The idea that death comes to all human beings, whatever their rank, is driven home with sad directness by the rhyming of 'dust' and 'must' at the end of each of the three stanzas. The final six lines are a series of charms and spells, invoking protection for the departed spirit from evil influences.

LANGUAGE

Much of the power and interest of the song derives from the way in which the dominant ideas are brought to life in terms of concrete illustrations. Instead of generalising about the threats posed to everyday mortals by those in power,

Shakespeare suggests their menace in 'the *frown* o' the great' and 'the tyrant's *stroke*'. People and their offices are identified by reference to significant items associated with them: kings, learned men and doctors become 'sceptre, learning, physic'. The final two lines of the first stanza are particularly impressive: 'Golden lads and girls all must / As chimney-sweepers, come to dust'. The essential contrast here is between privileged boys and girls endowed with both beauty and wealth ('golden' suggests both the glow of youth and beauty and the possession of wealth and privilege) and those who, like chimney-sweeps, are neither beautiful nor rich. There is a disturbing pun on 'dust' in line 6. By virtue of their trade, chimney-sweepers, who were boys, necessarily 'came to dust', but the real purpose of the lines is to remind us that the most beautiful and prosperous youths and maidens have no better defence against becoming dust in the grave than have the poor dusty chimney-sweeps.

QUESTIONS

1 Two ways of looking at death are considered in this song. Describe them.
2 Examine the way in which the images in this song help to convey contrasting attitudes to death.
3 Discuss the relationship between general statements and the way in which these are brought home to the imagination by Shakespeare.
4 Consider the song as an illustration of Shakespeare's fondness for wordplay.
5 Is this an entirely sad poem?

PERCY BYSSHE SHELLEY

1792–1822

BIOGRAPHY

Shelley was born in Sussex. He had a privileged childhood. From his earliest years he was rebellious, showing little respect for authority or convention. At Eton he was known as 'mad Shelley' and the 'Eton Atheist'. At Oxford he was influenced by radical authors and dedicated himself to a campaign against Christianity. He was the joint author of a pamphlet called *The Necessity of Atheism* and was expelled from Oxford for refusing to discuss its contents with the university authorities. He eloped to Scotland with the sixteen-year-old Harriet Westbrook, whose unhappiness at school drove him to rescue her. Shelley regarded schools as centres of oppression.

Shelley's lifelong vocation was to emancipate the human spirit from the bondage of all kinds of authority and convention. In Dublin in 1812, he distributed tracts calling for Catholic emancipation from the Penal Laws and for the repeal of the Act of Union. Back in England, he attacked Christianity and defended the right of free speech. In 'Queen Mab', a poem which appeared in 1813, he denounced kings and priests as agents of divine tyranny. He soon tired of his young wife and formed an attachment to Mary Wollstonecraft, the sixteen-year-old daughter of the radical author William Godwin, who disapproved of marriage as a constraint on human liberty. In 1816, when Harriet drowned herself, Shelley immediately married Mary, whose principal claim to fame was to rest on her authorship of *Frankenstein* (1818).

In 1818, Shelley left England for Italy, where he spent the rest of his life. There he composed all the poetry for which he is now remembered: 'Ode to the West Wind', 'To Liberty', 'The Masque of Anarchy' and some fine sonnets, including 'Ozymandias'.

In August 1822, Shelley was drowned at sea and his body was cremated. He never abandoned his radical impulses and remained an anarchist to the end. His political and religious views, together with his unconventional private life, have tended to obscure his achievements as a poet, which soon earned him a secure place, along with Wordsworth, Coleridge, Keats, Blake and Byron, among the great English Romantics.

OZYMANDIAS

I met a traveller form an antique land
Who said: Two vast and trunkless legs of stone
Stand in the desert … Near them, on the sand,
Half sunk, a shattered visage lies, whose frown,
And wrinkled lip, and sneer of cold command,   5
Tell that its sculptor well those passions read
Which yet survive, stamped on these lifeless things,
The hand that mocked them, and the heart that fed:
And on the pedestal these words appear:
'My name is Ozymandias, king of kings: 10
Look on my works, ye Mighty, and despair!'
Nothing beside remains. Round the decay
Of that colossal wreck, boundless and bare
The lone and level sands stretch far away.

GLOSSARY

title *Ozymandias*: The statue in the poem, which stands in the desert at Thebes in Egypt, is that of Rameses II. Rameses was given the name Ozymandias by a Greek historian

1 *antique land*: a country which boasted an ancient civilisation

4 *visage*: face

6–8 *Tell that its sculptor … fed*: the sculptor has expressed the passions of Ozymandias on the face of the statue. These passions, stamped on stone, still survive the hand of the sculptor and the king

8 *The hand that mocked them*: the hand is that of the sculptor. He has mockingly recorded the cruel passions of Ozymandias on the face of the statue

8 *the heart that fed*: the heart is that of Ozymandias. Passions, emotions and feelings were supposed to have their origin in the heart

11 *Look on my works, ye Mighty, and despair!*: when Ozymandias ordered this inscription, he must have hoped that even the mightiest kings would feel despair when they saw his achievements, since they could never hope to equal them. Now that these works have all but vanished, the inscription has a different meaning. Rulers and great men of the world looking at the pedestal now will feel despair that their best achievements will meet the same fate as those of Ozymandias

GUIDELINES

The setting of this poem is the Middle-Eastern desert. Shelley wrote it during a period when there was a growing interest throughout Europe in the antiquities of the Middle East, and particularly those of Egypt. The statue described in the poem is based on the colossal statue of the ancient Egyptian ruler Rameses II.

Many of Shelley's contemporaries were overwhelmed by the magnificence of Egyptian monuments, which were many times larger than life, and by the contemplation of the power and prestige enjoyed by kings of antiquity. Shelley, however, had a different view. He was an anarchist, opposed on principle to kingship and to all forms of tyranny, which he regarded as hostile to the welfare of the human race. This attitude helps to explain his attitude to the ruined statue described in the poem. For him, the contemplation of the wrecked statue of a once magnificent monarch is not an occasion for regret or pity. Instead, it is a source of gratification to him that even the mightiest tyrannies are doomed to decline and fall, the only memorial of their greatness being some large fragments of stone in a desert which has buried all the other evidence of the past.

SUBJECT MATTER

The speaker of the poem is recording the experience of a traveller who has been visiting a country in which the remains of an ancient civilisation are still to be found. The traveller has been particularly impressed by the sight of two enormous legs of stone, the only parts of a once great statue standing after thousands of years. The trunk of the statue is no longer to be seen. On the desert sand, half-buried, the traveller finds the enormous head of the statue. He is struck by the expression on its face. It is not a happy or a pleasant expression. The frown, the wrinkled lip and the sneer are those of a tyrant who was used to giving commands and having these commands obeyed. The face suggests a cold heart and a pitiless nature. It also suggests that the tyrant had a high sense of his own importance and that he felt contempt for those he ruled. The sculptor who made the statue was highly skilled. He could read the heart of the tyrant and understand the passions that this heart fed: the cruelty, the anger, the lust for power and authority. In showing these passions on the face of the statue, the sculptor was at the same time mocking them.

The tyrant's sense of his own importance is suggested by the inscription on the base of the statue. The tyrant boasts of being not merely a king, but 'king of kings'. The inscription invites the other great men who look at the statue, and at the other great works found throughout the tyrant's kingdom, to despair of ever achieving such magnificence. The tyrant would like everyone to see him as the envy of the world. Nothing, however, remains for anyone to envy. The once proud statue is a great ruin. The tyrant's kingdom, with all its magnificence, has vanished, buried under an endless stretch of desert. The words on the pedestal take on a new, disturbing meaning.

FORM OF THE POEM

The poem is a sonnet. Shelley makes a broad division between the first eight lines and the last six. This division is an important structural feature. In the first eight lines we are invited to imagine a desert scene at the centre of which are the remains of a great statue. The emphasis is on description. The final six lines suggest a reflection on what has gone before. Shelley uses them to draw a moral from what the traveller has seen. The emptiness of pomp and power are revealed. The boastful inscription is mocked by the passage of time as well as by the boundless desert. The moving description in the final lines encourages us to reflect that time does not distinguish between the great and the humble: the desert eventually covers all.

THEMES

Various connected themes may be traced in the sonnet. One prominent theme is the destructive power of time, also a common theme in Shakespeare's sonnets. In 'Ozymandias', time is seen to mock the greatest achievements and hopes of the world's most powerful men.

Another theme of the sonnet is the emptiness of power. The tyrant Ozymandias once lorded it over kings and made slaves of his subjects. He could boast of immense achievements. Now no trace remains of him or his achievements except a broken statue in the desert.

A third theme is a favourite one among poets – the immortality of art. Human life passes away, but civilisations are remembered mainly in their works of art. Here all that survives of an impressive ancient civilisation is a work of sculpture. Without the broken statue and its inscription, even the name of the great Ozymandias would be lost to memory. As it is, his cruel passions have been made immortal through the art of the sculptor.

IRONY

There is a fundamental irony in the poem. All irony involves some form of contrast. The great contrast of this poem is between the magnificent works which once proudly dominated the desert and the poor remains of those ruined pieces of sculpture which the traveller contemplates. A powerful kind of irony is centred on Ozymandias. One must assume that at the height of his power, thousands of years ago, he gave orders for the inscription on the pedestal: 'My name is Ozymandias, king of kings, / Look on my works, ye Mighty, and despair'. When the inscription was carved by the sculptor, it was intended to glorify Ozymandias. It was meant to convey to other rulers that they should despair of ever creating such mighty works as Ozymandias had. Now, thousands of years later, the inscription takes on a new, ironic meaning. If modern rulers read it, they will indeed despair, but their despair will not be caused by envy of Ozymandias. Instead, they will feel despair at the thought that even the works of the mightiest kings are doomed to meet the same fate as those meted out at the orders of Ozymandias.

There is irony in the notion that if Ozymandias could return to the scene of his former greatness, he would find a totally new meaning in the original inscription. He himself would be the one to feel despair rather than inspire it in others. Irony can be found in the following:

> Half sunk, a shattered visage lies, whose frown
> And wrinkled lip, and sneer of cold command,
> Tell that its sculptor well those passions read
> Which yet survive, stamped on thee lifeless things,
> The hand that mocked them, and the heart that fed.

The sculptor's hand once ironically mocked the king's passions by depicting them on the statue's face. The king's heart once fuelled the same passions. It is ironic that these passions have survived both sculptor and king.

LANGUAGE AND IMAGERY

The language of the sonnet is mainly descriptive, and impressive in the simplicity of its diction. Shelley is content to set a scene, describe the face of the statue and record the words of the inscription. He allows the imagination of the reader to do the rest. The most impressive piece of description is at the end: 'Round the decay / Of that colossal wreck, boundless and bare / The lone and level sands stretch far away'. Here the sounds of the words are a perfect echo of their meanings. The slow rhythms and broad vowels, especially in the final line, help to convey a remarkable impression of endless stretches of empty desert.

QUESTIONS

1 Discuss the use of contrast as a structural feature of 'Ozymandias'.
2 Describe the speaker's attitude to what he is recording in the poem. How is this attitude reflected in the tone of his comments?
3 Is it possible to feel pity for Ozymandias?
4 Consider the significance of the desert landscape as part of the meaning of the poem.
5 Discuss the sonnet as a meditation on the theme of time, the great enemy.

RICHARD WILBUR

B. 1921

BIOGRAPHY

Richard Wilbur was born in New York in 1921. He was educated at Amherst College and Harvard University. The son of a commercial artist, Wilbur was interested in painting in his youth, but he eventually chose to become a writer, possibly because of the strong literary influence of his maternal grandfather and great-grandfather, both of whom were editors. His writing career began after he had served in the US Army during the Second World War.

He has been a lecturer, professor of English and writer-in-residence at a number of universities in the USA, including Harvard, Wellesley College, Massachusetts and Smith College, Massachusetts. In 1961 he was the cultural exchange representative of the USA in the former Soviet Union. He has translated French classical plays, in particular those of Racine and Molière, which have been successfully produced in New York. He is also a distinguished critic. Wilbur has won many major literary awards, including the Pulitzer prize. In 1987–88 he was named as the United States' Poet Laureate. His *New and Collected Poems* was published in 1989.

THE PARDON

My dog lay dead five days without a grave
In the thick of summer, hid in a clump of pine
And a jungle of grass and honey-suckle vine.
I who had loved him while he kept alive
Went only close enough to where he was   5
To sniff the heavy honeysuckle-smell
Twined with another odor heavier still
And hear the flies' intolerable buzz.
Well, I was ten and very much afraid.
In my kind world the dead were out of range   10
And I could not forgive the sad or strange
In beast or man. My father took the spade
And buried him. Last night I saw the grass
Slowly divide (it was the same scene
But now it glowed a fierce and mortal green)   15
And saw the dog emerging. I confess
I felt afraid again, but still he came
In the carnal sun, clothed in a hymn of flies,
And death was breeding in his lively eyes.
I started in to cry and call his name,   20
Asking forgiveness of his tongueless head.
..I dreamt the past was never past redeeming:
But whether this was false or honest dreaming
I beg death's pardon now. And mourn the dead.

GUIDELINES

The poet remembers a childhood experience which he found traumatic, namely the death of his pet dog. He confesses to us that he left the dog unburied for five days during a hot summer. Clearly he feels sorry and guilty for this, even after all this time. In the poem he recaptures the scene in strong sensuous images that make us see, hear and smell the situation.

In the third stanza he comments on the event. As an adult now he knows that his failure to deal with the dog's death was due to childish innocence. Death had no place in his 'kind world'. He hints too at another emotion he felt at the time: anger at the dog for having died. He found it hard to 'forgive' him.

His father's burial of the dog might appear to have brought the experience to an end. But the poet reveals that it has haunted him ever since. Now an adult, he dreams of his dog in a similar situation and yet changed, as is the way in dreams. As in dreams, too, everything – colours, the dog himself – is exaggerated. His old fear returns.

This time, however, he overcomes his fear and begs the dog's pardon.

In the last three lines he suggests a possible interpretation of the dream. Mistakes may be put right; the past may be atoned for. Although the poet does not know exactly whether this is true – is it 'false' or 'honest' dreaming? – it is an essentially optimistic and comforting moment of insight, especially if applied to human relationships. What we can certainly do, the poem suggests, is express regret for the mistakes we have made, no matter how late it is.

QUESTIONS

1 Would you agree that the child's fear of his dead dog is very well portrayed in the poem?
2 Apart from fear, what other feelings does the child experience?
3 What sort of childhood did the speaker have, in your opinion?
4 Is the dream sequence convincing, in your opinion? Support your view with reference to the poem.
5 'I dream the past was never past redeeming.' Would you agree that this is the main idea or theme of the poem?
6 How does this poem make you feel? Give a reason for your answer.
7 Why did the poet choose the title 'The Pardon' for this poem? Refer to the poem in your answer.
8 You want to make a short film of this poem. Describe the sort of atmosphere you would like to create. And say what music, sound effects and images you would use.

READING
UNSEEN POETRY

Reading a poem is an activity in which your mind, your beliefs and your feelings are called into play. As you read, you work to create the poem's meaning from the words and images offered to you by the poet. And the process takes a little time, so be patient. However, the fact that poems are generally short – much shorter than most stories, for example – allows you to read and reread a poem many times over.

Begin with the title. What expectations does it set up in you? What does it remind you of? As you read a poem, jot down your responses. These jottings may take the form of words or phrases from the poem which you feel are important, although you may not be able to say why this is so. Write questions, teasing out the literal meaning of a word or a phrase. Write notes or commentaries as you go, expressing your understanding. Record your feelings. Record your resistance to, or your approval of, any aspect of the poem – its statements, the choice of words, the imagery, the tone, the values it expresses.

Jot down any association brought to mind by any element of the poem, such as a word. Note any ideas suggested by any part of a poem – a word, a phrase, an image, the rhythm or tone, or the title. Be alert to combinations of words and patterns of repetition. Look for those words or images that carry emotional or symbolic force. Try to understand their effect. Note down other poems which the unseen poem reminds you of. In this way, you create a territory in which the poem can be read and understood.

Don't feel that you have to supply all the answers asked of you by a poem. In a class situation, confer with your fellow students. Words and images will resonate in different ways for different people. Readers bring their own style, ideas and experiences to every encounter with a poem. Sharing ideas and adopting a collaborative approach to the reading of a new poem will open out the poem's possibilities beyond what you, or any individual, will achieve alone.

Poems frequently work by way of hints, suggestions or associations. The unstated may be as important as the stated. Learn to live with ambiguity. Learn to enjoy the uncertainty of poetry. Don't be impatient if a poem doesn't 'make sense' to you. Most readers interpret and work on poems with more success than they know or admit! Learning to recognise your own competence and trusting in it is an important part of reading poems in a fruitful way. Remember that reading is an active process and that your readings are provisional and open to reconsideration.

In an examination, you will not be able to talk with your fellow students or return to the poem many times, over a couple of days. Trust yourself. In an examination the poem may be new to you, but the reading of poems is not. Draw on your experience of creating meaning. Poetry works to reveal the world in new ways. D. H. Lawrence said: 'The essential quality of poetry is that it makes a new effort of attention and "discovers" a new world within the known world'. In an examination, you are looking to show how a poem, and your reading of it, presents a new view of the world. Read the poem over, noting and jotting as you do so, and then focus on different aspects of the poem. The questions set on the poem will help direct your attention.

Here are some suggested ways into a poem. They are not exhaustive or definitive.

THE WORDS OF THE POEM

Remember that every word chosen by a poet suggests that another word was rejected.

In poetry some words are so charged with meaning that literal or everyday meaning gives way to their figurative or poetic meaning. Often there are one or two words in a poem that carry a weight of meaning: these words can be read in a variety of ways that open up the poem for you.

Here are some questions you can ask:

1 Are the words in the poem simple or complex, concrete or abstract?
2 How are they clustered into phrases?
3 Are there any obvious patterns of word usage, for example words that refer to colours, or verbs that suggest energy and force?
4 Is there a pattern in the descriptive words used by the poet?
5 Are there key words – words that carry a symbolic or emotional force – or a clear set of associations? (Does the poet play with these associations by calling them into question or subverting them?)
6 Do patterns of words establish any contrasts or oppositions, for example night and day, winter and summer, joy and sorrow, love and death?

THE MUSIC AND MOVEMENT OF THE POEM

In relation to the sounds and rhythms of the poem, note such characteristics as the length of the lines or the presence or absence of rhyme. Consider how sound patterns add to the poem's texture and meaning. For example, do the sound patterns create a sense of hushed stillness or an effect of forceful energy?

Ask yourself some or all of the following questions:

1 What is the pattern of line length in the poem?
2 What is the pattern of rhyme?
3 Is there a pattern to vowel sounds and length? What influence might this have on the rhythm of the poem or the feelings conveyed by it?
4 Are there patterns of consonant sounds, including alliteration? What is their effect?
5 Are there changes in the poem's rhythm? Where and why do these occur?

THE VOICE OF THE POEM

Each poem has its own voice. When you read a poet's work, you can often recognise a distinctive poetic voice. This may be in the poem's rhythms or in the viewpoint it expresses. Sometimes it is most evident in the tone of voice of the poem. Sometimes you are taken by the warmth of a poetic voice, or its coldness and detachment, or its tone of amused surprise. Try to catch the distinctive characteristic of the voice of the poem as you read. Decide if it is a man's voice or a woman's voice and what this might mean. Try to place the voice in a context. This may help you to understand the assumptions in the poem's statements, or the emotional force of those statements.

THE IMAGERY OF THE POEM

Images are the descriptive words and phrases used by poets to speak to our senses. They are mostly visual in quality (word pictures) but they can also appeal to our senses of touch, smell and hearing. Images and patterns of imagery are key elements in the way that poems convey meanings. They create moods, capture emotions and suggest or call out feelings in the readers.

Ask yourself these questions:

1 Are there patterns of images in the poem?
2 What kind of world is suggested by the images of the poem – familiar or strange, fertile or barren, secure or threatening, private or public, calm or stormy, generous or mean? (Images often suggest contrasts or opposites.)
3 What emotions are associated with the images of the poem?
4 What emotions, do you think, inspired the choice of images?
5 What emotions do the images cause in you?
6 If there are images which are particularly powerful, why do they carry the force they do?
7 Do any of the images have the force of a symbol?
8 What is the usual meaning of the symbol?
9 What is its meaning in the poem?

THE STRUCTURE OF THE POEM

There are endless possibilities for structuring a poem. The obvious structures of a poem are the lines and the stanzas. Short lines give a sense of tautness to a poem. Long lines can create a conversational feel and allow for shifts and changes in rhythm. Rhyme and the pattern of rhyme influence the structure of a poem.

The poem is also structured by the movement of thought. This may or may not coincide with line and stanza divisions. Words like 'while', 'then' and 'and' help you trace the line of thought or argument as it develops through the poem.

In narrative poems, a simple form of structure is provided by the story itself and the sequence of events it describes. Another simple structure is one in which the poet describes a scene and then records his/her response to it. Or a poem may be built on a comparison or a contrast. The structure may also come from a series of parallel statements or a series of linked reflections.

However, the structure of a poem can be quite subtle, dependent on such things as word association or changes in emotions. Be alert to a change of focus or a shift of thought or emotion in the poem. Quite often there is a creative tension between the stanza structure – the visual form of the poem – and the emotional or imaginative structure of the poem. For this reason, be alert to turning points in poems. These might be marked by a pause, by a change in imagery or by a variation in rhythm.

EXAM ADVICE FROM THE DEPARTMENT OF EDUCATION AND SCIENCE

The Department of Education and Science published this advice to students on answering the unseen poem in the Leaving Certificate Examination:

> *As the unseen poem on the paper will more than likely be unfamiliar to you, you should read it a number of times (at least twice) before attempting your answer. You should pay careful attention to the introductory note printed above the text of the poem.*

Other advice from the Department of Education includes the following explanation of terms and questions, which are relevant to the answering of the questions on the unseen poem:

Do you agree with this statement?

You are free to agree in full or in part with the statement offered. But you must deal with the statement in question – you cannot simply dismiss the statement and write about a different topic of your choice.

Write a response to this statement (or Discuss)

As above, your answer can show the degree to which you agree or disagree with a statement or point of view. You can also deal with the impact the text made on you as a reader.

What does the poem say to you about …?

What is being asked for here is **your** understanding/reading of the poem. It is important that you show how your understanding comes from the text of the poem, its language and imagery.

LAST WORD

The really essential part in reading a poem is that you try to meet the poet halfway. Bring your intelligence and your emotions to the encounter with a poem and match the openness of the poet with an equal openness of mind and heart. And when you write about a poem, give your honest assessment.

GUIDELINES FOR ANSWERING QUESTIONS ON POETRY

Questions may be phrased in different ways in the Leaving Cert English exam. Some examples include:

- Do you like the poetry of Poet U?
- Poet V: a Personal Response.
- What impact did the poetry of Poet W have on you as a reader?
- Write an introduction to the poetry of Poet X.
- Compile a selection of the poems of Poet Y for an anthology, giving reasons for your choices.
- Give a short talk on the poetry of Poet Z.

Whatever way the question is phrased, you will need to show that you have engaged fully with the work of the poet under discussion.

FORMING A PERSONAL RESPONSE TO A POET'S THEMES

Each and every reader responds to a poem individually. It may be that the work of a particular poet moves us in ways that we can never hope to understand fully. But having said that, if your answer is to become more than just a series of vague impressions, there are aspects of a poet's work that you should consider in your answers. You must look closely at the poet's choice of **themes.** Illustrate them with examples but don't just write out a list of themes! Your answer should show that you have considered this aspect of the poet's work carefully. Questions you should ask yourself include:

- do you find the themes appealing because they reflect your personal concerns and interests?
- do the themes offer an insight into the life of the poet?
- do the themes enrich your understanding of universal human concerns, love or death, for example?
- do you respond to the poet's themes because they are unusual or unfamiliar?
- do you respond to themes that appeal to the intellect as well as the emotions, such as politics, religion or history, for example?

Bear in mind that themes may be complex and open to more than one interpretation. In fact this is often the aspect that we respond to most.

In your answer you should consider how the poet develops the themes, what questions are raised in your mind and how they may or may not be resolved.

THE POET'S LIFE, PERSONALITY OR OUTLOOK

Since poems are often written out of a poet's inner urgency, they can reveal a great deal about the personality of the poet:

- poems can be as revealing as an autobiography. Read the work of each of the poets carefully with this in mind. Can you build up a profile of each poet from what he or she has written, from his or her own personal voice?
- is this voice honest, convincing, suggesting an original or perceptive view of the world?
- it may also be that you like the work of a particular poet for a contrasting reason – that he or she goes beyond personal revelation to create other voices, other lives. Many poets adopt a different persona to recreate a particular experience. Might this enrich our understanding of the world? Your response may take this aspect into account, too.

THE POET'S USE OF LANGUAGE

Your response to a poet's work will be influenced by how he or she uses language. In your answer you should include an exploration of language.

In preparing for the examination you should examine carefully the individual **images** or **patterns of imagery** used by each of the eight poets on your course.

When you write about imagery, try to analyse how the particular poet you are dealing with creates the effects he or she does:

- does he or she appeal to our senses – our visual, tactile and aural senses, and our senses of taste and smell? How do you respond? Do you find the images effective in conveying theme or emotion?
- do the images appeal to you because their clarity and vividness allow you to visualise the scene or because they leave you baffled and puzzled in an exciting way?
- are the images created by the use of **simile** and **metaphor?** Can you say why these particular comparisons were chosen by the poet? Do you find them precise, surprising, fresh …?
- if the poet made use of **symbol** or **personification,** consider how these devices might have added to a poem's richness, so that it acquires a universal significance
- you may find you like the way a particular poet blends poetic and conversational language, or how a poet uses language both to **denote** (to signify) and to **connote** (to suggest).
- you may respond positively to a poet's simplicity of expression or to a sense that a poet's use of complex language reflects complex ideas.

An exploration of language may include style, manner, phraseology and vocabulary, as well as imagery and techniques mentioned above.

THE SOUNDS OF POETRY

Many people find that it is the sound of poetry that they respond to most. It is an ancient human characteristic to respond to word patterns like **rhyme** or musical effects such as **rhythm**. This may be one of the aspects of a particular poet's work that appeals to you most.

Poets use sound effects such as **alliteration, assonance, consonance** and **onomatopoeia** for many reasons – some thematic, some for emotive effect, some merely because of the sheer pleasure of creating pleasant musical word patterns.

Look carefully at how each of the poets you have studied makes use of sound. Your response will be much richer if based on close reading and attention to sound patterns and effects.

POETRY AND THE EMOTIONS

We may respond intellectually to the themes of a poem, but very often it is the emotional intensity of a poem that enables us to engage with it most fully. At their best, poems celebrate what it is to be human, with all that being human suggests, including confronting our deepest fears and anxieties.

The **tone** of a poem conveys the emotions that lie behind it. All of the elements in a poem may be used to convey tone and emotion. A poet's choice of imagery and the language he uses can be very expressive. Remember, too, that the use of sound conveys emotions well. Do look at the work of the different poets with this in mind.

What corresponding emotions does the work of each poet on your course create in you as a reader? Do you feel consoled, uplifted, disturbed, perhaps even alienated? Does the poet succeed in conveying his or her feelings, if indeed that is what is intended in the poem? These are questions you should consider in preparing to form your response.

CONCLUSION

It is worth remembering that you will be rewarded for your attempts to come to terms with the work of the poets you have studied in a personal and responsive way. This may entail a heartfelt negative response, too. But even a negative response must display close reading and should pay attention to specific aspects of the poems. Do not feel that you have to conform to the opinions of others – including the opinions expressed in this book!

Read each question carefully. Some questions may direct your attention to specific elements of a poet's work. Make sure you deal with these in your answer. Other questions may simply invite you to include some aspects of a poet's work in your response. It would be unwise to ignore any hints as to how to proceed!

You will be required to support your answer by reference to or quotation from the poems chosen. Remember that long quotations are hardly ever necessary.

The Department of Education and Science has published the following advice to students on answering the question on poetry:

It is a matter of judgement as to which of the poems will best suit the question under discussion and candidates should not feel a necessity to refer to all of the poems they have studied.

As in all of the questions in the examination, you will be marked using the following criteria:

1 *Clarity of purpose (30% of marks available)* This is explained by the Department of Education and Science as 'engagement with the set task' – in other words, are you answering the question you have been asked? Is your answer relevant and focused?

2 *Coherence of delivery (30% of marks available)* Here you are assessed on your 'ability to sustain the response over the entire answer'. Is there coherence and continuity in the points you are making? Are the references you choose to illustrate your points appropriate?

3 *Efficiency of language use (30% of marks available)* The Department of Education and Science explains this as the 'management and control of language to achieve clear communication'. Aspects of your writing such as vocabulary, use of phrasing, and fluency – your writing style – will be taken into account.

4 *Accuracy of mechanics (10% of marks available)* Your levels of accuracy in spelling and grammar are what count here. Always leave some time during the exam to read over your work – you are bound to spot errors.

Good luck!

GLOSSARY
OF TERMS

ALLITERATION

This is a figure of speech in which consonants, especially at the beginning of words, are repeated. The term itself means 'repeating and playing upon the same letter'. Alliteration is a common feature of poetry in every period of literary history. It is used mainly for emphasis, to reinforce a point. A good example is found in John Donnes's sonnet 'Batter My Heart', where the speaker asks God to 'bend / Your force, to break, blowe, burn, and make me new'. Robert Frost uses alliteration in his poem 'Birches': 'When I see birches bend to left and right'.

ALLUSION

An allusion is a reference to a person, place or event or to another work of art or literature. The purpose of allusion is to get the reader to share an experience which has significant meaning for the writer. When a writer makes use of allusion, he or she takes it for granted that the reader will possess the background knowledge necessary to understand its significance in the context of the work. In many cases, the significance of the allusion becomes clearer as the poem evolves. The title of Elizabeth Bishop's poem 'The Prodigal' is an allusion to Christ's parable of the prodigal son told in the Gospel of St Luke. The poem alludes to some of the themes of that parable.

AMBIGUITY

Ambiguous words, phrases or sentences are capable of being understood in two or more possible senses. In many poems, ambiguity is part of the poet's method and is essential to the meaning of the poem. The tile of Philip Larkin's poem 'Church Going' involves a suggestive ambiguity. It means both 'going to church' and 'the church going' (i.e. disappearing, going out of use, or becoming decayed).

ASSONANCE

This is the repetition of identical or similar vowel sounds, especially in stressed syllables, in a sequence of nearby words. Assonance can contribute significantly to the meaning of a poem. An example is 'That night the slow sea washed against my head' from Derek Mahon's 'Day Trip to Donegal'.

BALLAD

Ballads were originally songs, transmitted orally. They commented on life by telling stories in a popular style. In ballads, the attention of the readers is concentrated on the story and the characters. Every ballad must have a meaning that can easily be grasped by the reader. 'Sir Patrick Spens' is one of the most celebrated of all ballads. Its first two stanzas exemplify the main features found in almost all ballads: the abrupt and arresting opening, the economical sketch of the setting and action and the sharp transition from narrative to dialogue and back again. Other features of ballads are refrains, repetitions and simplicity of diction.

COLLOQUIALISM

A colloquial word or phrase is one that is used in everyday speech and writing. The colloquial style is plain and relaxed. At the end of the eighteenth century, Wordsworth declared that his aim was to imitate, as far as possible, what he called 'the very language of men'. In much poetry of the twentieth and twenty-first centuries, there is an acceptance of colloquialism, even slang, as a medium of poetic expression. The poems of Philip Larkin frequently exemplify this idea.

CONCEIT

The term 'conceit' is generally used for figures of speech that establish arresting parallels between objects or situations which, at first glance, seem to have little or nothing in common. All comparisons discover a likeness in things unalike. A comparison becomes a conceit when the poet forces us to concede likeness, while at the same time we are strongly conscious of unlikeness. The conceit is a characteristic device of the seventeenth-century metaphysical poets, among them

Donne and Herbert. Sometimes an entire poem can be a long conceit. An example is Donne's 'The Anniversarie', which consists of a series of comparisons and contrasts between two lovers and two royal persons.

CONVENTION

This is the name given to any aspect of a literary work which author and readers accept as normal and to be expected in that kind of writing. For example, it is a convention that a sonnet has fourteen lines that rhyme in a certain pattern. By convention, the ballad has a particular kind of diction. Sometimes conventions are abandoned or replaced. Eighteenth-century poetic diction, for example, gave way to a more 'natural' form of expression.

DICTION

Diction is the vocabulary used by a writer – his or her selection of words. Until the beginning of the nineteenth century, poets wrote in accordance with the principle that the diction of poetry had to differ, often significantly, from that of current speech. There was, in other words, a certain sort of 'poetic' diction which, by avoiding commonplace words and expressions, was supposed to lend dignity to the poem and its subject. This is entirely contrary to modern practice.

GENRE

The term is used to signify a particular literary species or form. Traditionally, the important genres were epic, tragedy, comedy, elegy, satire, lyric and pastoral. Until modern times, critics tended to distinguish carefully between the various genres and writers were expected to follow the rules prescribed for each. For example, if a poet wrote an epic, it was assumed that his or her language would be dignified, in keeping with the heroic nature of the subject, and that he or she would use epic similes, often many lines in length. Epics were also expected to feature long descriptive passages.

IMAGERY

This is a term with a very wide application. When we speak of the imagery of a poem, we refer to all its images taken collectively. The poet C. Day Lewis puts the matter well when he describes an image as 'a picture made out of words'. If we consider imagery in its narrow and popular sense, it signifies descriptions of visible objects and scenes, as, for example, in Robert Frost's 'Birches' the trees are 'Loaded with ice a sunny winter morning'. In its wider sense, imagery signifies figurative language, especially metaphor and simile.

LYRIC

Originally a lyric was a song performed to the accompaniment of a lyre. The term is now used to signify any relatively short poem in which a single speaker, not necessarily representing the poet, expresses feelings and thoughts in a personal and subjective fashion. Most poems are either lyrics or feature large lyrical elements.

METAPHOR AND SIMILE

These are the two commonest figures of speech in poetry. A simile contains two parts – a subject that is the focus of attention, and another element that is introduced for the sake of emphasising some quality in the subject. In a simile, the poet uses some such word as 'like' or 'as' to show that a comparison is being made. The opening lines of Sylvia Plath's 'Finisterre' feature a striking metaphor: 'This was the land's end: the last fingers, knuckled and rheumatic, / Cramped on nothing'.

Metaphor differs from simile only in omitting the comparative word ('like' or 'as'). If in a simile someone's teeth are like pearls, in a metaphor they *are* pearls. While in the case of a simile the comparison is openly proclaimed as such, in the case of a metaphor the comparison is implied. A metaphor is capable of a greater range of suggestiveness than a simile and its implications are wider and richer. The simile, by its very nature (with the 'like' or 'as' formula), is limited to a comparatively small area of suggestion. One advantage of metaphor is its tendency to establish numerous relationships between the two things being compared. In John Montague's 'Windharp', the poet imagines a hand combing and stroking the landscape 'till / the valley gleams / like the pile upon / a mountain pony's coat'.

ONOMATOPOEIA

This involves the use of words that resemble, or enact, the very sounds they imitate. If a poet tries to make the sound reflect the meaning, he or she is using onomatopoeia. In 'The War Horse', Eavan Boland uses a simple form of onomatopoeia when she writes about the 'the clip, clop casual / iron' of the horse's shoes.

PARADOX

This is an apparently self-contradictory statement which, on further consideration, is found to contain an essential truth. Paradox is so intrinsic to human nature that poetry rich in paradox is valued as a reflection of the central truths of human experience. John Donne is one of the great masters of paradox. In his sonnet 'Batter My Heart', he is addressing God in a series of paradoxical demands: 'Take mee to you, imprison mee, for I / Except you enthrall mee, never shall be free'.

SIMILE

See 'metaphor and simile'.

SONNET

This is a single-stanza lyric, consisting of fourteen lines. These fourteen lines are just long enough to make possible the fairly complex development of a single theme, and short enough to test the poet's gift for concentrated expression. The poet's freedom is further restricted by a demanding rhyme scheme and a conventional metrical form (five strong stresses in each line). The greatest sonnets are those in which the poet has overcome the limitations of the form and achieved the great aim of reconciling freedom of expression, variety of rhythm, mood and tone and richness of imagery with adherence to a rigid set of conventions.

English poets have traditionally written one of two kinds of sonnet – the Petrarchan and the Shakespearean. The Petrarchan sonnet, favoured by Milton and Wordsworth, falls into two divisions – the octave (eight lines rhyming abba, abba) and the sestet (six lines generally rhyming cde, cde). The octave generally presents a problem, situation or incident; the sestet resolves the problem or comments on the situation or incident. In contrast, the Shakespearean sonnet consists of three quatrains (groups of four lines rhyming abab, cdcd, efef) and a rhyming couplet (gg).

STYLE

This may be defined as the manner of expression characteristic of a writer – that is, his or her particular way of saying things. Consideration of style involves an examination of the writer's diction, figures of speech, order of words, tone and feeling, rhythm and movement. Traditionally, styles were classified according to three categories: high (formal or learned), middle and low (plain). Convention required that the level of style be appropriate to the speaker, the subject matter, the occasion which inspired the poem and the literary genre. A modern critic, Northrop Frye, suggests that styles could be classified under two broad headings: (a) demotic style, modelled on the language, rhythms and associations of everyday speech, and (b) hieratic style, involving formal, elaborate expression, with the aim of separating literary language from ordinary speech.

SYMBOL

A symbol is anything that stands for something else. In this sense, all words are symbols because they signify things other than themselves. Literary symbolism, however, comes about when the *objects* signified by the words stand in turn for things other than themselves. At a simple level, symbolism is familiar to almost everybody because certain conventional symbols are universally popular. Objects commonly associated with fixed ideas or qualities have come to symbolise these: for example, the cross is the primary Christian symbol, and the dove is a symbol of peace. Colour symbols have no fixed meaning, but derive their significance from a context: green may signify innocence or Irish patriotism or envy. The literary symbol is not a token with a precise meaning to be pinned down and accurately described. Some poets use symbols as essentially private tokens so that even the context can do little to help them to generate their meanings. When Yeats, for example, does this, he sets his readers some difficult problems of interpretation. In John Montague's poem on his father, the cage inside which the latter works, as well as being an actual place, is also symbolic – not only of the father's trapped existence, but of the human condition in general. Montague is suggesting that we are all captives in cages, whether these are our own weaknesses, our own bodies, or the societies which make us prisoners of the convictions they impose.

TONE

When one is trying to describe the tone of a poem, it is best to think of every poem as a spoken, rather than a written, exercise. A poem has at least one speaker who is addressing somebody or something. In some poems, the speaker can be thought of as meditating aloud, talking to himself or herself. We, the readers, catch him or her in the act and overhear them. Every speaker must inevitably have an attitude to the person or object being addressed or talked about, and must also see himself or herself in some relationship with that person or object. This attitude or relationship will determine the tone of the utterance. Tone may thus be defined as the expression of a literary speaker's attitude to, and relationship with, the listener or the subject. In real life, a person's attitude to another is often revealed in the tone of voice of that person and in the words chosen. A sensitive reading aloud of most poems will soon reveal the tone of a speaker's utterance. Philip Larkin's poems present an interesting study in tone. He approaches his subject-matter in a matter-of-fact way, and this is reflected in the casual, unpretentious tone.